Lincoln, Seward, and US Foreign Relations in the Civil War Era

LINCOLN, SEWARD, AND US FOREIGN RELATIONS IN THE CIVIL WAR ERA

JOSEPH A. FRY

UNIVERSITY PRESS OF KENTUCKY

Scholarly publisher for the Commonwealth,
serving Bellarmine University, Berea College, Centre
College of Kentucky, Eastern Kentucky University,
The Filson Historical Society, Georgetown College,
Kentucky Historical Society, Kentucky State University,
Morehead State University, Murray State University,
Northern Kentucky University, Transylvania University,
University of Kentucky, University of Louisville,
and Western Kentucky University.

Editorial and Sales Offices: The University Press of Kentucky
663 South Limestone Street, Lexington, Kentucky 40508-4008
www.kentuckypress.com

Library of Congress Cataloging-in-Publication Data

Names: Fry, Joseph A., 1947– author.
Title: Lincoln, Seward, and US foreign relations in the Civil War era / Joseph A. Fry.
Description: Lexington, Kentucky : University Press of Kentucky, [2019] | Includes bibliographical references and index.
Identifiers: LCCN 2018047826| ISBN 9780813177120 (hardcover : alk. paper) | ISBN 9780813177144 (pdf) | ISBN 9780813177151 (epub)
Subjects: LCSH: United States—Foreign relations—1861–1865. | United States—Foreign relations—1865-1898. | Lincoln, Abraham, 1809–1865. | Seward, William H. (William Henry), 1801-1872. | United States—Politics and government—1861–1865. | United States—Politics and government—1865–1869.
Classification: LCC E469 .F79 2019 | DDC 327.73009/034—dc23

This book is printed on acid-free paper meeting
the requirements of the American National Standard
for Permanence in Paper for Printed Library Materials.

Manufactured in the United States of America

Member of the Association
of University Presses

Dedicated to Ron Kyle.

CONTENTS

INTRODUCTION

The North's victory in the American Civil War had profound domestic and international significance. By prevailing in this epic conflict, the United States preserved both the nation's territorial integrity and its experiment in republicanism and democracy. Sustaining territorial integrity and republicanism enabled the nation to continue its ascent toward world power status and to emerge in the twentieth century as the world's foremost democratic government. The South's secession and forceful defense of slavery challenged US nationalism, liberalism, and sense of providential destiny. The young nation had been an independent country for fewer than eighty years, and neither its survival nor its form of government was firmly established in 1861. To the contrary, at the midpoint of the nineteenth century, it was unclear that the "nation state—as opposed to empires or confederations—would define the political organization of Europe and the Americas" or that democratic government would not fall before monarchial or aristocratic rule in the western world. Therefore, the Union's victory provided a great boost to both nationalism and liberalism in the Americas and Europe and reinforced the American self-image as a chosen people.[1]

The South's secession also interrupted the march of American imperialism, and the United States' victory empowered the nation to resume that march and its path to becoming a great power. US territorial expansion after 1787 embodied an imperial process in which white Americans had overcome opposition from European opponents such as the British, French, and Spanish and New World foes such as Native Americans and Mexicans. The United States had imposed its will on weaker peoples, often forcefully seized territory, and ruled others without their consent. As it expanded across the continent, the United States had also practiced a pre-twentieth-century form of globalization, and foreign trade was a continuous concern for American farmers, manufacturers, and merchants. After 1820, this US territorial expansion had spawned an "imperial competition" between the North and South in which the two regions battled over control of the New West and disagreed over the merits of further US expansion into the tropical areas of the Western Hemisphere. The victory of Abraham Lincoln and the Republican Party in the 1860 presidential election signaled that the South and slavery would be excluded from the New West and would not expand into the tropics. Dixie had lost its persistent influence over US foreign policy—a foreign policy that had frequently been proslavery over the previous six decades. Faced with this new reality, the South seceded and attempted to form an independent country with its own foreign policy and imperial aspirations.[2]

Just as foreign policy considerations played a central role in the coming of the Civil War, the North's superior foreign policies were crucial to the conflict's outcome. Richard Current cited the North's significant advantages in population, industrial and military capacity, and natural resources and concluded, "As usual, God was on the side of the heaviest battalions." The war's outcome was, of course, ultimately decided on the battlefields, but the seemingly stronger nation does not always win civil wars. Military, economic, and political intervention by outside third parties on behalf of the weaker side can tip the balance and could have done so in the American conflict. That no European power intervened on the South's behalf to offset the North's advantages ensured Confederate defeat.[3]

President Abraham Lincoln and Secretary of State William Henry Seward, two most unlikely partners, formulated and implemented the US foreign policies that forestalled European intervention. Lincoln and Seward had come to their respective offices from vastly different personal backgrounds and had been keen rivals for the Republican presidential nomination in 1860. When Lincoln won the nomination, Seward was left bitter and temporarily disillusioned. Still, their post-1860 partnership in many ways embodied what Joshua Wolf Shenk has characterized as the "powers of two," or a relationship in which a pair of exceedingly talented, complex, alpha personalities forged a highly productive alliance—one that succeeded because of "power clarity" and a clear "*hierarchical*" order that defined who functioned as the senior partner. Lincoln definitively established, and Seward accepted, that order in early 1861, and the partnership functioned superbly and without serious incident over the course of the war.[4]

Lincoln and Seward both recognized, and the president brilliantly articulated, the war's domestic and international significance. The United States' grand republican experiment and the nation's ability to defend its territorial integrity hung in the balance and carried enormous implications for the future viability of democratic government and the maintenance of US international influence. Both partners agonized over whether the nation would emerge from the war as a coherent continental nation or a balkanized group of smaller, rival countries, such as those in South America and Europe, that invited persistent outside interference. The two leaders agreed that preserving the Union was essential to realizing these US ideological and geopolitical objectives, although they periodically differed on the best foreign policy steps for defeating the Confederacy. For example, Seward promptly realized that the United States had no alternative but to succumb to British demands during the *Trent* affair in December 1861, and he provided the diplomatic and public explanation for that decision in contrast to Lincoln's less timely willingness to bow to London's dictate. Six months later, the president grasped the military and diplomatic necessity for the Emancipation Proclamation, despite the secretary's ambivalence and reluctance to take this decisive action linking US victory to the freeing of the slaves. In both instances, the more reluctant partner acknowledged the stronger argument and provided supportive affirmation.

After Lincoln rejected Seward's ill-advised recommendation in April 1861 to incite a "foreign crisis" designed to induce the South to rejoin the Union, the foreign policy duo agreed to make "one war at a time" the foundation of US foreign policy. They understood that despite the North's advantages in population and material assets, the Union could not be preserved if the United States simultaneously fought the Confederacy and another powerful nation. To avoid such a calamity, while blocking European intervention and restricting Confederate access to European-produced war materiel, required considerable diplomatic finesse. Seward's principal contribution was to convince British and French leaders that diplomatic recognition of the South or building additional ships for the Confederacy after mid-1863 would lead to war with the United States. Lincoln, in turn, fully understood that Seward's purposeful bluster and threats would be credible only if the United

States steadily augmented its military power and defeated the South on the battlefield. The president never lost sight of the connection between foreign relations and US military success as he exercised his powers as commander in chief and steadily enhanced his grasp of military strategy. Even though the United States won no decisive military victories prior to Gettysburg and Vicksburg in mid-1863, the major European powers were persistently apprehensive about a possible military confrontation with the North.[5]

Both policymakers also understood that US threats had to be combined with strategic caution and timely compromises. Hence, the Confederate diplomats taken from the *Trent* were surrendered, and the United States responded in a relatively restrained way to Britain's sale of ships and war materiel to the Confederacy; to British, French, and Spanish aid in the South's efforts to run the US naval blockade of Dixie; to Confederate raids on the United States from Canada; and to French Emperor Napoleon III's attempt to install a European monarch in Mexico. On balance, the Lincoln-Seward policies, a combination of threat, caution, and compromise, worked well. The United States avoided involvement in a second war, and there was no decisive European intervention on behalf of the Confederacy.

As Lincoln and Seward formulated and implemented these successful foreign policies, they skillfully practiced "public diplomacy" designed to influence both their domestic US audience and foreign nations. Through his public addresses and pronouncements, messages to Congress, and letters dispatched abroad and meant for publication, Lincoln eloquently articulated what has been called the "American Creed," with its providential overtones, and adroitly framed the war's significance and US objectives. His speeches, such as the Gettysburg Address; pronouncements, such as the Emancipation Proclamation; and letters, such as those published in British newspapers in early 1863, emphasized that the Union fought to defend republicanism, nationalism, and freedom. Seward made no such grand or eloquent declarations, but he worked closely and effectively with friendly northern newspaper editors and selectively published diplomatic correspondence to explain and garner sympathetic coverage of administration policies, rebut domestic critics and political opponents, and reemphasize essential US foreign policy positions and goals to the major European powers.[6]

When these Lincoln-Seward foreign policies helped secure the North's victory, the United States could turn its attention back to imperial expansion. Seward clearly spearheaded this effort from 1865 to 1869 following

Lincoln's assassination. Although the president had exhibited a much "more modest" expansionist agenda when looking beyond the North American continent, the two partners had agreed on many key features of the US imperial perspective. Both deemed the United States exceptional; ideologically and institutionally equipped to instruct other nations and peoples (particularly nonwhites); and destined for international greatness with American institutions "spread to their ultimate limits." Both favored US expansion across the North American continent, as long as slavery was excluded from the New West; both endorsed homestead legislation, the transcontinental railroad, land grant colleges, and the Department of Agriculture, all of which were meant to promote the westward migration of white, free-labor settlers and their political, economic, and cultural institutions; and Lincoln, as commander in chief, deployed military forces to remove Native Americans from the settlers' path. This Whig-Republican program for continental expansion has been aptly characterized as "a more slowly unfolding and densely interconnected empire" than the one advocated during the 1840s and 1850s by contemporary "Democratic counterparts." Nevertheless, the program was profoundly imperial, particularly for American Indians and indigenous Alaskans, whose experiences were strikingly similar to those of the native Hawaiians, Filipinos, and Puerto Ricans who subsequently came under US rule.[7]

Left to direct US foreign relations on his own following the president's death, Seward sought to implement his more highly developed conception of US imperial growth—a vision he had initially propounded in the 1850s and returned to following the war. The secretary continued to promote territorial expansion on the North American continent, where he successfully purchased Alaska but failed to acquire British Columbia. He devoted even greater attention to US commercial expansion, with a primary emphasis on trade with East Asia. Acquisition of Alaska expanded US frontage on the Pacific, and the addition of British Columbia would have served the same purpose. Seward also attempted to annex Hawaii and islands in the Caribbean and to build an isthmian canal; these steps were intended to provide ports, coaling stations, and a shorter route for trade with China and Japan, where he promoted an Open Door trade policy affording the United States equal commercial access. Save the purchase of Alaska, none of these projects came to fruition in the 1860s, but Seward's vision and efforts embodied the shift of US imperial focus from territorial to commercial expansion during the late nineteenth century and forecast the nation's burst of imperialism in the 1890s and the early twentieth century.[8]

Seward made another observation that exhibited remarkable foresight. In the course of his 1871–1872 trip around the world, he visited a prominent English library where a researcher was at work "surrounded by great piles" of books. The widely read American statesman declared that the author was engaged in the all-too-familiar, and perhaps not overly intellectual, process by which books were produced from previously published works—an endeavor whereby "the great mass of . . . facts and ideas" were "selected, copied, and rearranged with more or less skill" from earlier publications.[9] It is a bit disconcerting to have been "found out" by Secretary Seward some 145 years in advance of this project, which is an unapologetic synthesis of the rich literature on Lincoln, Seward, and US foreign relations preceding, during, and following the American Civil War. Hopefully, I have arranged these materials and ideas with more rather than less skill in this book intended for college classes and general readers.

My study of Civil War diplomacy began with an undergraduate senior thesis in 1968–1969 that examined US-British relations during 1861. This research on the 1860s continued with a PhD dissertation and biography of Henry Shelton Sanford, the US minister to Belgium from 1861 to 1869. Although my biography of John Tyler Morgan, an Alabama secessionist, Confederate general, and US senator, focused especially on late nineteenth-century US imperial expansion and did not treat Civil War diplomacy, it did lead me to examine the South as a region and its influence on foreign relations. That project also reinforced my interest in the nexus of biography and US foreign policy and led to sustained efforts to understand nineteenth-century US imperialism. A subsequent study of the South and US foreign relations from 1789 to 1973 included chapters on the coming of the Civil War and Confederate foreign relations. There followed more than a decade of research and writing about the South and the Vietnam War. Given the latter emphasis, it has been an enjoyable and stimulating intellectual experience to return to the nineteenth century, biography, US imperial expansion, and the foreign policy of the 1860s.[10]

1

ORIGINS OF THE FOREIGN POLICY PARTNERSHIP, 1801–1861

I.

On February 23, 1861, President-elect Abraham Lincoln slipped covertly into Washington, D.C., at 6 a.m., nearly ten hours before his scheduled arrival time. In response to reports of an assassination plot, the new president traveled in semi-disguise, bereft of his signature stovepipe hat and accompanied by only his private bodyguard and Allan Pinkerton, a railroad detective. Lincoln's welcome party at the Baltimore and Ohio Railroad depot consisted of one person, Republican congressman Elihu B. Washburne from Illinois, who promptly whisked him away to the Willard Hotel. After being shown to his quarters, Lincoln had his first substantive meeting in the nation's capital over breakfast with William Henry Seward, the incoming secretary of state. Thus began an unlikely, but highly successful, partnership that oversaw US foreign relations over the ensuing four years and contributed directly to the North's victory in the Civil War by forestalling European intervention on the side of the Confederacy.

Lincoln and Seward came to their meeting at the Willard from starkly different backgrounds: Seward from prosperity and privilege and Lincoln from a past of poverty and deprivation. Seward was born on May 16, 1801, into a family of five siblings in upstate New York. Young Henry's father, Samuel Swezy Seward, was the postmaster in the village of Florida and, at various times, also a doctor, lawyer, merchant, county judge, and state legislator. The family lived in what townsfolk called the "Seward mansion," and the elder Seward owned seven slaves in 1820 and left an estate valued at

1. Abraham Lincoln. Courtesy of the National Archives and Records Administration.

$300,000 at his death in 1849. Although a hard, demanding parent (in contrast to Henry's kinder mother), Samuel provided the best possible education for his son. This included attendance at Farmers' Hall Academy, a boarding school in nearby Goshen, and Union College, the second-oldest college in New York, from which Seward graduated Phi Beta Kappa in 1820 at the age of nineteen. This level of education and accomplishment placed Seward among a tiny minority of young men in early nineteenth-century America, demonstrated his intellectual capacity and personal drive, and spoke clearly to the family's economic and social standing.[1]

Following his graduation from Union, Seward read law in Goshen for a year before he moved to New York City to work in a prominent law firm. Back in Goshen in the fall of 1822, he was admitted to the state bar. Still only twenty-two years old, Seward continued his legal career in Auburn, New York, some 150 miles west of Albany, by joining a firm headed by Elijah Miller, a retired judge. Seward quickly emerged as an extremely social, ambitious, energetic, and talented attorney. He also courted Frances Adeline Miller, the daughter of his boss, and married her in October 1824. Seward married for love, but also for financial reasons, since Frances was one of only two daughters and was, therefore, likely to command a substantial inheritance. A beautiful woman with black hair and eyes, Frances stood slightly over five feet six, the same height as her thin, red-haired husband. Well-educated and well-read, she was devoted to Henry but was also independent minded, sometimes critical of his political positions, and far less enthralled with entertaining and socializing than her new husband, who delighted in parties and the consumption of ample quantities of wine and cigars.

By 1830, two of the couple's five children (Augustus and Frederick) had arrived, and the pattern of Henry's long absences in the pursuit of business and politics was firmly established. This pattern intensified over the ensuing decades as Seward's political career took off and he scrambled to earn the income needed to support their lavish lifestyle. Frances was essentially a single parent during Henry's extended absences. His five-month trip to Europe with his father in 1833 provided a telling example of his priorities and the family's personal and fiscal dynamics.

Nearly eight years Seward's junior, Abraham Lincoln was born on February 12, 1809, in a one-room log cabin with a dirt floor near Elizabethtown, Kentucky, approximately sixty miles south of Louisville. Lincoln's father, Thomas, was an honest, moral, and hardworking man whose labors never yielded prosperity or family security. The family moved to remote, densely forested Spencer County, Indiana, in 1816, where Lincoln's mother, Nancy, died two years later. The following year, Thomas married Sarah Bush Johnston, a widow whom he had known for many years in Kentucky. Upon her arrival in Indiana, Sarah brought order and love to a household in disarray. Perhaps most important, she, in contrast to Thomas, encouraged young Abraham's love of learning and his pursuit of an education.[2]

As befitted a boy, and then a young man, living on the frontier, much of Abraham's education took a decidedly practical bent. He learned to clear land, plant and tend crops, split fence rails, and build flat boats. By the age of thirteen or fourteen, Lincoln had begun to work for neighboring farmers; he was essentially hired out, and the bulk of his pay went to his father and the family. In 1828, Lincoln, not yet twenty years old, joined another man in floating a flat boat of produce down the Ohio and Mississippi rivers to New Orleans, where he first encountered a more cosmopolitan environment and witnessed slavery.

Lincoln grew to be a sinewy and powerful man of six feet four inches and 180 pounds; although renowned for wrestling and rail-splitting exploits, he much preferred, and eagerly pursued, book learning. According to his stepmother (and much to his father's consternation), he "didn't like physical labor," but "was diligent for Knowledge." His stepsister agreed that "Abe was not Energetic Except in one thing—he was active & persistent in learning." He attended school for a few months at the age of ten, the first of three similarly brief sessions, the last coming when he was fifteen. All told, this formal schooling totaled less than a year and contrasted starkly with Seward's instruction from private tutors and matriculation at Farmers' Hall Academy and Union College. Lincoln was self-taught, a remarkable process he continued even after he became president. As a youth in backwoods Indiana, Lincoln "begged, borrowed, and then devoured a small library of books," among them *Aesop's Fables, Robinson Crusoe, The Arabian Nights,* the King James Version of the Bible, a collection of *Hymns and Spiritual Songs,* Shakespeare, and an 1820 history of the United States. This emphasis on education in a society that placed such great value on physical prowess set Lincoln apart, as did his abstention from drinking, smoking, gambling, hunting, and swearing. Although none of his Indiana neighbors could have imagined his future accomplishments, they certainly recognized that young Abe was different.[3]

His neighbors in New Salem, Illinois, reached similar conclusions after Lincoln left his family and moved there in 1831. In this village of approximately one hundred people, where he worked as a store clerk and was appointed postmaster in 1833, Lincoln amused customers and friends with his unending supply of hilarious stories. He also continued his self-education and once again elicited bewildered responses from many townsfolk as he devoted all of his free time to studying law. John Stuart, a prominent Springfield attorney, granted Lincoln free access to his law library, and, after Lincoln passed the Illinois bar in 1836, he moved to Springfield to join Stuart's firm in 1837. As a junior partner, Lincoln handled a wide variety of cases and rode on horseback to county seats around the Eighth Judicial District. In some years, he spent up to six months "riding the circuit," which allowed him to cultivate a broad range of business and social contacts that proved politically beneficial. In 1841 Lincoln moved on to another Springfield firm, headed by Stephen T. Logan.

Friends and acquaintances noted the young man's often-gloomy disposition. Another of Lincoln's law partners, William Herndon, declared, "His melancholy dripped from him as he walked." Lincoln struggled with depression throughout his life, most acutely in 1835 and 1840–1841. According to the closest student of his struggle, Lincoln gradually and successfully managed his "blue spells" through his humor and storytelling and by focusing on his ambition, his sense of calling, and his determination to be part of great events. In decided contrast to the twenty-first-century political environment, neither Lincoln's constituents nor his opponents thought his melancholy should disqualify him from public office. They seemed to agree with him when he wrote that "melancholly [*sic*]" was a "misfortune not a fault."[4]

Lincoln's two most serious bouts with depression resulted from his relations with women. Although he was socially awkward around the opposite sex, Lincoln had made strides in this milieu and was in love with and engaged to Ann Rutledge when she died in August 1835. This led to his first bout with depression. The second incident, in 1840–1841, followed the breaking off of his engagement to Mary Todd. After he suffered a year of great emotional distress, Lincoln and Todd rekindled the relationship and were married in November 1842. Todd, a well-educated and intelligent woman from a prominent and prosperous Lexington, Kentucky, family, possessed all the social graces Lincoln lacked and shared his relentless ambition. She subsequently told a friend that she had been convinced he would become president: "If I had not thought so, I never would have married him, for you can see he is not pretty." By 1846, two of the Lincolns' four sons were born (Robert Todd and Edward Baker). When at home, Lincoln was a doting father; but, he, like Seward, was gone for extended periods throughout the 1840s and 1850s, which left Mary Todd Lincoln, similar to Frances Seward, responsible for most of the parenting.[5]

By the early 1840s, Seward and Lincoln were married and well-established attorneys. But their economic circumstances were as different as their personal histories. Following their marriage, Abraham and Mary had rented a single room above the Globe Tavern in Springfield. Two years later, they purchased for $1,200 the home in which they lived until moving to Washington in 1861. At the time of that move, Lincoln was earning approximately $2,000 per year, and his assets totaled $17,000. By contrast, after their 1824 wedding, which was attended by several hundred guests, Henry and Frances had moved into her father's large home set on four acres near Auburn, where they resided for several decades. In 1842, as the Lincolns rented their single room, Seward ended his second term as governor of New York, with personal debts that amounted to at least $200,000. Although the bulk of this sum derived from his participation in a western New York land speculation, the family's lifestyle, replete with champagne, caviar, Henry's Cuban cigars, and Frances's Tiffany glassware, was also telling. Over the remainder of the 1840s, Seward's lucrative patent law practice and returns from the Holland Land Company enabled him to reestablish fiscal solvency even as he sent two of his sons to college and remained politically active. Clearly, his ongoing personal and professional life operated at a level far removed from Lincoln's.[6]

II.

Despite that disparity, Seward and Lincoln had both benefited from and prospered in the context of a remarkable period of US territorial, demographic, and economic growth. By seizure, purchase, or negotiation, the United States acquired more than 2 million square miles of land during the first sixty years of the nineteenth century. From 5.3 million in 1800, the nation's population had increased to 31.4 million in 1860, some 4.4 million of whom were African American. American economic growth kept pace; the gross national product doubled every fifteen years, and average per capita income increased by 102 percent during the century's first six decades. A "transportation revolution" undergirded this phenomenal economic expansion. More than 3,700 miles of canals were constructed by 1837, only to be eclipsed by railroads. Commercial railroad building began with the Baltimore and Ohio in 1828; and, by 1860, total US railroad mileage of thirty thousand exceeded that of the remainder of the world combined. The telegraph simultaneously ushered in a "communication revolution." Developed in the 1830s and first employed commercially in 1844, the telegraph provided instantaneous communication. By 1850, fifty thousand miles of wire crisscrossed the nation, conveying economic, political, and even strategic and military information.

This new market economy featured clear sectional specializations. Manufacturing was most prominent in two northern areas: the section stretching from Boston to Baltimore and the Great Lakes area around Buffalo, Cleveland, Pittsburgh, and Chicago. As commercial agriculture replaced subsistence farming, the Midwest became the foremost producer of foodstuffs and animals, and the South focused on tobacco, sugar, and, especially, cotton. Over the sixty years that preceded the Civil War, Dixie remained overwhelmingly agricultural. In 1860, 80 percent of southerners toiled in agriculture, and more than 90 percent of the nation's manufactured goods were produced in the North and Midwest.[7]

During this period, the United States was an active and enthusiastic participant in what has come to be called globalization. US exports were valued at $52.5 million in 1815, $124.3 million in 1839, and $333.6 million in 1860. Significantly, the cotton trade was the largest subdivision of the global economy, and the proceeds from Dixie's exports of raw cotton were critical to US economic growth. Cotton accounted for 33 percent of the dollar value of all American exports in 1815, 57 percent in 1836, and 58 percent in 1860. These dollars then went toward the purchase of products from the North and Midwest and allowed the United States to maintain a favorable balance of trade.[8]

The two young attorneys also came of age amid dramatic political developments; by the 1830s, both had joined the Whig Party, which opposed President Andrew Jackson's Democratic Party. The Jacksonians feared that rapid industrialization and urbanization would render the new working class overly dependent on their employers and relegate them to city slums. To avoid such calamities, the Democrats advocated territorial expansion and enhanced foreign markets for US agricultural exports. New, cheap lands and ample markets would, they argued, enable self-employed working people to maintain their economic and political independence in a rural, agricultural setting. While pushing for territorial and commercial expansion, the Jacksonians favored a restrained federal government, which opposed concentrated wealth such as that invested in banks, stimulated "free trade" by implementing low tariffs, and refrained from building public projects such as roads, railroads, and canals.

The Whigs, who took their name from opposing "King" Andrew, were far less apprehensive regarding the industrial and urban segments of the exploding US economy and were far more inclined to take active, positive federal actions to promote those changes. Although the Whigs also favored aggressive economic expansion abroad, they were much less enamored of territorial growth, especially if that growth detracted from efforts to improve existing institutions and society or extended the institution of slavery. Instead, they endorsed banks, which they deemed necessary to a more sophisticated, diverse economy; a higher tariff to aid US manufacturing and enhance job opportunities for workers; internal improvements to provide the transportation and communication networks designed to bolster economic growth; and public education to improve the prospects for all Americans. Whig reform proclivities also derived from the evangelical religious movements that swept the nation by the 1820s. Evangelicals, who joined the Whigs, favored an activist state that opposed slavery and worked to combat sin by promoting reforms, such as prohibition and Sunday closing laws.[9]

According to the historian James McPherson, the "people who subscribed to these Whig-Republican principles tended to be those who had succeeded in the market economy, or aspired to." Seward and Lincoln met these criteria, and both gravitated toward politics at an early age and, ultimately, into the Whig Party. As was true of their social standing and legal careers, Seward's political ascent easily surpassed Lincoln's. The young New Yorker became politically active at the age of twenty-one when he moved to Auburn. After associations with Martin Van Buren's Albany Regency, which, by the end of the 1820s supported Jackson and opposed the National Republicans led by John Quincy Adams, Seward moved in 1829 to the Anti-Masonic Party, the most viable local opponent of the Regency. The anti-Mason movement originated in western New York in response to the mysterious disappearance of a former member of this secretive organization. The movement emphasized social equality, initiated political activities in 1827, and evolved into an institutional successor to the National Republicans.[10]

Beginning in 1830, Seward served two terms as an Anti-Mason in the state senate, where he endorsed the Second Bank of the United States, generally voted for railroad and canal projects, and supported public education for both boys and girls. Even more significant, he formed a lifelong political partnership with Thurlow Weed, a brilliant political operative and newspaper editor, whom Seward considered a "real wizard" in politics. The two first met in the early 1820s when the tall, muscular Weed helped the diminutive

Seward drag his carriage and its passengers from a muddy ravine. Subsequently, Seward helped finance Weed's *Albany Evening Journal* in 1830, and Weed oversaw all of his friend's election campaigns through the run for the presidency in 1860.[11]

During the winter of 1833–1834, Seward and Weed moved from the dying Anti-Masonic Party to the fledgling Whigs. After an unsuccessful run for governor as a Whig in 1834, Seward was elected to New York's highest office in 1838. Consistent with his Whig proclivities and service in the state senate, Seward oversaw the expansion of the Erie Canal and other internal improvement projects and lobbied successfully for improved, more accessible public education, especially in New York City. His attempt to enhance access to education incited nativist outrage when the governor suggested that some public funds might be directed to Catholic, largely immigrant parochial schools. This pro-immigrant stance would come back to haunt Seward politically in the 1850s.[12]

He also provoked great controversy, this time with southerners, by his responses to slavery-related issues. Henry, and even more strongly Frances, deemed slavery morally and politically evil. These sentiments were evident in his response to demands by the state of Virginia that three black seamen, who were New York citizens, be extradited to the Old Dominion for their alleged attempt to help a slave escape. Seward refused on the grounds that since slavery was illegal in New York, no crime had been committed. The governor also refused to return fugitive slaves to Dixie and denounced Secretary of State Daniel Webster for his handling of the *Creole* affair in 1842. Webster had criticized British authorities in the Bahamas for freeing slaves who had taken control of the ship and landed it in Nassau. In an assertion that foreshadowed his outspoken positions in the 1850s, Seward declared that no person could "by the force of any human constitution or laws be converted into chattel or a thing in which another being like himself can have property."[13]

Seward had also risen to national prominence and clashed with Webster over the trial of Alexander McLeod, a Canadian citizen. During a rebellion by some Canadian residents against British rule, British loyalists had crossed the US border and destroyed the *Caroline,* a ship being used by the rebels. McLeod was subsequently arrested in 1840 and charged with participation in the raid that burned the *Caroline* and resulted in the death of an American citizen. Webster sought to have the charges dropped to avoid disrupting Anglo-American relations. The secretary also aided McLeod's legal defense, but Seward stubbornly upheld the state's right to conduct the trial. The governor was prepared to pardon McLeod if he had been convicted, but the jury found the Canadian not guilty, allowing Seward to maintain his politically popular position uncompromised.[14]

Seward chose not to run for reelection to a third term in 1842. Against an ominous backdrop of divisions within the New York state Whig Party, persistent Democratic charges of Whig budgetary extravagance, and his staggering personal debts, Seward moved back to Auburn and his law practice. But he was hardly ready to leave the political fray permanently. Soon after departing Albany, he observed, "It is seldom that persons who enjoy intervals of public life are happy in their periods of seclusion"; and, as he remarked later, he could hardly be content "to go back to Auburn and amuse myself with writing history the rest of my life."[15]

Like Seward, Lincoln dove into politics as a young man when he ran for the Illinois state legislature in 1832 at the age of twenty-three. Despite the strong support of his New Salem neighbors, Lincoln's relative obscurity across the remainder of the district led to his defeat. By 1834, he had remedied that defect while working as a storekeeper, postmaster, and surveyor, and he was easily elected to the legislature as a member of the newly formed Whig Party. Lincoln was thereafter reelected in 1836, 1838, and 1840. Consistent with Seward and other Whigs across the nation, he favored the Second Bank of the United States (and Illinois State Bank), a protective tariff, and improved public education, and was an especially aggressive proponent of internal improvements—even when they nearly bankrupted the state. Over the course of these five campaigns and eight years in the legislature, Lincoln developed into a skilled stump speaker who never failed to highlight his humble origins and used humor, sarcasm, and engrossing storytelling to great advantage. Standing well over six feet, he also presented an impressive physical presence—albeit one with wild unkempt black hair and ill-fitting clothes. Notwithstanding his appearance, which persistently led others to underestimate him, Lincoln's intellect, political passion, and party loyalty earned the respect of Illinois Whigs, who made him the party's floor leader and chairman of the Finance Committee in just his second term.[16]

Lincoln's physical attributes, oratorical skills, and searing wit did not always redound to his credit. Although the crowd responded positively when he tossed a man "10 or 12 feet, Easily" whose fighting had interrupted his stump speech, two other incidents were much less satisfying. In 1840, his "skinning" or searing mockery of Jesse Thomas, a Springfield Democrat, was so harsh that Thomas fled the stage in tears. Lincoln later acknowledged his "deepest chagrin" over this event. He was equally ashamed of an anonymous letter he sent to the *Sangamo Journal* in 1842 attacking James Shields, the Democratic state auditor. The letter, together with another written by two of Lincoln's women friends, prompted Shields to challenge Lincoln to a duel. Lincoln, in turn, selected cavalry broadswords as the weapons—hardly a chivalrous choice by a man whose height and reach far exceeded those of his adversary. Although his friends intervened to settle the matter peacefully, Lincoln was exceedingly embarrassed by his shameful behavior.[17]

Lincoln's legislative service also occasioned his first public pronouncement on the increasingly controversial issue of slavery. In January 1837 he and six others voted against a resolution, which had seventy-seven supporters. The resolution upheld the South's "right of property in slaves" and asserted that the federal government did not have the power to abolish slavery in the District of Columbia. Lincoln and another Whig attorney from Springfield later entered into the House Journal a "protest against the passage" of the resolution. They declared that "the institution of slavery" was "founded in both injustice and bad policy," that Congress had the "power under the Constitution" to abolish slavery in D.C., but "that power" was to be "exercised" only at the "request" of District residents. This antislavery statement was neither as robust nor as nationally prominent as Seward's, but both men had proclaimed clear positions on the nation's most controversial and explosive issue.[18]

Like Seward, Lincoln declined to run for reelection in 1842, following his fourth term in the legislature. He had tired of leading the Whig minority and of Democratic abuse that linked the state's fiscal woes to his pet projects—the construction of roads, canals, and railroads. Just as Seward had become the most prominent New York Whig, Lincoln had risen from poverty and complete obscurity to the front rank of his Illinois party. Although he left public office, his intense ambition and commitment to politics were undiminished.

III.

As these two rising Whigs returned to their law practices, the United States began a decade of remarkable and consequential territorial expansion. Under the leadership of two southern presidents, John Tyler, a Virginia Democrat who masqueraded as a Whig, and James K. Polk, a Tennessee Democrat, the United States acquired Texas, the Oregon Territory, and the northern third of Mexico—acquisitions that totaled 1.2 million acres, including all or parts of the current states of Washington, Oregon, Idaho, Montana, California, Nevada, and Utah, and parts of Arizona, New Mexico, Colorado, and Wyoming. Reflecting long-held beliefs in American exceptionalism; political, moral, and racial superiority; and providential destiny to become a great nation and spread republican institutions, John L. O'Sullivan, the editor of the *Democratic Review,* endorsed the nation's "onward march" toward the "boundless future . . . of American greatness" and "the right of our manifest destiny to overspread and to possess the whole continent which providence has given us for the development of the great experiment of liberty and federalist self government."[19]

Tyler, Polk, and O'Sullivan embodied Democratic enthusiasm for the territorial expansion and free trade that were ostensibly needed to preserve an agricultural economy tied to world markets and populated by thriving, independent yeomen. The Whigs were far less enthralled with rapid territorial expansion, particularly if it required the use of military force or jeopardized national coherence. Rather than looking outward for national development and solutions to domestic problems, they contended that the United States should lead by example and advocated pacific territorial expansion instead of belligerent attacks on neighboring countries such as Mexico. Acting on these assumptions, Whigs endorsed the aggressive pursuit of markets for American products and negotiations with Great Britain to obtain Oregon but were apprehensive over the annexation of Texas and were highly critical of the patently aggressive war with Mexico.[20]

Seward and Lincoln faithfully advocated these Whig positions. True to the pattern of their previous careers, Seward remained a far more prominent political actor. Even as he condemned most of the Tyler-Polk foreign policies, Seward subscribed to much of the Manifest Destiny ideology. He declared in the mid-1840s that Americans were destined to march in "resistless waves to the icy barriers of the north, and to encounter Oriental civilization on the shores of the Pacific." The United States had been chosen, he asserted, to "renovate the condition of mankind" by spreading republicanism worldwide.[21]

Two considerations tempered Seward's seemingly open-ended aspirations: his opposition to expanding the United States through force directed at foreign adversaries and his mounting concern over extension of slavery into newly acquired territory. These considerations led him to endorse the peaceful Oregon settlement in a region devoid of slavery, but to decry the annexation of Texas and the "bastard war" with Mexico. As he campaigned for Henry Clay in the 1844 presidential election, he branded the Democrats the slavery party and warned that the acquisition of Texas would lead to war with Mexico, the potential addition of one to five slave states, and ever-greater demands from the South—demands, he warned correctly, that "will be made the ground for secession . . . and disunion." As war with Mexico loomed in 1846, he linked his distaste for slavery and the use of force: "I want no war. I want no enlargement of territory, sooner than it would come if we were contented with a 'masterly inactivity.' I abhor war, as I detest slavery. I would not give one human life for all the continent that remains to be *annexed*."[22]

To Seward's chagrin, more than seventeen thousand Americans and at least twenty-five thousand Mexicans were killed or wounded before the Mexican-American War ended in February 1848, with the United States acquiring over 529,000 square miles of Mexican territory. Following the war, Seward campaigned actively in New York, Massachusetts, Pennsylvania, and Ohio for the Whig presidential candidate, General Zachary Taylor. Ironically, Taylor, a Louisiana slaveholder, had become a viable Whig nominee based on his service in the war and the absence of any political record for the Democrats to attack. During the campaign, Seward sustained his outspoken antiwar positions. After he belabored the Democrats for promoting the "cause of Slavery . . . by war" and "the acquisition of useless territory by conquest," he voiced much more controversial positions. First, Seward condemned Ohio's Black Codes, which precluded African Americans from voting, serving on juries, or holding office. He then declared, "Slavery can be limited to its present bounds, . . . it *can* and *must* be abolished, and you and I can and must do it." Thurlow Weed worried that Seward's radical assertions on the war, black rights, and slavery had jeopardized his political future, but he was elected one of New York's US senators in 1849. The new senator's blunt rhetoric had not derailed his political career, but it attracted the attention of southerners, one of whom warned him, "If we ever find you in Georgia, you will forfeit your odious neck."[23]

While campaigning for Taylor, Seward met Abraham Lincoln for the first time when both addressed a great crowd of Whigs in Boston on September 21, 1848. As Seward was about to return to public life as a senator in March 1849, Lincoln was on the eve of concluding his one term as a Whig congressman. The two men, who would jointly oversee US foreign relations during the Civil War, did not meet again until October 1860, after Lincoln had defeated Seward in the contest for the Republican Party presidential nomination. After voluntary retirement from the Illinois legislature in 1842, Lincoln had failed in his pursuit of the Whig nomination for Congress in the state's Seventh District the following year. He thereafter convinced the party to rotate the nomination among its leading members. Profiting from this procedure, Lincoln aggressively pursued and successfully secured the Whig nomination in 1846 and essentially ignored slavery as an issue as he soundly defeated his Democratic opponent.

By the time he took office in December 1847, the Mexican-American War and slavery had moved to the forefront of American politics. During the second half of the 1850s and his presidency, Lincoln articulated a sophisticated, influential conception of the nation's international destiny and significance, the importance of its republican institutions, and slavery's burden on US foreign relations. But this worldview was largely unformed, or at least unstated, in the 1840s. Lincoln admitted that he had limited interest "in the Texas question" since he "never could very clearly see how the annexation would augment the evil of slavery." Unlike the majority of northern Whigs, the Illinois congressman was not convinced the war with Mexico had been "originated for the purpose of extending slave territory"; and, with his state at the "center of western pro-war fervor," declared that seizing some Mexican land was "a sort of necessity." Well into his two-year congressional term, he perceived slavery as a "distracting question" that diverted attention from Whig economic issues.[24]

Operating from these assumptions, the freshman legislator focused his critique of the war on President Polk's dubious contention that Mexico had initiated the conflict when its forces aggressively crossed the established border into US territory and attacked American soldiers. Lincoln disagreed. He deemed the war "*unnecessary*" since "Mexico was in no way molesting, or menacing" the United States and "*unconstitutional* because the power of levying war" resided with Congress, not the president. This conception of the commander in chief's powers would evolve significantly after he became the nation's chief executive. On December 22, 1847, and in a subsequent speech on January 3, 1848, Lincoln harshly criticized Polk's motives, veracity, and actions. In what critics labeled his "spotty" resolutions, he demanded "a full knowledge of all the facts . . . to establish whether the particular spot of soil on which the blood of our *citizens* was so shed, was, or was not, *our own soil*." He dismissed Polk's account as "sheerest deception" and described the president as "a bewildered, confounded, and miserably perplexed man" who felt "the blood of this war, like the blood of Abel . . . crying to Heaven against him." Lincoln's law partner, William Herndon, warned him that it was risky to criticize an American war in progress and worried that Lincoln had committed "political suicide," but the congressman refused to acquiesce in Polk's contention that "every silent vote given for supplies" equaled "an endorsement of the justice and wisdom of his conduct."[25]

Herndon's apprehension was prescient, as Illinois Democrats repeated the charge over the subsequent decade that Lincoln was a "Benedict Arnold" who had adopted a "traitorous course" by siding with the "enemy against his own country" and failing to support America's soldiers in the field, and the Whigs lost this seat in the next election. His political epitaph, critics predicted, would be: "Died of Spotted Fever." Lincoln, after he became president, acknowledged the political lesson when he agreed, only partly in jest, with another Whig's observation: "I opposed one war. That was enough for me. I am now perpetually in favor of war, pestilence and famine."[26]

As Lincoln completed his congressional term according to the rotation system he had devised, he campaigned for Zachary Taylor. He did so because he agreed with his Whig colleagues that Taylor was electable, not because the general stood for principles or issues that Lincoln had championed. The lanky, ill-kempt, midwesterner's signature speaking style was on full display in a July congressional speech in which he sarcastically assailed Lewis Cass, the Democratic nominee. In response to Democratic criticism of Taylor's nonexistent political record, Lincoln mocked Cass's service in the War of 1812 by comparing it to his own participation in the Black Hawk War of 1832. Lincoln informed other members of the House that he too was "a military hero": "Yes, sir; in the days of the Black Hawk war, I fought, bled, and came away." He continued, "Speaking of Gen. Cass' career, reminds me of my own." As at least his Whig colleagues laughed uproariously, he concluded, "If he saw any live, fighting Indians, it was more than I did; but I had a good many bloody struggles with musquetoes."[27]

Lincoln may have elicited momentary merriment in Congress, but there was little joy in the nation as the 1840s concluded. Instead, the issue of slavery's expansion into the New West evoked great consternation. From the beginning of the nineteenth century until the mid-1840s, US territorial annexations had facilitated the geographic expansion of slavery as an institution. Although this dynamic had been challenged in 1819–1820 with the debate over Missouri's entrance into the Union as a state, the resulting compromise allowed the nation to sidestep this explosive issue for the next quarter century. The Missouri Compromise balanced the incorporation of Missouri as a slave state with the simultaneous acceptance of Maine as a free, or nonslave, state. The agreement also stipulated that slavery would be excluded from the remainder of the Louisiana Purchase north of 36°30'. For the first time since the American Revolution, territorial expansion had threatened to come at Dixie's expense; and southerners emerged from this debate acutely sensitive to any negative reflections on the region's honor and to potential changes in the sectional balance of power in Congress, especially in the Senate.[28]

Both these concerns provided an ominous backdrop to US foreign relations, particularly the nation's imperial expansion at the expense of Native Americans and Mexicans, over the ensuing twenty-five years. These southern apprehensions came to the fore in August 1846 when David Wilmot, an obscure Pennsylvania Democratic congressman, offered a proviso stating that "neither slavery nor involuntary servitude" should be allowed in any territory acquired from Mexico. The proviso was not adopted, but the debate over its merits initiated the transition of the disagreement over territorial expansion from one primarily of Whigs versus Democrats to one between the North and South. Slavery was the core issue as the nation's most fundamental disagreement shifted ominously from parties to sections. The debate also prompted southerners to voice their longstanding fears. Senator John C. Calhoun from South Carolina warned that if deprived of the fruits of national expansion, the South would be left "a mere handful" of circumscribed states with their fate left "entirely . . . in the hands of the nonslaveholding States." And Georgia Whig Alexander Stephens rejected this "*insult* to the South," this "expression to the world" that Dixie warranted "public censure and national odium."[29]

Over the subsequent fourteen years, an "imperial competition between North and South" over control of the New West tore the nation asunder. Although the Compromise of 1850 ostensibly reinforced slavery by strengthening the Fugitive Slave Law, California entered the Union as a free state, and settlers in the Utah and New Mexico Territories were empowered to exercise "popular sovereignty" or to decide for themselves on the legality of slavery. Most observers assumed correctly that these settlers would opt to become free states. The South was similarly disappointed by the aftermath of the Kansas-Nebraska Act of 1854, which repealed the Missouri Compromise and its prohibition of slavery north of 36°30' in the Louisiana Purchase. What initially appeared to be the recognition of southern equality and an opportunity to expand slavery to the remaining areas of the New West turned into another disheartening defeat for the South. There followed political maneuvering in Washington and the newly formed territories of Kansas and Nebraska, outright warfare in Kansas, and the Supreme Court's Dred Scott decision, which ruled unconstitutional the Missouri Compromise and its restriction of slavery to areas south of 36°30'; but both Kansas and Nebraska voted to become free states. Much to Dixie's distress, US territorial expansion across the continent no longer strengthened and expanded the institution of slavery. Instead, the South's principal economic institution, political equality, and sense of honor were imperiled.[30]

Had these developments not raised sufficient alarm in the South, they were accompanied by the formation of the Republican Party in 1854–1855. Drawing primarily from northern Whigs, but also antislavery northern Democrats and former members of the American Party, an anti-immigrant coalition, the Republicans organized in response to the blatantly pro-southern Kansas-Nebraska Act and gained followers and influence as they reacted to the violence in Kansas and the Dred Scott decision. The nation's first purely northern party, the Republicans were dedicated to the containment of slavery to states and territories where it was legal in the mid-1850s and to denying its expansion into the New West. Those lands were to be reserved for free white as opposed to African American slave labor. The new party also adopted the Whig preference for an activist central government that favored a protective tariff, internal improvements, homestead legislation to help settle the New West with free labor, and national support for education—all federal policies popular in the North but not in the South. As Republicans worked energetically and effectively to block Dixie's expansion of slavery and proposed a domestic agenda long opposed in the South, southerners felt ever more endangered.[31]

With their access to the New West denied, southerners, especially those from the Deep South states of Alabama, Louisiana, and Mississippi, looked outside the United States for additional territory to offset northern gains. Their search, which focused on Cuba and Central America and included parts of Mexico, "increasingly took the form of imperialist military action" and was accompanied by calls to reopen the international slave trade. Over the course of the 1850s, southerners supported failed attempts to purchase Cuba or to seize it militarily through unauthorized filibustering expeditions conducted by private citizens. Dixie's residents were similarly disappointed by abortive filibustering efforts in Nicaragua. In 1858 Senator Albert G. Brown of Mississippi directly proclaimed Dixie's goal to expand slavery and the South's political power: "I want Cuba, and I know that sooner or later we must have it. . . . I want Tamaulipas, Potosi, and one or two other Mexican States; and I want them all for the same reason—for the planting or spreading of slavery." *DeBow's Review,* a New Orleans magazine, was even more ambitious, proclaiming, "We [the South] have a destiny to perform, 'a manifest destiny' over all Mexico, over South America, over the West Indies." Acquiring Cuba was equated to Britain's "march of conquest in India," to the "tendency of the age" to absorb "weaker Powers" and their "inferior races." Many southerners also asserted that reopening the slave trade was essential to counterbalance the flow of white European immigrants into the North and to provide the labor needed to develop any southern states added in the tropics.[32]

IV.

Amid these explosive developments in the 1850s, Seward and Lincoln followed similar paths: they prominently opposed these southern objectives, further developed their foreign policy perspectives, moved from the Whig to the Republican Party, and competed for their new party's presidential nomination in 1860. Each man undertook these actions with the conviction that the South had dominated the national government since the adoption of the Constitution in 1789. Southern slaveholders served as president for two-thirds of the seventy-two years until the Civil War began in 1861, with John Tyler "arguably . . . the most active proslavery president" in the antebellum period. During this same period, two-thirds of the Speakers of the House and twenty of the thirty-five members of the Supreme Court had been southerners. Southern justices always constituted a majority on the high court before 1861. John Quincy Adams complained as early as 1820 about "Southern domination which has swayed the Union for the last twenty years," and historian Don E. Fehrenbacher has asserted that "in the actual conduct of diplomacy from 1789 to 1861, the federal government habitually assumed the role of protector, and sometimes even as a vindicator, of slavery." Over the two decades immediately preceding the Civil War, southerners had conducted a "foreign policy of slavery" designed to further the interests of slaveholders within the United States and across the Western Hemisphere. This sustained regional influence also prompted Seward, Lincoln, and other northern Republicans to apprehend in the 1850s a "slave power conspiracy" dedicated to sustaining that domination.[33]

Upon taking his Senate seat as the decade began, Seward succeeded the recently deceased John Quincy Adams as the "outstanding political leader of the anti-slavery forces of the North" when he delivered two major speeches that addressed the proposed Compromise of 1850. The New Yorker endorsed the admission of California as a free state and opposed the expansion of slavery into the other territories of the New West since the peculiar institution was incompatible with "the security of natural rights, the diffusion of knowledge, and the freedom of industry." He argued further that the Constitution reserved the public domain "to union, to justice, to defense, to welfare and to liberty"; and, in an exceedingly controversial assertion, Seward declared that there existed an even "higher law than the Constitution" by which "the Creator of the Universe" set aside these lands for these same purposes.[34]

For the duration of the 1850s, Seward combatted the South's "challenge" to "the cause of freedom"; remained adamantly opposed to slavery's extension into the New West and the tropics; warned that a more politically powerful South would block free labor's access to the new territories and work to reopen the slave trade; cautioned that compromise with southerners was impossible since they would always increase their demands; and denounced the Democratic Party, whose strength and allegiance were located in the South. The feisty New Yorker cited the Dred Scott decision as evidence of the slave power conspiracy and denounced the "judicial usurpation" in which President James Buchanan had inappropriately influenced the court "to undermine the national legislature and the liberties of the people." In 1858 he declared the existence of an "irrepressible conflict" between "two radically different political systems." One was based on "slave labor" and the other on the "free labor of free men." The United States would, Seward contended, "become entirely either a slave-holding nation, or entirely a free-labor system." Although the senator envisioned a peaceful ending of slavery, both his "higher law" and "irrepressible conflict" speeches marked him as a comparatively radical opponent of the South and its institutions.[35]

Seward's opposition to slavery and its expansion did not mean that he considered African Americans the equal of whites. He had defended two black men accused of murder in a controversial New York case in the early 1840s; he and Frances covertly aided runaway slaves as they passed through Auburn on the "underground railway" to Canada; and he financially aided black antislavery activists Frederick Douglass and Harriet Tubman. All of these actions required moral and political courage and set him apart from the vast majority of northerners. He and Frances also employed black servants whom they treated with respect, and he believed that African Americans deserved the right to social and economic liberty and opportunity. Still, he deemed the "African race . . . incapable" of "assimilation and absorption" into the dominant white population and bound to "remain distinct . . . inferior masses." Seward could not conceive of an integrated society and readily relegated black welfare to a lower priority than that of whites or the nation.[36]

Just as Seward's antislavery views did not elevate blacks to equal standing with whites, his antislavery foreign policy perspectives did not limit his conception of international relations to circumscribing southern territorial, political, or economic growth. To the contrary, the future secretary of state had by the 1850s developed an elaborate and prescient conception of America's place in the world and its future international role. Voicing a fundamental assumption that he shared with Lincoln and that would help guide their policies in the 1860s, Seward declared that the United States should "take up the cross of republicanism and bear it before the nations." To "qualify" for this "mission" as a "living offense to . . . despotic powers elsewhere" and to fulfill its responsibility for "promoting liberty" at home and abroad, the United States had to meet clear moral standards. Only by "maintaining the democratic system of government" and containing and eventually eliminating slavery could the nation earn the right to pursue its noble calling. US moral standing was especially important since Seward stipulated that the United States should promote republicanism through the force of example and commerce rather than military might. As others were drawn to US institutions and trade by "a process of osmosis," there would follow the "ultimate regeneration and reunion of human society throughout the world."[37]

Seward, who fully grasped the significance of the evolving globalization of commerce and communication, declared the "real empire" was the "empire for the seas." Foreign trade and commerce would be "the chief agent" of US "advancement in civilization and enlargement of empire," since "political supremacy" would follow "commercial supremacy." Therefore, "as the United States became the strongest power in the world, and its influence promoted the spread of democratic institutions, its geographical limits would be steadily enlarged."[38]

If the United States were to dominate "the commerce of the world," Seward emphasized the need for national coherence—hence the need to end slavery—and the centrality of Whig domestic programs. A transcontinental railroad and other internal improvements to link the nation's sections, a protective tariff to stimulate manufacturing and job creation, a homestead act to promote the agricultural development of the New West, federal aid for education, and a liberal immigration policy were essential, since "the nation that draws the most materials and provisions from the earth, fabricates the most, and sells the most of productions and fabrics to foreign nations . . . will be, the great Power of the earth." Once fabricated or grown, the American products had to be transported abroad. To facilitate this, the New York senator called for an expanded merchant marine, backed federal funding for Cyrus West Field's transatlantic cable, and endorsed the Collins steamship line designed to promote trade with Europe, and proposed the acquisition of "even distant islands in either ocean."[39]

Although trade with Europe was crucial, Seward placed even greater emphasis on commerce with East Asia, the foremost "prize," the "chief theater of events in the world's great hereafter." By the 1850s, the senator perceived the United States as "a Power of the Pacific Ocean," as "practically the only real Power . . . that dwells upon the Pacific ocean." Therefore, a transcontinental railroad was vital to link the East and Midwest to the Pacific Coast; California's incorporation as a free state provided the essential ports and naval repair facilities on the Pacific; and US naval surveys should be conducted to ascertain the best sea routes to China and Japan. As the 1850s closed and the Civil War loomed, Seward was the most visionary proponent of US commercial expansion, a project to which he would return at the epic conflict's conclusion.[40]

While Seward solidified his prominent position in national politics during the early 1850s, Lincoln settled back into relative obscurity by practicing law in Springfield and Illinois's Eighth Judicial District. His political career seemed to have ended with the conclusion of his congressional term. From 1849 through 1853, he devoted the bulk of his time to his law practice, now shared with William Herndon. Still dogged by persistent depression and characterized by his haphazard, badly worn, and ill-fitting wardrobe, Lincoln continued his regimen of self-education by mastering Euclid's geometry. Although he declined overtures to run again for Congress or for governor in Democratic-dominated Illinois, he still longed for a role in public life and explained that longing to Herndon: "How hard, oh, how hard it is to die and leave one's country no better than if one had never lived for it!" As if in preparation for an escape from this exile from public life, Lincoln subscribed to and voraciously read major Whig papers, such as the Washington *National Intelligencer* and *Chicago Tribune,* together with several abolitionist and even southern papers.[41]

The passage of the Kansas-Nebraska Act in 1854 provided the occasion for Lincoln's escape. By repealing the Missouri Compromise and delegating the question of slavery in the territories to the "decision of the people residing therein," or to popular sovereignty, this measure raised the specter of slavery's expansion into the New West and set off a national political revolution that led to the formation of the Republican Party during 1854–1855. The prospect of slavery's extension into the territories spurred Lincoln's return to public life. He also felt compelled to challenge Senator Stephen Douglas, the leader of Illinois's Democratic Party, who had long been the bête noire of the state's Whigs and had sponsored the Kansas-Nebraska law. Indeed, Lincoln's confrontations with Douglas, a major political player nationally, were the key to his rise to national prominence during the second half of the decade.[42]

On October 4, 1854, in the hall of the Illinois House of Representatives in Springfield, Lincoln responded directly to Douglas and to the threat of slavery's expansion via the Kansas-Nebraska Act. In this speech, he acknowledged the legality of slavery in the South but adamantly opposed its "EXTENSION" to any other US territories. This was a change from his previous emphasis on Whig economic issues to a concentration on the peculiar institution. Lincoln based his opposition to "the spread of slavery" on its "monstrous injustice." "No man," he asserted, was "good enough to govern another man, *without that other's consent.*" This was the "leading principle—the sheet anchor of American republicanism." And, in a perceptive insight that would continue to inform his foreign policy perspective as president, Lincoln noted that slavery "deprives our republican example of its just influence in the world—enables the enemies of free institutions, with plausibility, to taunt us as hypocrites."[43]

Based on this and numerous similar speeches he delivered in the fall of

1854, Lincoln was once again elected to the Illinois legislature and emerged as one of the primary contenders for a US Senate seat to be determined in February 1855. Since the anti-Nebraska forces had carried the legislature and were poised to elect one of their own, rather than a Douglas Democrat, Lincoln promptly resigned his newly won legislative seat to avoid the Illinois constitutional prohibition against sitting legislators being chosen as a US senator. When the unyielding opposition of several former Democrats to the election of a Whig dashed his hopes, Lincoln threw his decisive support behind Lyman Trumbull. Although exceedingly disappointed, Lincoln had made a most successful return to public life. By early 1856, he moved to the Republican Party and, the following June, received the second-highest number of votes for the new party's vice-presidential nominee. This was "validation" of his standing as "a national Republican leader," and he solidified that standing by delivering more than fifty speeches on behalf of John C. Fremont, the unsuccessful Republican presidential candidate.[44]

When neither Lincoln's speeches nor other Republican efforts forestalled Democrat James Buchanan's election, Lincoln joined Seward and other Republicans in denouncing the Dred Scott decision and the new administration's proslavery actions in Kansas. As he prepared for another run for the US Senate, Lincoln delivered "the most important address of his political career" to the Republican state convention on June 16, 1858. He admitted the difficulty of proving a slave-power conspiracy but declared, "We find it impossible to not *believe*" that Douglas, President Buchanan, former President Franklin Pierce, and Chief Justice Roger Taney "all understood one another from the beginning, and all worked upon a common *plan*." Lincoln warned that the Taney Supreme Court might soon make slavery "lawful everywhere," in the New West and even the North, that Illinois could become "a *slave* State." And, in language he had used often since 1855, he declared that "a house divided against itself cannot stand," that the United States "government" could not "endure permanently, half *slave* and half *free*." Lincoln did not "expect the Union to be *dissolved*" or the "house to *fall*," but he did foresee that it would "cease to be divided." "Either the *opponents* of slavery" would "arrest the further spread of it," and put it on "the course of ultimate extinction" or it would become a national institution. Reminiscent of Seward's "irrepressible conflict" speech, Lincoln's imagery of a house divided, half slave and half free, attracted widespread press attention but did not cause northern antislavery figures to view him as a radical.[45]

The Illinois Republican convention's enthusiastic nomination of Lincoln as the party's Senate candidate led to his celebrated debates with the Democratic incumbent, Stephen Douglas. The seven direct confrontations, during which the two candidates shared the stage and aggressively lambasted one another, drew crowds ranging from four to twenty thousand. Douglas claimed that Lincoln was a "Black Republican" whose radical views threatened to disrupt the Union; that he favored African American equality with whites; and that he opposed any territorial acquisitions "unless slavery therein shall be forever prohibited." Given Douglas's previous support for proslavery filibusterers such as William Walker in Nicaragua and his calls for the annexation of Cuba, the senator's last charge clearly addressed territorial expansion and the extension of slavery into both the New West and the tropics.[46]

While addressing the territorial question, Lincoln reiterated his claim that Douglas had participated in the slave-power conspiracy with Buchanan and Taney to nullify the Missouri Compromise. Lincoln also maintained his unbending opposition to the extension of slavery into either the New West or any tropical areas south of the United States—a fundamental and decisive foreign policy position that he would sustain through the secession crisis in April 1861. He rejected annexing Cuba with its 1.5 million slaves and predicted that Douglas's pro-southern policies would lead to "a grab for the territory of poor Mexico, an invasion of the rich islands of South America, then the adjoining islands will follow, each one of which promises additional slave fields" and greater southern political power. These acquisitions would further inflame the controversy over slavery and thereby endanger national unity.[47]

Lincoln, like Seward, inflexibly opposed any westward continental expansion or additional territorial acquisitions that would bolster the institution of slavery and southern political power, but he also subscribed to the belief that the United States was an exceptional republican nation destined for great international influence. In 1856 Lincoln told a Michigan audience, "We are a great empire. We are eighty years old . . . the wonder . . . of the whole world" because of American "prosperity"—a condition based on the opportunity for "every man" to "make himself." Three years later, he trumpeted the nation's "immancipation [*sic*] of thought, and the consequent advancement of civilization and the arts," a process he perceived to be moving westward and occurring most readily in a "new country" like the United States. Lincoln located much of the US opportunity for individual achievement and collective economic and cultural advancement in the New American West. Therefore, his opposition to slavery's expansion into the territories, like his determination to keep these areas open for "*free white people everywhere,*" was a "*western* as well as an *antislavery* position." Richard Etulain has written that Lincoln was an "expansionist of another kind," who, as president, would further the imperial process of US westward expansion by supporting homestead legislation, a transcontinental railroad, land grant colleges, and Indian removal. Although Lincoln's expansionist vision did not rival Seward's, he agreed that national coherence was essential for the United States to fulfill its destiny as a powerful, creative republican country and to become a model for the international community. Lincoln would not have perceived westward expansion in imperial terms, but its impact on American Indians foreshadowed the US colonial system imposed on Hawaiians, Filipinos, and Puerto Ricans at the turn of the twentieth century.[48]

Although Lincoln's racial attitudes toward Indians would play an important role in his decisions regarding westward expansion in the 1860s, his immediate challenge was to respond to Senator Douglas's race-baiting charges. Douglas asserted that Lincoln believed blacks had been "created equal," favored African American "citizenship" and "social equality" with white "wives and daughters," and threatened the "inalienable rights of the white men." These accusations put the Republican candidate on the defensive and forced him to elucidate his positions on race. Lincoln, like Seward, did not consider blacks the equal of whites "in color, size, intellect, moral development, or social capacity," and he did not intend "to bring about social and political equality" between the races. Lincoln similarly rejected any policy "making voters or jurors of negroes, nor of qualifying them to hold office, nor to intermarry." Even so, again like Seward, Lincoln's racial attitudes were far more advanced than the great majority of contemporary American whites, including Douglas. He argued that African Americans were entitled to the rights of "life, liberty, and the pursuit of happiness," as enumerated in the Declaration of Independence, and the "right to eat the bread . . . which his own hand earns." The Republican candidate also rebuked Douglas by condemning slavery's immorality and situating it as part of the "eternal struggle between . . . right and wrong." Douglas, who made apologies for slavery and ostensibly advocated its expansion, was on the wrong side of this struggle, on the side of "tyrannical principle" versus the "common right of humanity."[49]

Despite his comparatively laudable racial views, Lincoln agreed with the "universal feeling" among white Americans that black inferiority and "physical differences" would "probably forever forbid" the two races from "living together upon the footing of perfect equality." This led him to favor colonization of free blacks to Liberia and, later in the 1860s, to Latin America. Dispatching African Americans abroad ostensibly offered a way to restore "a captive people to their long-lost father-land" and to allow whites to avoid having to live with a despised minority. Even as he endorsed this preferred outcome in the mid-1850s, Lincoln recognized its limited utility. Neither the necessary funding nor ships existed to implement the plan, and virtually no blacks wanted to return to Africa. Seeming to ignore such realities, Lincoln resurrected this fanciful scheme after he became president.[50]

V.

Although Lincoln had more than held his own against the formidable Douglas in the debates and campaign, the Little Giant's Democratic followers prevailed in the legislature by 54 to 46. After they voted to reelect the senator, Lincoln correctly described the outcome as "*a slip and not a fall*" for his political career. The battle with Douglas made Lincoln into a national figure; and soon after the election, papers from Illinois and Ohio began to endorse his nomination as the Republican candidate for president in 1860. To become the Republican standard bearer, he would have to defeat Seward, the acknowledged frontrunner.[51]

Lincoln recognized that defeating the energetic and accomplished New Yorker posed a daunting challenge. Before the 1858 senatorial campaign, he asked an old friend, "What's the use of talking of me for the Presidency whilst . . . such men as Seward, [Salmon P.] Chase, and others are so much better known to the people? . . . Nobody, scarcely, outside Illinois, knows me." Lincoln had achieved much greater national prominence by battling Douglas, even if that prominence fell far short of Seward's standing. To bolster that public standing, Lincoln traveled more than four thousand miles in 1859 and delivered twenty-three speeches in Ohio, Wisconsin, Illinois, Iowa, and Kansas Territory. In February 1860 he spoke at Cooper Union in New York City at the invitation of New Yorkers who sought an alternative to Seward, and he followed this well-received and much-discussed appearance with invited speeches in New Hampshire, Rhode Island, and Connecticut. In these talks and extensive personal correspondence, Lincoln maintained his adamant opposition to the expansion of slavery, while endeavoring to claim a moderate middle ground between the ostensibly more radical Seward and Chase and the clearly more conservative Edward Bates. With an emphasis on his humble origins, he lauded the merits of the free labor system and carefully avoided offending former Know Nothing Party nativists on the issue of immigration. He complemented this shrewd messaging by deftly maneuvering to maintain the unity and support of the Republican Party in Illinois and to have the Republican national convention held in Chicago.[52]

In stark contrast to Lincoln's vigorous and effective actions, an overconfident Seward spent the final eight months of 1859 on a leisurely tour of Europe and the Middle East. His time in Britain, France, Belgium, the Netherlands, Austria, Italy, and Egypt enhanced his qualifications to be secretary of state but did nothing to bolster his presidential candidacy. At Weed's suggestion, Seward had left the country to avoid any misstep that might jeopardize the nomination they felt sure would be forthcoming. A friend agreed with this strategy, assuring Seward that "everything looks well now for 1860, and as no mistake will be made next winter, I feel as if the thing [nomination] was pretty much finished." Upon his return, Seward delivered a much-lauded Senate address designed to counter the lingering charges of radicalism derived from his "higher law" and "irrepressible conflict" speeches, but his nomination was far from secure.[53]

To the contrary, Lincoln and his Illinois followers dashed Seward's hopes. Acknowledging Seward as the clear favorite, Lincoln's strategy was "to give no offense to others" and to become everyone's second choice. His representatives at the national convention executed this strategy to perfection. They jammed the galleries of the convention hall with thousands of boisterous partisans, who were often admitted on counterfeit tickets, and seated other crucial state delegations near the Illinois contingent. Led by Illinois District Judge David Davis, they also disregarded Lincoln's direction to "make no contracts that will bind me" and, instead, made promises of patronage to Pennsylvania, Indiana, New Jersey, and probably to Missouri and Maryland. Davis and the Illinois operatives had outmaneuvered the legendary Weed with these backroom deals. Asked if he had "prevaricated somewhat" when he denied having made such deals, Davis responded, "PREVARICATED? . . . We lied, lied like hell."[54]

Perhaps even more important than these promises was the perception that Lincoln was more electable than Seward—that he was more likely to carry the essential states of Pennsylvania, Illinois, Indiana, and Ohio. According to historian William E. Gienapp, "His selection was purely a triumph of availability." Lincoln was viewed as more moderate on slavery, had not offended former Know Nothings on immigration, was a solid supporter of traditional Whig economic issues, and was well-known and respected among midwesterners in the key battleground states. After Seward led on the first ballot, these cumulative considerations produced a stampede to Lincoln on the third. The Lincoln strategy had worked beautifully. The man who had begun life in such humble circumstances, had lived on the edge of poverty for many years, had virtually no formal education, and had held office beyond Illinois for only two years—a record consistently less impressive than that of William Henry Seward—had moved to the forefront of his party and would soon be elected president.[55]

Seward was devastated. Even as he accepted his place in Lincoln's cabinet several months later, he graphically revealed the depth of his anguish: "Disappointment!" he blurted out to a startled congressman, "You speak to me of disappointment. To me, who was justly entitled to the Republican nomination for the presidency, and who had to stand aside and see it given to a little Illinois lawyer." But, after briefly declining to campaign on Lincoln's behalf, Seward made crucial contributions to the Republican victory. He remained intensely ambitious and committed to public life, assumed correctly he would be offered a position in Lincoln's cabinet, and expected to play an important, even dominant, role in the new administration. Acting from these motives, Seward embarked on an arduous, month-long speaking tour that took him from New York to Detroit, Milwaukee, St. Paul, Dubuque, St. Louis, and finally Chicago. Upon his return to Auburn, he and Weed helped carry their vital home state. In total, he had "campaigned for Lincoln in fifteen different states and territories," and, according to one historian, "in the final weeks of the campaign," did "more than any other man" to ensure the Republican victory.[56]

That victory was realized when Lincoln carried all the northern states, save New Jersey. In essence, Lincoln had run against Douglas and the northern wing of the Democratic Party in the North, where his 1.8 million votes equaled 54 percent of the regional total and translated into 180 electoral votes—which surpassed those garnered by all other candidates and earned his election. Lincoln prevailed in no southern states, where a parallel election featured a southern Democratic Party led by John C. Breckenridge and the

Constitutional Union Party, which nominated John Bell. Breckenridge, who represented the dominant southern position that slavery had to be expanded into and legally guaranteed in the New West, won the electorally irrelevant contest in Dixie.[57]

By winning the presidency with no southern votes, Lincoln and the exclusively northern Republican Party threatened the South's well-being. According to historian Matthew Karp, "With men like Lincoln and Seward in power, slavery's greatest champion . . . the United States, had abruptly switched sides." Given the Republicans' unyielding opposition to the extension of slavery into the New West or the tropics and the party's pro-northern economic policies, southerners concluded that their political, economic, and social equality; their material interests; and their personal and sectional honor were no longer safe within the Union. The *Richmond Enquirer* declared representatively, "the Northern people, by a sectional vote, have elected a President for the avowed purpose of aggression on Southern rights." Lincoln's election constituted "*a declaration of war.*" A New Orleans paper added that the election's outcome was "*a deliberate, cold-blooded insult and outrage*" to Dixie's honor. Alabama congressman Jabez L. M. Curry pronounced that "the [political] bond of brotherhood between the North and South" had been "broken," and claimed southerners were being "stigmatized and *pilloried* and reduced to inferiority" over their "possession of slave property." These perceptions led South Carolina to vote on December 20, 1860, to secede from the Union; and the other Lower South states of Mississippi, Florida, Alabama, Georgia, Louisiana, and Texas followed suit over the next forty days.[58]

From the secessionists' vantage point, Lincoln was a "*foreign* tyrant," and the South could not "submit to the government of a foreign and hostile people" and in essence become "part of the great Northern Empire." This widely shared perception, and the founding of the Confederate States of America during the first week of February 1861, rendered the secession crisis the Lincoln administration's first foreign policy challenge. Several key assumptions guided the president-elect as he confronted this challenge. Most fundamentally, he was determined to preserve national unity and the nation's republican experiment. Secession was the "essence of anarchy"; if minority rule were to prevail over a fairly expressed majority voice in the 1860 election, then what he would later call "the last best hope of earth" would be destroyed. Fully cognizant of previous southern domination of the federal government and Dixie's relentless pursuit of new slave territories, Lincoln rejected any compromise of the Republican platform's opposition to the expansion of slavery into the New West or the tropics. He feared "the same old trick by which the South breaks down every Northern victory." If he, the Republican Party, and the North were to "surrender" to southern threats of secession, it would be "the end of us, and of the government." Dixie would simply "repeat the experiment upon us. . . . A year will not pass, till we shall have to take Cuba as a condition upon which they will stay in the Union." The new president would not "*pay* for being inaugurated" or allow the "Republican party [to] become a mere sucked egg, all shell and no principle in it" by conceding to southern demands. The issue of national finances reinforced Lincoln's determination to preserve the Union. Successful southern departure from the United States would preclude the collection of customs duties in southern ports and threaten national solvency by diverting this vital source of US income.[59]

Lincoln's misreading of the strength of secessionist sentiment in the South buttressed his refusal to compromise. Although he believed his Kentucky background gave him insight into the South's attitudes, responses in his native border state diverged greatly from those in the Lower South and even from Upper South states such as Virginia and North Carolina. Moreover, Lincoln had no close personal associations with any politicians from the Deep South. In August 1860 he had opined, "People of the South have too much of good sense, and good temper, to attempt the ruin of the government." Three months later, he continued to doubt that "the Disunionists can work their people up to the point of consummating their threatened treason." Apprehensive that his public statements would further provoke southern unrest or cause divisions among Republicans, Lincoln essentially withheld public comment from the time of his election until his inaugural address on March 4, 1861. He tried to reassure Dixie that he had no intention of attacking slavery where it currently existed, but went no further in addressing the mounting crisis.[60]

Behind the scenes, he was far less conciliatory. Through an extensive private correspondence, Lincoln rejected all compromise proposals that expanded slavery's territorial reach. On December 18, Senator John J. Crittenden, a Kentucky Whig, proposed the most prominent and potentially acceptable of the propositions floated over the secession winter. Crittenden suggested six permanent Constitutional amendments; the central one would have reinstituted the old Missouri Compromise line through all remaining US territories to the Pacific Ocean. Slavery would have been prohibited north of 36°30' but protected south of this line in all US land "now held, or hereafter acquired." In short, slavery could expand not just across the continental United States, but also into any areas of the tropics subsequently annexed. John Breckenridge immediately cited the "hereafter" clause as "vital" to the South, which could not "afford to be shut off from all possibility of tropical expansion." Focusing on this same clause, Lincoln flatly rejected the Crittenden Compromise. It would, he advised other Republicans, encourage "filibustering and extending slavery," "put us again on the high-road to a slave empire," and "lose us every thing we gained by the election."[61]

As Seward and most contemporaries expected, Lincoln asked the New Yorker to serve as secretary of state. The president extended the invitation in early December, Seward accepted at the end of the month, and Thurlow Weed announced the appointment in the *Albany Evening Journal* on January 9, 1861. Consistent with his public statements during the 1840s and 1850s, the incoming secretary of state completely agreed with Lincoln's belief that the success of the US experiment in republican government carried great historical and international significance—that the "hopes of the world" rode on the preservation of the Union and its practice of self-government. Preservation of the Union was also vital to national security and to the realization of Seward's vision of commercial empire and international influence. If the United States were subdivided into two smaller, competing countries, he feared they would "like Italy, Turkey, India, and China, become the theatre of transatlantic intervention and rapacity." Ongoing rivalry between the two American nations might also lead to the "surrender of liberty" in favor of the ostensible protection provided by "military despotism." Any smaller, less politically, economically, and militarily coherent and powerful nation would be far less likely to become the commercial and political juggernaut he envisioned.[62]

Seward concurred with Lincoln on the need to preserve the union and its republican form of government, but he disagreed with the president-elect on three other critical issues. First, Seward and Weed believed the senator's greater public standing and political experience compared to Lincoln's would naturally make the secretary of state the "premier," with decisive authority in the new administration. By April 1, Seward would be disabused of this erroneous assumption. Second, Seward, based on much greater personal experience with southern political leaders, deemed their threat of secession entirely credible rather than a strategic bluff. Third, given this assessment, Seward was much more inclined than Lincoln to compromise, even on the issue of slavery in the territories. He based this inclination on his belief that compromise could buy essential time and convince Upper South states, especially Virginia, North Carolina, and Tennessee, to remain in the Union and thereby defeat the Lower South's secession project. But, just as Lincoln had underestimated the commitment of secessionists in the Lower South, Seward overestimated the strength of unionism in the crucial Upper South states.[63]

During the four months between Lincoln's election in November 1860 and the Confederate attack on Fort Sumter in the Charleston Harbor on April 12, 1861, Seward advocated a conciliatory policy. In mid-November he advised Republicans to demonstrate "magnanimity" toward the South; in late December he portrayed the secession crisis as a "family" quarrel and predicted that sixty days of patient restraint would produce "a more cheerful atmosphere." Although Weed publicly endorsed the extension of the Missouri Compromise line and Seward may have privately agreed, he adhered to Lincoln's instructions and voted against the Crittenden Compromise in the Senate. Still, he continued to pursue his strategy of forestalling the nation's complete division through an appeal to Upper South unionism. This approach and his presumption in seeming to speak for the new administration were apparent in his much-discussed speech to the US Senate on January 12, 1861. In this talk, which Seward failed to clear with Lincoln in advance, he proposed several steps intended to placate the South. They included the repeal of northern laws designed to prevent the pursuit of runaway slaves; a constitutional amendment forbidding future congressional interference with slavery in the South; the admission of Kansas as a free state; and the organization of the remaining New West into two states. Most listeners assumed that this division would allow New Mexico to enter the Union as a slave state, which was contrary to Lincoln's absolute opposition to slavery's expansion into the remaining US territories.[64]

Lincoln, who was "not overpleased with Seward's speech," had a mixed response to the self-styled premier's January 27 letter. Seward urged the president-elect to be "forebearing and patient" and to compose a "wise and winning" inaugural address. While seeking to capture that tone, Lincoln ultimately accepted several of Seward's suggested amendments designed to soften the inaugural address. In a direct response to Seward's letter, Lincoln advised that he cared "little" about the issues of fugitive slaves, slavery in the District of Columbia, and other matters that arose "of necessity from the fact that the institution is amongst us." He even seemed to agree with Seward's New Mexico proposal. The president did not "care much about New Mexico, if further extension [of slavery] were hedged against." But, Lincoln's "inflexible" stance "on the territorial question, that is, the question of extending slavery under the national auspices," and especially to areas "hereafter acquired" negated this momentary and private flexibility regarding the desert Southwest.[65]

Undeterred, Seward continued to assume that as the "leader of the ruling party" he would dominate the administration and that his policy of reconciliation and patience would appeal to unionism in the Upper South and defuse the secession crisis. Both assumptions were apparent in his seven pages and forty-nine specific suggested amendments to the draft of Lincoln's inaugural address and his sudden resignation as secretary of state on March 2. The latter was intended to help force Lincoln to moderate his speech and to keep the president from appointing Salmon P. Chase, a former Democrat and more radical antislavery figure, as Secretary of the Treasury. Although Lincoln accepted a number of Seward's suggestions to soften the speech's tone, he rejected the New Yorker's attempt to dictate the composition of the cabinet. Lincoln explained to his private secretary that he could not "afford to let Seward take the first trick." But he also wanted to retain Seward at State and quietly persuaded him to withdraw his resignation.[66]

With Lincoln's inauguration, the president and his cabinet turned their attention to Fort Sumter, which was under siege in the Charleston, South Carolina, harbor. In his inaugural address, Lincoln had pledged to "hold, occupy and possess" all federal property. In two cabinet meetings on March 9 and 29, the president and his advisers debated whether to reprovision the fort, which was being threatened by southern soldiers and was rapidly running out of supplies, or to evacuate and surrender the fort to the Confederacy. During both meetings, Seward argued for evacuation on the grounds that attempted resupply would incite armed conflict and nullify his conciliatory policy. As these deliberations progressed, the secretary also promoted his policy of appealing to southern unionism by communicating with Stephen Douglas, Crittenden, and a broad array of southern politicians, including Jefferson Davis. Seward informed these southerners and the New York press that Fort Sumter would be surrendered.[67]

These assurances proved to be unauthorized and incorrect when Lincoln announced at the March 29 cabinet meeting that he would resupply Sumter. Several considerations prompted his decision. The president declared that relinquishing the fort could prompt European diplomatic recognition of the Confederacy. Recognition and the possible material and military aid that might follow would have been "utterly ruinous." Lincoln's decision also responded to the majority of the Republican Party that opposed any further appeasement of the South and reflected the US need to retain control of southern ports and their customs revenues. Finally, the president had come to doubt that turning over the fort would either induce the Upper South to remain in the Union or the Lower South to return to the fold.[68]

Lincoln's ultimate responses to the administration's first foreign policy crisis flatly rebuffed Seward's policy advice. Unreconciled to either the rejection of his faith in southern unionism or his presumed role as premier with dominant power in the new administration, Seward responded in a decidedly unwise manner. On March 31 he composed a long memorandum titled "Some Thoughts for the President's Consideration," which his son delivered to Lincoln on April 1. He declared correctly that after a month the administration was essentially "without a policy either domestic or foreign." He acknowledged that unavoidable attention to the distribution of offices and the special session of the Senate explained this policy vacuum but asserted that a host of pressing issues demanded attention. Seward reiterated his arguments for the surrender of Sumter, advocated the defense and retention of all other US "forts in the Gulf [of Mexico]," and endorsed the recall of the US Navy "from foreign stations to be prepared for a blockade" of the southern coast. He contended that removing Sumter, a partisan political issue, from public view and concentrating on these other installations would convert the question before the nation from "*one upon slavery*" to the issue of "*Union or Disunion*" and the spirit of patriotism. Save the evacuation of Fort Sumter, these proposals were all subsequently adopted.[69]

In a further effort to change the national conversation to one of patriotic loyalty and to appeal to southern unionism, Seward also recommended that the United States demand explanations from Spain regarding its recent intervention in San Domingo and from France for its cooperation with Spain in the latter's potential interference in Haiti. If satisfactory responses were not forthcoming, Congress should be summoned to declare war on these two countries. Seward also wanted to request similar explanation from Great Britain and Russia regarding their prospective policies if civil war were to ensue between the Union and Confederacy. Were these collective suggestions not sufficiently provocative, the secretary concluded his April 1 memorandum by exhorting Lincoln to act more energetically: "Either the President must do it himself . . . or devolve it on some member of the Cabinet. . . . It is not my especial province. But I neither seek to evade nor assume responsibility."[70]

Seward was correct, as many other contemporaries observed, in his assertion that the administration had gotten off to a slow, somewhat ill-defined start. In addition to the matters the secretary noted, Lincoln was feeling his way as a first-time executive grappling with a host of complex issues. However, the secretary erred on his other main points. His final effort to secure the surrender of Fort Sumter failed when Lincoln sustained his decision for resupply and, in so doing, adroitly forced the South to fire the first shots of the war. By calculating that a foreign crisis would have reunited the United States, Seward badly misjudged the strength of southern unionism in both the Upper and Lower South. His stern warnings to Europeans who contemplated some form of intervention in the American conflict would prove more effective; but an unintended foreign war would have gone far toward insuring Confederate success and southern independence—a realization on which Lincoln and Seward based their foreign policy throughout the Civil War.

Despite the inflammatory language in his April 1 memorandum, Seward sought a "foreign crisis" rather than a foreign war. He understood the contemporary international environment too well and was far too opposed to war as an instrument of foreign policy to have thought otherwise. Still, both his language and envisioned crisis were reckless and would not have restored the Union. To the contrary, major problems with one or more European countries would have proved a major distraction for the North and a potential boon for the South on both the political and military fronts. Finally, the secretary's suggestion that Lincoln surrender control of his administration was misguided and mistaken.[71]

In his response to Seward's memorandum, Lincoln effectively took the second, and ultimately the decisive, trick in their relationship. Two days after Seward submitted his March 2 resignation, William Cabell Rives of Virginia met with Lincoln. Based on this meeting, Rives concluded that the new president had "been misjudged and misunderstood by the Southern people" who deemed him "incapable of independent judgment" and "willing to be used as a tool by more able men." "This is all wrong," the veteran Virginia politician declared. “He will be the head of his administration, and he will do his own thinking.” Lincoln confirmed this assessment in his deft handling of Seward’s latest presumptuous power play. The president quickly drafted a counter statement, but never sent it, preferring instead to meet privately with his secretary of state. Lincoln contested Seward’s portrayal of a policy vacuum and refused to alter his no-compromise policy on territorial expansion or his unwillingness to bow to southern pressure at Fort Sumter. Both the effort at resupply and the war followed. Finally, Lincoln bluntly reasserted his control over the administration by informing Seward that if a different policy were needed, “I must do it.” When Seward accepted Lincoln’s primary authority, the crucial partnership for the management of US foreign policy was cemented, as was the identity of the senior partner.[72]

2

THE FIRST PERILOUS YEAR, 1861

I.

As the Civil War loomed ever more likely in early March 1861, President Lincoln attended a dinner party at the Washington home of Rudolph Schleiden, minister of the German city-state of Bremen. In response to questions regarding prospective US foreign policy, Lincoln declared, "I don't know anything about diplomacy," and continued, "I will be very apt to make blunders." Later in June, the president advised John Lothrop Motley, who was about to assume his duties as US minister to Austria, on how best to influence administration foreign policy: "It does not so much signify what I think, you must persuade Seward to think as you do." Lincoln stated as much to Seward, asserting, "I shall have to depend upon you for taking care of these matters of foreign affairs, of which I know so little, and with which I reckon you are familiar."[1]

Lincoln's self-deprecating remarks suggesting that Secretary of State Seward would be given relatively unrestrained control over the North's foreign policy were misleading. Lincoln has been appropriately described as "an innate and consummate diplomatist," and the nation's chief executive exercised critical, and ultimately decisive, control over Union foreign relations. The president had signaled his definitive, senior partner role when he rejected Seward's inclination to compromise on the expansion of slavery into the territories and quashed the secretary's April 1 memo and its foreign war panacea. Assured that "Seward knows I am his master," Lincoln reasserted his senior status in this foreign policy partnership at critical junctures over the ensuing four years. Still, the Lincoln-Seward working relationship was very

2. William Henry Seward. Courtesy of the Library of Congress.

much a partnership, to which the well-traveled, cosmopolitan, and politically savvy Seward made indispensable contributions as he handled day-to-day foreign policy administration, offered the president thoughtful counsel on domestic and foreign policies, skillfully situated foreign policy within a highly charged domestic political context, and effectively exploited European anxieties and balance of power concerns.[2]

That Lincoln and Seward became "useful friends" and worked in "close harmony" was hardly a foregone conclusion, given their vastly disparate personal backgrounds, their previous political rivalry, their fundamental policy disagreements during the secession winter, and Mary Todd Lincoln's intense dislike of the secretary of state, whom she derided as a "hypocrite" and a "dirty abolitionist sneak" who sought to claim credit for all administration successes. At first glance, the two appeared to be a classic, incompatible odd couple: the tall, ungainly, self-taught, humble, often self-effacing, ostensibly provincial midwesterner who neither smoked nor drank and had virtually no experience navigating Washington's political and foreign policy milieu versus the college-educated, well-traveled, cosmopolitan, vain, transparently ambitious, hyperactive five feet six inch New Yorker who consumed significant quantities of cigars, brandy, and wine, swore with great gusto, and delighted in hosting and attending lavish dinner parties.[3]

Upon closer examination, the president and secretary of state had much in common, and many of their personal differences proved more complementary than conflicting. Most important, they shared a sense of US nationalism and destiny that envisioned the United States as the world's foremost exemplar of political democracy and representative government. They further agreed that preserving the Union was essential to fulfilling that US destiny and duty to mankind. Only a powerful, united North American nation could successfully conduct the republican experiment and fend off potential European interventions.

By the time they assumed office in 1861, both men had difficult relationships with their wives. Tortured by the death of two sons, intensely ambitious for her husband's career and legacy, and exceedingly uncomfortable in Washington society, Mary Lincoln was dubbed the "Hellcat" by a White House secretary and was known to have attacked Abraham with broomsticks and books. Frances Seward, like Mary Lincoln, was an intelligent and educated woman, who by 1860 had become a committed prohibitionist and abolitionist—neither of which aligned with Henry's inclinations. Even more fundamentally, she found Washington society dreadfully boring and, from the 1850s on, suffered from bouts of depression. During the Lincoln presidency, she lived at the family home in Auburn, New York, visited Washington only occasionally, and left all hostess duties in D.C. to their daughter, Fanny.[4]

On a much lighter note, neither Lincoln nor Seward paid careful or systematic attention to their habitually ill-fitting clothes or often rumpled hair, and both thoroughly enjoyed a good joke or story. Once, as the two rode in a mule-drawn wagon along a rough road, the driver began to swear excessively at the balky animals, which prompted Lincoln to ask if the man was an Episcopalian. The driver replied, "I ain't much of anything," but when attending services, "I go to the Methodist Church." The president then observed, "I thought you must be an Episcopalian for you swear just like Secretary Seward, and he's a churchwarden."[5]

Seward loved the joke and had Lincoln-related anecdotes of his own. A visitor to the State Department recalled being regaled by the secretary who said the president had recently cautioned him not to let a story "be smutty," which prompted Seward to respond in precisely that fashion. He described a witness, who when asked in court if "you know this man?" had replied, "Why, I know him. I can't say I have carnal knowledge of him."[6]

Complementing this appreciation for storytelling and humor were the two men's ability to recognize one another's strengths and the importance of these attributes to achieving their shared objectives, their evolving and genuine personal fondness for one another, their strict personal honesty, their refusal to hold grudges, and their pleasure in discussing American history and past presidents' leadership qualities. Lincoln frequently walked across Lafayette Square from the White House to Seward's home, where the two talked late into the night. The president, who virtually never swore, found his friend's profanity-laced diatribes amusing, the secretary's hospitality relaxing, and the energetic, optimistic New Yorker's company a refreshing antidote to his own proclivity for intense self-reflection and depression and the burden of the war's daily carnage. Just as Lincoln came to value Seward's position as the most loyal and dependable member of his often-fractious cabinet, the secretary's estimate of his chief's abilities steadily increased. By mid-May, Seward judged Lincoln's "magnanimity . . . almost superhuman"; and, the following month, he declared, "Executive skill and vigor are rare qualities. The President is the best of us; but he needs constant and assiduous cooperation." During the war's first year, these shared personal qualities and the press of official business led Lincoln to spend more time with Seward than with any other public official or even the members of his own family—a practice that no doubt contributed to Mary Lincoln's loathing of the secretary of state.[7]

As Lincoln and Seward initiated their personal friendship and official partnership, they confronted southern secession and, with it, the nation's most serious foreign policy crisis since Great Britain had acknowledged US independence in 1783. When the shots rang out at Fort Sumter, the

North possessed seemingly insurmountable advantages in population, fiscal resources, and manufacturing capacity. The United States had twice as many people and railroad mileage, three times as much bank capital, and ten times as many manufactures. Northern industrial workers outnumbered southern laborers by 1.3 million to 110,000 and produced thirteen times as much cotton and woolen cloth, thirty times as many boots and shoes, twenty-four times as many railroad locomotives, and thirty-two times as many firearms.[8]

But the stronger side does not always win wars. America had prevailed against the British just eighty years earlier; and a century later, the United States, easily the strongest military power in world history, failed to defeat North Vietnam and the National Liberation Front in South Vietnam. Most civil wars, like the one that ensued between the North and South from 1861 to 1865, have attracted outside interventions, and those interventions have frequently been essential to the weaker side's victory. Without French aid, the United States could not have gained its independence from Great Britain; and without help from the Soviet Union and the People's Republic of China, Hanoi and the NLF could not have survived their confrontation with the United States.[9]

Forestalling such outside intervention in the American Civil War became Lincoln and Seward's principal foreign policy objective, and this crucial dimension of northern statecraft has led historian Howard Jones to assert that the conflict's outcome "rested as much on foreign affairs as it did on the battlefield." Great Britain, the world's most powerful nation, led by Prime Minister Henry John Temple, 3rd Viscount Palmerston, and Foreign Secretary Lord John Russell, received the bulk of the North's foreign policy attention. These two veteran statesmen presided over a tenuous and unstable Liberal Party majority in Parliament from 1859 through 1865. Their strong antislavery views and distrust of France and its leader, Emperor Napoleon III; Britain's nearly $440 million of investments and lucrative export markets in the United States; and Canada's strategic vulnerability reinforced the caution required to navigate the British domestic political situation.[10]

Other considerations prompted these English leaders to ponder intervention in the American maelstrom. Neither held American democracy in high regard, and they took some pleasure in the developments that produced what Palmerston termed the "Disunited States of North America." Moreover, as the war ground on, both came to doubt that the North could subdue the South, were appalled by the human suffering, and grew anxious over the impact of the dwindling supply of the South's raw cotton on the British economy. But these concerns arose later, and the pressures for caution and nonintervention held sway as the war began. Russell advised Parliament, "For God's sake, let us if possible, keep out of it!" Lord Palmerston, whose guiding foreign policy assumption was the pursuit of British national interest rather than "chivalrous enterprises," completely agreed—since, "They who in quarrels interpose, will often get a bloody nose."[11]

British restraint was fortunate for the North since Napoleon hoped to take advantage of the American Civil War to further much more aggressive and intrusive French interests in the Western Hemisphere. Napoleon "could not forget the overbearing insolence of the United States government in its days of prosperity" and, according to a French exile, sought "to weaken or destroy Democracy in the United States" and have that "vast republic disappear from the face of the earth." In addition to his desire for the demise of US democratic government, Napoleon believed the conflict offered an opportunity to implement his "Grand Design for the Americas," which included a French-sponsored monarchy in Mexico, a resurgence of the Catholic church, and a vastly expanded French commercial presence in the Western Hemisphere.[12]

Although the emperor faced far fewer popular constraints than Palmerston and Russell, he was not completely free to pursue this ambitious, pro-Confederate foreign policy. Most important, he had, since the mid-1850s, linked his foreign policy to cooperation with Britain and never dared to act independently regarding the American war. Ironically, his previous, ill-advised military adventures in Africa and Asia, and a mutual jealousy and suspicion of Britain, reinforced Napoleon's refusal to act on his anti-Union inclinations. He was further constrained by the divided nature of the French press and public opinion on the war, the interests of those segments of the French economy that profited from the conflict, far more pressing geopolitical issues in Europe, and the strictly neutral position of his Foreign Minister, Edouard Thouvenel, who favored cooperation with the British and opposed any clearly pro-southern French intervention.[13]

The leaders of Great Britain and France acted primarily upon these ideological, economic, and geopolitical considerations, but there was also a significant personal dimension to the first year of Civil War diplomacy. This facet of US-European relations derived from the European leaders' and diplomats' assessments of and interactions with Lincoln and Seward. These assessments, which materially influenced how British and French leaders and diplomatic representatives responded to the conflict, were often badly flawed. Although European misperceptions resulted in part from a lack of understanding of US domestic politics and their own elite, often condescending biases regarding American democratic government, faulty evaluations of these two complex Americans were hardly confined to foreigners. Lincoln's law partner, William Herndon, pronounced his old friend "a profound mystery—an enigma—a sphinx—a riddle," and Seward admitted, "I am an enigma even to myself."[14]

Like so many of Lincoln's fellow Americans, Europeans badly underestimated the new president's abilities. In April 1861 Lord Lyons, the British minister in Washington, informed Palmerston and Russell that the president "has not hitherto given proof of . . . any natural talents to compensate for his ignorance of everything but Illinois village politics." France's minister to the United States, Henri Mercier, agreed with this negative assessment. Mercier formed a "very poor opinion of Mr. Lincoln," whom he deemed obviously ill prepared to "play the leading role" to which he had been called. The president, Mercier opined patronizingly, was "one of those American types," with "energy and strong will," but who lacked the "qualities of mind" needed for real "character." Even Eduard de Stoeckl, who represented Russia, the one consistently pro-Union European nation, judged that Lincoln lacked the "capacity" or "talent and energy" that Republicans attributed to him."[15]

While these critically placed Europeans were dismissive of Lincoln, they expressed outright hostility and apprehension toward Seward. Lyons, with whom Seward had the most direct contact, could detect "little or no understanding in Mr. Seward" of the "power of the Great Countries of Europe" or of Washington's need "of conciliating" those nations. Instead, the "insolent" Seward sought to "excite the American mob" against the European powers. Lyons worried that the secretary of state might seek to provoke a foreign war as a means to reunite the United States, to advance his "personal ambition . . . to succeed Mr. Lincoln" as president, or to attempt to annex Canada as compensation for the South's departure from the Union. Mercier, a monarchist at heart with significant sympathy for the Confederacy, rendered a more severe evaluation. Seward, he contended, was "nothing but one of those demagogues who can sail only on the sea of popular emotion and who always try to stir up passion in order to exploit it." Stoeckl concurred and contended that Seward exhibited "complete ignorance of all that . . . concerns international relations."[16]

Russell and Palmerston shared Lyons's apprehension that Seward might seek to provoke tensions with Great Britain, and the foreign secretary warned that the impulsive secretary of state "must not be allowed to get us into a quarrel." Palmerston was more caustic. The prime minister castigated Seward as a "vapouring, blustering, ignorant Man" guilty of "foolish and uncalculating arrogance." When Palmerston told Queen Victoria that the United States was "not guided by reasonable men," he considered the secretary of state his primary example.[17]

Seward bore some responsibility for these negative assessments. The secretary loved to talk and to drink, and, at times, after significant quantities of wine or brandy, he talked too much or too loosely. One of these occasions had arisen in November 1860 when Seward spoke with the Duke of Newcastle at an Albany, New York, dinner party honoring the Prince of Wales. The stunned duke thereafter widely circulated the story that the future secretary of state had assured the Englishman that he would "take the first opportunity . . . to insult your country." Seward subsequently disputed this account, but the damage was done. In early January 1861 Lyons had reinforced Newcastle's impression when he warned Lord Russell that the secretary of state designee would be "a dangerous Foreign Minister . . . who would play the old game of seeking popularity at home by displaying violence toward us."[18]

Nearly three months later, Seward seemed to substantiate Newcastle's report and the British minister's prediction with a boisterous display at another dinner party. Against the tense backdrop of the Lincoln cabinet's debates over the reinforcement of Fort Sumter and rumors that Britain and France were leaning toward the diplomatic recognition of the Confederacy, Seward lost his temper, became "violent and noisy," and screamed at Lyons, Mercier, and Stoeckl that any such recognition would "mean war" with the United States and that the "whole world" would "be engulfed." Shortly thereafter, the secretary hosted William Howard Russell, the *Times* of London's Washington correspondent for dinner. The reporter, like his fellow countrymen, was appalled at the secretary's "arrogance and menace" and his threat that any European government that "received" Confederate diplomats would "risk . . . breaking off relations" with the United States.[19]

British noblemen, diplomats, and reporters were not the only contemporaries to portray Seward as hostile and irrational. Republican Senator Charles Sumner of Massachusetts aggressively propagated the same negative images to his wide circle of English friends, including Lord Lyons and John Bright.

A far more radical antislavery figure than Seward, Sumner had opposed any compromise with the South. By flirting with the Crittenden Compromise proposal and offering reassuring overtures to southern politicians, Seward had incited Sumner's boundless and self-righteous wrath. An expert in international law and an Anglophile with extensive English contacts, the Massachusetts senator had aspired to become secretary of state or US minister to London—only to see those positions filled by Seward and Charles Francis Adams, whom Seward had championed. From his position as chairman of the Senate Committee on Foreign Relations, and armed with additional information provided by Adam Gurowski, a clerk and translator in the State Department, Sumner repeatedly told his British friends that Seward planned "to force the country [US] into a foreign war." He further derided the secretary as an "evil influence" who was "not frank and straightforward; only a cunning contriver of little plots; and not a true man."[20]

II.

Lincoln had reason to share Sumner's concerns when he received Seward's inflammatory April 1 memorandum, "Some Thoughts for the President's Consideration." This paper, a call to intentionally provoke a foreign crisis by challenging British, French, and Spanish actions, was devised as an appeal to southern unionism and a strategy to head off secession. It was also grounded in legitimate foreign policy considerations. By late March, Lyons had threatened that US interference with international commerce would likely draw "the Powers of Europe into the quarrel," and the British minister suggested that his government's initial step might be to "recognize the Southern Confederacy." Seward also knew that Mercier had recommended joint French-British diplomatic recognition of the South based on his conviction that the North could not prevail and the imminent war's prospective damage to the French economy.[21]

Were these threats not sufficiently alarming, Lincoln and Seward received reports that Britain and France were outfitting major naval fleets destined for use in the Western Hemisphere; that those countries were contemplating a joint protectorate over Mexico; and that Spain was preparing to reestablish its imperial control over Santo Domingo. The latter scheme came to fruition on March 23 when Spanish troops sailed from Cuba to annex the former colony. At the cost of more than five hundred military deaths and another seven thousand to disease, the Spanish occupation failed miserably by 1865; but, in the spring of 1861, only the ominous, and perhaps precedent-setting, fact of European intervention was evident to Lincoln and Seward. Both feared that the Spanish colonial action would be the first of many—that, as the Boston *Daily Journal* apprehended, it marked "The Gathering of the Vultures," since the "terror of the American name is gone, and the Powers of the Old World are flocking to the feast from which the scream of our eagle has hitherto scared them."[22]

This confluence of foreign policy threats had helped prompt Seward's April 1 memorandum with its call for stern warnings, even threats of war, directed toward the European powers and the secretary's belligerent admonitions to Lyons, Mercier, and W. H. Russell from January through mid-April. These warnings and others to follow derived from more than a tongue loosened by too many glasses of wine. To the contrary, the New Yorker was, according to one observer, "a precious foxy old man" who told "no one his secrets." The secretary of state was consciously practicing a form of "brinkmanship" designed to forestall European imperial interventions in the Western Hemisphere and to block European inclinations to extend diplomatic recognition and material aid to the Confederacy. By threatening to break diplomatic relations or even resort to force, he hoped to elicit caution and restraint in London and Paris and thereby secure essential time for the Union to initiate its foreign and military policies. Although Lincoln had wisely vetoed Seward's plan for direct, official threats, the secretary's verbal pyrotechnics had hit home among British and French diplomats and policymakers—all of whom worried that an irrational, untutored, unpredictable, overly political Seward might involve them in an unwanted war with the North.[23]

Seward's bark was primarily calculated and certainly much harsher than his ultimate bite. He confessed as much to both the US minister in London, Charles Francis Adams, and to Lord Lyons. In July Seward instructed Adams, "You could do no greater harm, than by inducing an opinion that I am less decided in my intercourse with the British Minister than I am reputed to be or less determined to maintain the pride and dignity of our Government." Soon thereafter, the secretary privately assured Lyons that he "had used strong language in his earlier communications to Foreign Powers . . . from the necessity of making them clearly understand the state of Public Feeling here." As had been the case with the April memorandum, Seward's shrill warnings to the British and French and his publication of some of his dispatches had both foreign and domestic objectives. The secretary clearly understood the administration's need not only to block foreign interventions but also to maintain popular support for the administration at home. He explained that "the first business of a statesman and Minister here is to keep the confidence of his own countrymen," and he had taken "violent" foreign policy stands "to keep myself in the good graces of public opinion" and thereby "remain in office and stave off the radicals" within the Republican Party.[24]

Lincoln and Seward's decision to emphasize the preservation of the Union rather than the abolition of slavery during the war's first year complicated both this "first business" at home and the conduct of diplomacy abroad. Although decidedly antislavery, neither Lincoln nor Seward was an abolitionist, and both believed that preserving the Union took precedence over all other objectives. Both had opposed the expansion of slavery but had pledged not to interfere with the institution where it existed legally in the southern and border states. Lincoln had reiterated this pledge in his inaugural address; he stressed that he had no intention "directly or indirectly, to interfere with the institution of slavery in the States where it exists" and declared that he had "no lawful right" and "no inclination to do so." Seward had thereafter instructed Minister Adams in London to avoid discussion of "opposing moral principles" related to slavery since the institution's "condition . . . in the several States will remain just the same" regardless of the war's outcome.[25]

Several other compelling considerations reinforced Lincoln's belief in 1861 that he lacked the constitutional authority to abolish slavery where it legally existed. He recognized that making the abolition of slavery the war's justification threatened to undermine public support in the North. Large numbers of Democrats and other antiblack northerners would object to sacrificing themselves to liberate slaves. The president was also convinced that a focus on slavery would jeopardize the North's tenuous hold on public and military support in the border states. To explain his emphasis on preserving the Union rather than promoting black emancipation, Lincoln asserted, "To lose Kentucky is nearly . . . to lose the whole game. Kentucky gone, we can not hold Missouri, nor, as I think, Maryland. These all against us, and the job on our hands is too large for us. We would as well consent to separation at once, including the surrender of the capitol."[26]

Emphasizing preservation of the Union rather than the question of slavery may have helped retain the allegiance of many northern Democrats and the border states, but it caused serious discord among Republicans. More radical members of the party castigated the Lincoln-Seward position. A Connecticut Republican raged, "*Damn* the border states. . . . A thousand Lincolns cannot stop the people from fighting slavery"; and Sumner groused that it was "vain to have the power of a god" and "not to use it godlike." Others attributed the "honest" Lincoln's misguided policy to the fact that "he listens overmuch to Seward."[27]

Antislavery northern diplomats added their voices to this critical chorus. From Spain, Carl Schurz declared that the US failure to accentuate slavery had "stripped our cause of its peculiar moral force" and misled Europeans into thinking that the war simply pitted southerners who sought to become "free and independent" against northerners who "insisted on subjugating and ruling them." Schurz was convinced that "as soon as the war becomes distinctly one for and against slavery," European opinion would turn "overwhelmingly in our favor." Henry S. Sanford, the US minister to Belgium, agreed and advocated "AN ANTISLAVERY CRUSADE IN ENGLAND," as did Cassius M. Clay, who represented the North in St. Petersburg and insisted on "a higher tone of principle—*Liberty for ourselves—Liberty for the slave,* in all the *rebel states.*"[28]

Although Radical Republicans and these US diplomats failed to alter the Lincoln-Seward policy priority during 1861, they were correct to suggest that the focus on the Union confused Europeans and enabled the Confederacy to define the "terms of debate by emphasizing its desire for national self-determination and free trade—not slavery—as motives for secession." Initial responses among both policymakers and the majority of the public in Great Britain and France had posited slavery as the cause of the war and had sided with the North. When Lincoln and Seward insisted that preserving the Union took precedence over abolishing slavery, these European observers moved on to assess the political-constitutional question of whether the South had a right to peacefully pursue its independence and to evaluate the war's potential economic impact on neutral nations. By the fall of 1861, Lord Russell lamented that Lincoln's slavery position had muddied the diplomatic waters; and the president and secretary of state were puzzled when Europeans seemed unable or unwilling to acknowledge the seemingly obvious reality that the morality and fate of slavery constituted the fundamental differences between the North and South.[29]

The British foreign secretary's exasperation intensified after April 19 when Lincoln declared the US intention to blockade Confederate ports. In so doing, the president acted on his as yet ill-defined authority as "commander in chief of the army and navy in time of war . . . to take any measure" best suited for subduing the enemy "in time of war." When queried about the measure's constitutionality, Lincoln asked, "Was it possible to lose the nation, and yet preserve the constitution?" And answered, "By general law life *and* limb must be protected; yet often a limb must be amputated to save a life; but a life is never wisely given to save a limb. I felt that measures, otherwise unconstitutional, might become lawful, by becoming indispensable to the preservation of the constitution, through preservation of the nation." Citing the commander in chief's authority in wartime proved valid for domestic purposes, but the assumption of a war's existence was also required for the blockade to meet international legal standards. By proclaiming a blockade and, by implication, a state of war, Lincoln and Seward contradicted their contention that the conflict was purely a domestic matter into which foreign nations could not properly intrude. In short, the American leaders sought to employ the blockade, a tool of war, without admitting the war's existence.[30]

Neither Great Britain nor France was prepared to accept this contradictory position and its threat for their citizens and commerce. Both nations genuinely sought to avoid military involvement and dreaded the possibility that privateers, or ships licensed by the North or South, might attack neutral shipping. To avoid such complications and to establish official and legal neutrality in what was clearly an actual foreign war, Great Britain issued a Declaration of Neutrality on May 13. France followed suit on June 10. Lord Russell argued appropriately that the British declaration simply acknowledged an obvious war, as had Lincoln's call for a blockade. The British declaration extended recognition to both the North and South as "belligerents" in the war and invoked Great Britain's Foreign Enlistment Act of 1819. The latter forbade British citizens from enlisting in the service of either belligerent or "fitting out or equipping" vessels for use in the war. Although not an official part of the declaration, Britain also prohibited privateers and any captured ships or materiel from entering its ports. Slightly less than a month later, France issued a similar declaration that recognized the Confederates as belligerents, proclaimed strict neutrality between the two sides, and instituted comparable restrictions on its citizens and privateers.[31]

By proclaiming a state of war, Britain and France rejected the Lincoln administration's claim that the conflict was a purely domestic disturbance and therefore beyond those nations' purview. British and French recognition of both the North and South as belligerents conferred an equal legal status on the Confederacy and raised the prospect of progression to the next step of full diplomatic recognition and, with it, confirmation of the South's legal standing as an independent nation on the international stage. This recognition would have enabled the South to negotiate treaties, forge geopolitical and military alliances, and contract loans. That level of recognition, Don H. Doyle has asserted, "quite likely meant independence for the South."[32]

The British declaration outraged Seward and northerners generally. Issued the day before US minister Charles Francis Adams arrived in Great Britain, the measure was condemned as not just hasty and unwarranted by developments in America, but also intentionally mean-spirited. Even more disturbing to the secretary of state, it appeared to be the first step toward the South's full diplomatic recognition. While jubilant Confederates greeted the declaration with similar expectations, the British and French actions ultimately proved much more beneficial to the North. They recognized the legitimacy of the still-tenuous Union blockade, which, to be considered legal, had to be interpreted as actually effective rather than just a "paper" proclamation. In addition, British and French neutrality and evenhanded treatment of the two American foes greatly favored the North, given its vast superiority in population, fiscal resources, manufacturing capacity, and military equipment. Finally, as R. J. M. Blackett has demonstrated, once Britain's Palmerston-Russell government had opted for neutrality, Confederate diplomats and sympathizers faced a daunting and ultimately impossible challenge to mount the public pressure or demonstrate the geopolitical or military rationales necessary to force a policy alteration in favor of the South.[33]

As Seward agonized over the possibility of European diplomatic recognition of the Confederacy, he learned that both British and French foreign ministers had met with Confederate diplomatic representatives—Lord Russell with William Lowndes Yancey and A. Dudley Mann on May 3 and 9 in London and Thouvenel with Pierre A. Rost in early June in Paris. The secretary's initial outburst when informed of the Confederate meetings with Russell, "God damn them, I'll give them hell," applied equally to the French policymakers. Both Russell and Thouvenel had termed the meetings "unofficial," refused to accept the Confederate commissioners' credentials, and emphasized their nations' neutrality. Even had he known this in mid-May, Seward would not have been appeased.[34]

Instead, he was outraged and determined to do something "bold and decisive." On May 21, the secretary drafted Dispatch No. 10, which instructed Minister Adams to end all communications with the British government if Russell held further interviews with Yancey and Mann. Were the British to harbor Confederate privateers, the United States would respond with "an adequate and proper remedy." And, British diplomatic recognition of the South ensured that the United States and Great Britain would "cease to be friends" and immediately become "enemies."[35]

As was his practice with important diplomatic correspondence, Seward provided President Lincoln a copy of this dispatch. Consistent with his response to Seward's "Some Thoughts for the President's Consideration," Lincoln softened the language and directed that Adams use the dispatch as a guide, rather than reading the document verbatim to the foreign secretary. The president's intercession reflected his "acute political intelligence" and firm "grasp of strategic interests" and embodied one of his "several well-judged presidential interventions in foreign affairs." Still, it is important to note that Lincoln wisely sought to modify the tenor, not the substance, of Seward's firm warning against European interference in the American War. The two leaders agreed on the essentials of Union foreign policy.[36]

Seward accepted the most significant, but not all, of the president's amendments. Most important, he removed the strong language regarding the United States and Britain becoming enemies and consented to Adams's use of the dispatch as a guide for his discussions with Russell. The secretary subsequently informed Thouvenel that any additional official or unofficial French interactions with Confederate representatives would be "injurious to the dignity and honor of the United States" and, by extending the war, would help to "overthrow" the US government. The secretary further authorized US minister to France, William L. Dayton, to read the blunt admonitions in Dispatch No. 10 to the French foreign minister.[37]

Even the sanitized version of this dispatch shocked Adams in London. The New Englander had great respect for Seward but feared that his boss was "almost ready to declare war with all the powers of Europe." To clash with Great Britain would, Adams recognized, be "like throwing the game into the hands of the enemy." Fortunately for the Union cause, Adams acted much as Lincoln had intended; he skillfully conveyed Seward's essential message and eliminated the "sharp edges." This diplomatic task was facilitated by the near-immediate respect that emerged between Adams and Lord Russell—a respect that served the North well for the remainder of the war. Both of these short, stout, balding men were austere and formal, cared little for society or small talk, and were inclined instead to directness, honesty, and a calm, dispassionate manner. These qualities, together with their stubborn defense of their respective nations, fostered mutual regard and esteem. In mid-June, Russell confided to the British minister in Paris, "I like Adams very much, though we did not understand one another at first."[38]

President Lincoln and Minister Adams had dampened Seward's bluster, but the secretary remained indignant that Britain and France had acknowledged Confederate belligerence and was determined to have his forthright warnings heard in London and Paris. This was evident on June 15 when Ministers Lyons and Mercier arrived at the State Department to jointly reiterate that their nations were neutral and determined to protect their citizens and commerce. To forestall such European cooperation, which he deemed collusion, and perhaps to divide the two Great Powers, Seward refused to meet officially with the two of them. Instead, he accepted their written diplomatic communications separately and unofficially and stressed that he would receive no "communication founded on the assumption that the Southern rebels were to be regarded as belligerents."[39]

When combined with Seward's similarly ominous statements over the previous six months, the incident left these veteran diplomats, as well as their superiors in Europe, apprehensive. They feared the secretary might yet provoke a dangerous diplomatic crisis or even war for domestic political purposes or out of the misguided hope of reuniting the nation against a foreign adversary. Their resulting caution and determination not to be drawn into the American conflict validated Seward's overall policy of brinksmanship and calculated belligerence. Still, brinksmanship carried costs: the British responded with a show of strength and dispatched additional soldiers and weapons to Canada, and ongoing British-French anxiety increased the possibility of diplomatic or military miscalculation by either the United States or the Europeans.[40]

III.

Miscalculations were most likely to occur in the realm of US and Confederate naval operations. The controversy in May 1861 over the *Peerless,* a steamer reportedly purchased in Canada by Confederate agents for use as a privateer, was symptomatic. Seward requested through Lord Lyons that the governor general of Canada detain the ship. When Lyons refused, the secretary of state, with Lincoln's approval, warned the British minister that the United States would seize the vessel rather than allow it to attack US shipping. Seward also dispatched a covert agent into Canada to clarify the status of the *Peerless* and to obstruct Confederate acquisition of the ship. Seward's threat to seize the vessel and his use of an ostensibly secret agent enraged Lyons, who complained bitterly to Russell and Palmerston. The secretary of state's actions were consistent with his unyielding warnings against outside interference in the American war, and they contributed to the Canadian governor general's decision to detain the *Peerless* until it was clear the ship was not being converted into a privateer.[41]

Seward's *Peerless* policy was not limited to threats and the use of a spy in a neighboring, neutral country. As was true of his more general demeanor by early summer, the secretary's interactions with the British also included a more moderate, reassuring dimension in which he denied any "feeling of hostility against the government of Great Britain" and pledged to insure "full satisfaction" for Britain and other "parties aggrieved" by any unwarranted seizure of the ship. This moderate, less harsh tone, save on the issue of potential British and French recognition of the Confederacy, typified Seward's diplomacy by midsummer, especially regarding the far more explosive issue of the Union blockade of southern ports.[42]

Lincoln's decision, at Seward's behest, to blockade southern ports was a central facet of northern military strategy. It was designed to limit Dixie's exports and deny the South access to crucial resources, such as arms, munitions, and manufactured goods. The blockade prompted British and French recognition of the war's existence and the Confederacy's legal status as a belligerent. Thereafter, these countries nervously waited to see how the measure would be implemented. Seward argued, and Lincoln agreed, that the blockade should be proclaimed and enforced in accordance with the 1856 Declaration of Paris, which embodied accepted international law. Most important, for the blockade to be situated in this international legal context, it had to effectively thwart access to southern ports rather than present an ineffective, "paper" blockade."[43]

In addition to ensuring that the blockade was appropriately announced and instituted consistent with international law, Seward successfully opposed the efforts of Secretary of the Navy Gideon Welles and his congressional allies, led by Senator Sumner, to force adoption of an alternative means of enforcement. Welles's Navy Department report and its rapid adoption by Congress in early June authorized Lincoln to close southern ports as a domestic legal step and to collect customs duties offshore, if necessary, without establishing a formal blockade. Lyons and Mercier vigorously protested, and Russell and Palmerston agreed that closing a port by congressional edict constituted a paper, and therefore illegal, blockade that could lead to British and French military intervention. Having recognized a state of war, Britain and France could not simultaneously accept this declared US domestic legal authority over southern ports.[44]

Lincoln and Seward fully understood the port-closing bill's dangerous implications. The president signed the bill into law but accepted Seward's advice to remain silent regarding its enforcement. Seward, in turn, instructed Adams to inform Foreign Secretary Russell that the United States did not envision adopting the Welles approach, showed these instructions to Lyons, and conveyed the same message to the British minister verbally. Although not yet fully convinced of Seward's rationality or moderation, the stuffy English diplomat acknowledged that the secretary of state had demonstrated a "prudent and pacific mood" and deduced that Seward had blocked Welles's more inflammatory option.[45]

As Seward adopted his more cooperative, less belligerent posture, Lincoln initiated his brilliant commentary on the war's historical and international significance, and, in so doing, appealed to champions of republican government worldwide. Demonstrating his "profound sense of history," the president had declared in his inaugural address that the impending war's "central idea" was to prove that "popular government" was "not an absurdity." Were a southern "minority" allowed "to break up the government whenever they choose," it would "go far to prove the incapability of the people to govern themselves." In May the president accentuated the conflict's "deep import" in a letter to fellow republicans in San Marino, Italy. "It involves," Lincoln pronounced, "the question whether a Representative republic, extended and aggrandized so much as to be safe against foreign enemies can save itself from the dangers of domestic faction."[46]

The president was even more compelling in his July 4 address to Congress, when he declared that the conflict's importance involved "more than the fate of these United States." The "whole family of man" was waiting to see "whether a constitutional republic, or a democracy—a government of the people, by the same people can, or cannot, maintain its territorial integrity, against its own domestic foes." More than political democracy was at stake since the Union sought to maintain "in the world, that form, and substance, of government, whose leading object" was "to elevate the condition of men—to lift artificial weights from all shoulders . . . to afford all, an unfettered start, and a fair chance, in the race of life." Tellingly, amid this inspiring rhetoric, Lincoln made no reference to slavery; instead, he adhered to his and Seward's official position that the war's primary objective was to preserve the Union rather than abolish the peculiar institution.[47]

Two weeks later, the president, his secretary of state, and their northern constituents were shocked when Confederate forces routed Union soldiers on July 21 at the Battle of Bull Run in northern Virginia. The sight of northern troops and civilians, who had gone to the front expecting to revel in a US victory, hurriedly retreating the thirty miles back to Washington had a diverse and profound impact. Northerners were disabused of their assumption that the war would be easily won in a matter of months. Southerners were confident that this demonstration of Confederate military superiority displayed their political viability and would lead Europe to recognize Dixie's independence. British leaders Russell and Palmerston, the latter contemptuously sneering at the North's "Bull Run Races," grew even more convinced that the United States could not defeat and reintegrate the South. This conviction reinforced their inclination to contemplate intervention to forestall the prospective suffering and loss of life.[48]

In the wake of the Union army's disastrous performance, Lincoln turned his attention to becoming an informed and decisive commander in chief. This process would lead him to acquire a greater grasp of military strategy than virtually all of his generals and provided the power and constitutional rationale for not just the blockade but also subsequent, crucial foreign policy actions, such as the issuance of the Emancipation Proclamation. As he would declare in his second inaugural address, the president recognized that, on "the progress of our arms . . . all else chiefly depends." "All else" certainly included key foreign policy matters such as European recognition of Confederate independence, the abolition of slavery, and the ultimate preservation of the Union and its continued march toward great power status in the twentieth century. Precluding European recognition of the Confederacy was the most immediate of these concerns and the one on which the preservation of the Union and abolition of slavery depended.[49]

Lincoln's insight was particularly applicable since Palmerston, Russell, and Thouvenel acted on what historian Norman A. Graebner has characterized as "Europe's diplomatic tradition" of realism. This tradition led European nations to refuse to recognize or align with the Confederacy "until the South had demonstrated the power required to establish and maintain its independence." Establishing that independence depended, in turn, on sustained military success. Diverse observers discerned this reality and agreed with Lincoln's observation. By late August, William Yancey contended correctly that only Confederate battlefield victories would earn the South independence and international standing. British Lord Robert Cecil concurred and advised a northern correspondent: "Well, there is one way to convert us all—Win the battles, and we shall come round at once." Most important, Palmerston subsequently pronounced that only by the "Course of Events" could southern "independence . . . be converted into an Established Fact." Unless "their separate independence" was a "truth and fact," the state of the Confederacy would not be "a bit more independent for our saying so unless we followed up our Declaration by taking Part with them in the war"—which the prime minister and his foreign secretary very much sought to avoid.[50]

Against the backdrop of this crucial foreign policy reality, President Lincoln undertook a much more active role as commander in chief. Compared to his Confederate counterpart, Jefferson Davis, Lincoln clearly had much to learn. Davis had graduated from West Point, bravely led US soldiers in the Mexican-American War, and ably served as US secretary of war from 1853 to 1857. Lincoln's record of three months as a private and captain with no combat experience during the Black Hawk War in 1832 was comparatively insignificant. Undaunted, the self-educated attorney, who had studied Euclidian geometry for mental recreation, applied the same focus and determination to mastering military theory and strategy. According to John Nicolay, one of the president's private secretaries, Lincoln read widely in "stratigical works," closely scrutinized incoming military reports, and "held long conferences with eminent generals and admirals." Although initially deferential to these military leaders, by early 1862, Lincoln had acquired an impressive understanding of military strategy and had become a "hands-on commander in chief" who functioned as the "first and last authority in setting military policy."[51]

Two of Lincoln's post–Bull Run decisions forecast this emerging and expansive executive role. First, in a move that ultimately proved highly problematic, the president replaced his general in chief of the army, the seventy-five-year-old, overly cautious Winfield Scott, with thirty-four-year-old, reportedly aggressive George B. McClellan. Only later did Lincoln learn that "Tardy George" was even more strategically inert than his aged predecessor; but the president's decision and his frequent visits to McClellan's Washington headquarters during the remainder of the fall signaled his declining deference to the US military establishment. The chief executive exhibited this same assumption of authority when he countermanded General John C. Fremont's August 30 proclamation, which freed all slaves owned by Confederate supporters in Missouri. Lincoln explained that "liberating the slaves of traitorous owners" in Missouri jeopardized his and Seward's policy of prioritizing retention of the border states over abolition. Missouri, Maryland, and Kentucky could not be allowed to come under Confederate control.[52]

Just as Bull Run had focused Lincoln's attention on his military responsibilities as commander in chief, the unexpected southern victory reinforced Seward's more moderate tenor in his interactions with Britain and France. With hopes of a quick Union victory dashed, maintaining a stable, less provocative stance toward Europe's great powers became imperative. The secretary's decision for greater restraint also derived from his perception that his earlier stern warnings had been heard and heeded in London and Paris. From the British capital in late June, Minister Adams reported a "proportionate timidity" regarding interference in the war and a "British desire only to be perfectly neutral, giving no aid nor comfort to the insurgents." The British and French refusal to meet further with Confederate commissioners and the European recognition of the US blockade's viability substantiated Adams's assessment. By late September, Seward wrote his wife, Frances, "My fears of foreign intervention are subsiding. The prestige of secession is evidently wearing off in Europe." Although neither Adams nor Seward was privy to the correspondence, Lord Lyons soon thereafter confirmed these observations when he informed Russell that he was "anxious to avoid as far as possible giving any pretext to this government to take violent or offensive measures" against England.[53]

Relative restraint by all parties during the fall of 1861 did not eliminate incidents of diplomatic friction or erase the mutual suspicions and tensions that had arisen earlier in the year. The first of these incidents came in mid-August with the arrest in New York City of Robert Mure, a South Carolinian about to sail for London with an official British diplomatic pouch. Robert Bunch, the British consul in Charleston, had issued Mure a passport and entrusted him with the diplomatic papers. Seward demanded Bunch's recall and objected, correctly, that the consul had no independent authority to issue a passport, that the British official had inappropriately included "treasonable correspondence" to the Confederate commissioners in London in the official diplomatic pouch, and that these actions embodied a step toward British recognition of the South. The secretary grew even more convinced of the threat of such recognition when Russell reluctantly admitted that he had authorized Bunch to discuss enforcement of the Declaration of Paris with the Richmond government. Seward was aghast at Russell's duplicitous behavior; the British foreign secretary and Prime Minister Palmerston complained anew about Seward's unreasonable posture; and the recriminations continued through the end of November. Still, neither side desired a more serious confrontation; and both Seward and Lyons proceeded carefully, with the former strenuously objecting to any hint of British recognition and the latter consistently denying any such intention.[54]

Seward and Lyons exercised similar discretion in their handling of the US arrest of British citizens charged with sedition. On April 27, 1861, President Lincoln had suspended the right of habeas corpus, which guarantees that persons be presented with specific charges when they are arrested and be granted a court appearance to ascertain the legality of those charges. The subsequent arrest of those Lincoln termed "a most efficient corps of spies, informers, suppliers, and aiders and abettors" included some British citizens and other foreigners. Lord Russell complained that Lincoln had acted in a "despotic and arbitrary" fashion and had violated the US Constitution. Against his better judgment, Lyons followed Russell's directive to lodge a vigorous written protest, which Seward promptly published together with his response. He rebutted Russell's position and courted domestic nationalism by declaring Lincoln could hardly be expected to accept British interpretations of his nation's Constitution and laws. Duly chastised, Lyons thereafter confined his objections to private discussions rather than "spirited Notes," and Seward quietly released all of the imprisoned Englishmen. The two in essence agreed not "to kick up rows" over this issue.[55]

Two other matters occasioned relatively less demonstrative consternation during the second half of 1861 but proved far more consequential as the Civil War progressed. On October 31, France, Britain, and Spain signed the

Treaty of London, in which they agreed to a joint military expedition to collect unpaid debts from Mexico. These European powers invited the United States to participate but rejected Lincoln and Seward's offer to assume payment of the interest on Mexico's debts as an alternative to the tripartite European intervention in the Western Hemisphere. The US leaders were appropriately apprehensive since Napoleon III had an underlying "Grand Strategy" to dominate Mexico and expand French influence in the Americas. He planned to install a European monarch and, thereby, establish a major Gallic presence in the Western Hemisphere. Lincoln and Seward were also fearful that the intervention might become a precedent for future interference in the American war, despite assurances from Britain and Spain of military withdrawal after collection of the Mexican debts. Like the disputes over Bunch's recall and the arrest of British citizens, the European actions in Mexico were still being disputed as fall turned to winter.[56]

The Confederate purchase of war materials and construction of a navy in Great Britain would also become major diplomatic irritants. Having entered the war with very limited manufacturing capacity and neither a navy nor the shipyards needed to build one, the Confederacy had begun to buy war materials covertly on the continent and in Britain and to construct a navy in the latter. Led by Captain James D. Bulloch, a highly competent mariner and ingenious purchasing agent, the South had successfully dispatched the *Bermuda, Thomas Watson, Fingal,* and *Gladiator* from Britain, loaded with cannons, rifles, munitions, uniforms, blankets, and medical supplies for use by southern soldiers. Bulloch also contracted with Laird Brothers in Liverpool for the construction of two vessels that became the *Alabama* and *Florida*. These ships served the South as blockade runners and raiders that preyed on northern commerce. A Union secret service operation, overseen by US consul in Liverpool Thomas H. Dudley and US minister to Belgium Henry S. Sanford, discovered and observed these Confederate activities, but the British government took no action in response to Adams's protests. Lord Russell and his legal advisers concluded that Adams's evidence was insufficient to invoke the Foreign Enlistment Act, which prohibited British citizens from aiding either side in the war. As was true of the other frictions plaguing Anglo-American relations in late 1861, distress over these Confederate purchases and naval operations was eclipsed by the far more pressing crisis surrounding the American seizure of Confederate diplomats from the *Trent,* a British mail steamer.[57]

IV.

The *Trent* affair occurred when Captain Charles Wilkes, the commander of the USS *San Jacinto,* forcibly stopped the *Trent* and captured James M. Mason and John Slidell, Confederate diplomats en route to Europe to solicit diplomatic recognition of the South. The incident happened on November 8 off the coast of Cuba. Wilkes, a notoriously cantankerous and impetuous leader, sought the military fame that had eluded him during a long career and acted on his own authority. Since the *Trent* had forfeited its neutral status by carrying Confederate diplomatic dispatches, Wilkes could have taken the ship and its papers for trial in a US prize court. Instead, the commander seized Mason and Slidell, whom he termed the "embodiment of dispatches," and allowed the *Trent* to continue on its journey to England. In so doing, he violated accepted international law, directly challenged British national honor, and incited the gravest threat of an Anglo-American military clash during the Civil War era.[58]

Wilkes's actions were initially greeted with resounding public approval in the North. Following the embarrassing loss at Bull Run and no subsequent compensatory Union military accomplishments, northerners were grateful for any development that could be construed as a victory. Although Mason and Slidell were not the equivalent of diplomatic dispatches, the two former US senators and ardent secessionists did personify the advocacy of political separation and defense of slavery that northerners credited with destroying the nation. Most northern newspapers applauded Wilkes's bold action and agreed with the Boston *Transcript*'s assertion that the captain had "dealt a heavy blow—at the very vitals of the conspiracy threatening our national existence." Prominent northerners, such as Edward Everett and Caleb Cushing, who had compiled esteemed records as legislators and diplomats, endorsed the legality of Wilkes's retention of Mason and Slidell, as did Attorney General Edward Bates. Secretary of the Navy Gideon Welles sent the captain a congratulatory letter expressing the department's "emphatic approval"; the House of Representatives passed a resolution praising his "brave, adroit and patriotic conduct"; and dinners and public meetings were held in Wilkes's honor in Boston and New York.[59]

News of the *Trent* affair elicited a decidedly different response in Great Britain. The British press was harshly critical and belligerent. According to the London *Times,* only Mason and Slidell's release, accompanied by a "sufficient apology," could atone for such an "unjustifiable outrage." Other papers were even more vehement. The London *News* condemned this "wanton folly" by the "imbecile" Lincoln administration, and the Birmingham *Daily Post* opined, "England can put up with bluster, but not with blows." From the British capital, an American informed Seward that Londoners were "frantic with rage, and were the country polled, I fear 999 out of 1,000 would declare for immediate war."[60]

Palmerston and Russell agreed upon a hard-nosed policy. The foreign secretary declared "the United States Government are very dangerous people to run away from," and the prime minister instructed his cabinet, "I don't know whether you are going to stand this, but I'll be damned if I do!" As the formulators of British foreign policy reflected on how to manage the crisis, they assumed the worst about Lincoln and Seward. Prompted by Lyons's communication of a rumor from Washington that Seward had ordered the capture of the Confederate envoys without the president's approval, Palmerston speculated that the administration had purposely provoked the crisis to divert attention from military and political failures. The prime minister was also convinced that Seward was determined to attack Canada. As tensions between the two nations mounted, Palmerston told Queen Victoria that the United States was "not guided by reasonable men," and forecast that Lincoln and Seward could not stand up to the belligerent American public. The "masses," he declared, would "make it impossible for Lincoln and Seward to grant our demands," rendering "war . . . the probable result." Russell opined, "The best thing would be if Seward could be turned out and a rational man put in his place." Perhaps, the foreign minister added sarcastically, General "McClellan could be made DICTATOR."[61]

Acting on this genuine fear of armed conflict, Palmerston and his cabinet prepared for war. They banned the export of arms, munitions, and saltpeter, an essential ingredient for making gunpowder. During early December, London also strengthened its Atlantic fleet and dispatched more than 11,000 troops aboard eighteen transport ships to Canada, which increased the forces sent since summer to nearly 14,500. These troops and the Canadian militia were provided 50,000 arms and 2.25 million rounds of ammunition. Governor General Charles Monck was given specific directions to activate 38,000 Canadian militia and to defend key strategic locations. These actions appeared more ominous for the Union when combined with assurances from Napoleon III, whom Palmerston and Russell always distrusted, that France agreed with the British response to the crisis.[62]

Still, given the ongoing threats of war in Europe, the need for British troops in New Zealand, Japanese restiveness in Asia, and Canada's continuing vulnerability, Britain's geopolitical situation was not as strong as it appeared. Most important, as historian Robin Weeks has observed, "The British army was inadequate for dealing with a war on two fronts," and European considerations always took precedence. Since the United States was even more incapable of a two-front war, this geopolitical environment argued for peace.[63]

Financial considerations in both countries reinforced the mutual need for a pacific outcome. In 1861 the overall US debt totaled $444 million, 90 percent of which was owed to British banking houses. A war with the Union would have devastated these investments, Britain's most significant commercial market, and accompanying shipping interests. The *Economist* had such a disaster in view when it declared in June 1861, "A war with either of the belligerents would be a calamity, but a war between England and the *Northern* states of America would be the most affecting misfortune which could happen to civilization." Fear of such a calamity prompted a 10 percent drop in the price of US bonds in the London stock market and led Baring Brothers and the Rothschilds to suspend operations in the United States.[64]

The *Trent* affair's financial impact was even greater in the United States, where investors moved their money from stocks and bonds to commodities such as gold and gunpowder and depositors' panicked withdrawals forced bank closures. The diplomatic crisis and possible war also jeopardized the Lincoln administration's ability to finance the Union government and its war. At the time of Mason and Slidell's capture, Secretary of the Treasury Salmon P. Chase projected that national borrowing would fund 90 percent of northern expenditures over the ensuing year. Chase and the other members of the cabinet recognized that it would be virtually impossible to induce investors to purchase US government bonds in the shadow of an imminent, or worse, an actual Anglo-American war. Again, the *Economist* was incisive: "Is it possible that a nation whose finances" are so precarious, "who is engaged in a civil war—can venture on a war with Great Britain?"[65]

Against this backdrop of nationalist fervor, geopolitical and military calculation, and financial crisis on both sides of the Atlantic, Palmerston and Russell formulated the official British response to Wilkes's rash and ill-advised actions. After the royal consort, Prince Albert, had risen from his deathbed to moderate British demands, the prime minister and foreign secretary pronounced the *Trent* affair "an affront to the British flag and a violation of international law." Great Britain demanded the release of the Confederate agents and "a suitable apology for the aggression which has been committed." Lyons was instructed to give the United States a strict seven-day deadline to respond, and Russell required a "plain Yes or a plain No" answer—although he did allow the British minister the flexibility to remain in Washington beyond the seven days if Lyons judged that Seward and Lincoln were making a genuine effort to meet these demands.[66]

Lord Lyons reported, perhaps with some satisfaction, that Wilkes's actions forced Seward and Lincoln to confront a "very painful dilemma": they had to endure the "humiliation of yielding to England" or spark "a disastrous Foreign War." As events demonstrated, the alternatives were not quite so stark. Still, the principal formulators of US foreign policy unquestionably faced the greatest international relations crisis of the Civil War's first year. Both the president and secretary of state have been portrayed as initially agreeing with their victory-starved constituents' approval of the capture of Mason and Slidell. If so, Lincoln and Seward quickly moved beyond any momentary euphoria and recognized the real possibility of a destructive war with Great Britain. Lincoln's more sober and guiding principle echoed his earlier reaction to Seward's April 1 thoughts for the president; he could not have "two wars on his hands at a time."[67]

During the month between November 16, when news of Wilkes's seizure of the Confederate envoys reached Washington, and December 19, when Lord Lyons unofficially presented Seward with the British ultimatum, the president proceeded in a decidedly cautious fashion. He confided to a journalist on November 16, "I fear the traitors will prove to be white elephants"; in his annual message to Congress on December 3, the president omitted any mention of the *Trent* affair; on December 4, the chief executive assured Alexander T. Galt, the Canadian minister of finance, that the crisis "could be arranged"; and on December 10, he conveyed a similar message to Senator Orville Browning, an old friend from Illinois, by emphasizing that there "probably would be no trouble." In response to the opinion of some that John Bull was registering idle threats, the president told the story of a reportedly friendly Springfield bulldog: "I know the bulldog will not bite. You know he will not bite, but," Lincoln asked, "does the bulldog know he will not bite?"

A cautious policy, he suggested, was essential to avoid war and a severe British bite.[68]

With one notable exception, Seward was equally cautious as he charted a path between war and humiliation and adhered to Lincoln's guiding principle of avoiding two simultaneous wars. Seward said virtually nothing publicly, save a belligerent outburst on December 16 during a dinner party at the home of the Portuguese minister. Clearly distressed over the difficult choices the United States faced, and perhaps invoking his studied bravado, Seward warned that if pushed into war, the United States would "wrap the whole world in flames!" "No power," he declared, would escape "the fire of our battle." William H. Russell, the London *Times* correspondent, overheard this threat and assumed the secretary of state was intent on war, but another guest intervened, "That's all bugaboo talk. When Seward talks that way, he means to break down." This assessment was confirmed when Russell visited Seward's home the following day for dinner. He was greeted cordially and told that "everything consistent with US honour would be done" to avoid armed conflict. The secretary conveyed the same sentiment to French minister Mercier, who was assured, "We shall not have a war; great nations like England and the United States do not make war from emotion."[69]

As Lincoln and Seward searched for a peaceful solution to the *Trent* affair, Sumner continued to complicate their working relationship and their pursuit of a remedy that would preserve both the administration's domestic support and the nation's international standing. Throughout 1861, the senator had undermined the secretary's standing with Lyons and prominent British statesmen. When the *Trent* crisis arose, Sumner promptly attributed it to Seward's "fatal mismanagement" of US foreign policy and implied that his political rival was a "great impediment to Peace." After Seward refused to discuss *Trent* matters with Sumner, the senator focused his attention on Lincoln and warned him, "You must watch him and overrule him."[70]

Unlike Everett and Cushing, Sumner had immediately recognized that Wilkes had violated international law and that Mason and Slidell should be surrendered. To reinforce the legal arguments, he emphasized the practical necessity of avoiding war and shared with Lincoln private letters from pro-Union Englishmen John Bright and Richard Cobden, who emphasized the need for compromise. However, when he sensed that Lincoln was ambivalent about giving up the despised southerners, the chairman of the Senate Foreign Relations Committee reversed course and supported Lincoln's inclination to submit the matter to international arbitration. In contrast to Sumner's prior argument for immediate compromise and freedom for Mason and Slidell, arbitration would have prolonged the crisis, challenged Russell's seven-day deadline, and in so doing, increased the possibility of miscalculation and ruinous war.[71]

Amid great tension in Washington and London, Lyons received Russell's ultimatum on Wednesday, December 18, and met with Seward at the State Department the following day. At Seward's request, the British minister provided him an unofficial copy of the demands on the condition that only the secretary and President Lincoln were to see them. Lyons further agreed to give Seward until Saturday the twenty-first to study the dispatch. When they met on Saturday, Lyons consented to postpone the formal presentation of the British position until Monday the twenty-third. He "was very glad [to] . . . give Mr. Seward (who is now on the peace side of the Cabinet) time to work with the President." At their Monday meeting, Lyons revealed Russell's seven-day deadline for the US response and reiterated that an unacceptable reply would lead to the severing of Anglo-American diplomatic relations and his departure for London.[72]

As Lyons's placement of Seward on the "peace side" of Lincoln's cabinet suggests, the secretary of state had decided to surrender Mason and Slidell. Seward's earlier pacific assurances to W. H. Russell and Mercier had indicated this, as had the decidedly more temperate tone of major Washington and New York newspapers—a "sudden conversion," according to one informed member of the Washington diplomatic corps, "generally attributed to the inspiration of the secretary of state." Seward was also fully aware that the administration had made no significant preparations to enhance the nation's capacity to fight Great Britain, that Union finances were precarious, and that all of his news from Europe dictated the Confederates' release. Thurlow Weed, whom Seward had sent to Europe in November to promote the Union cause, advised his old friend from London, "such prompt and gigantic preparations" for war "were never known." Failure to release Mason and Slidell, Weed warned, "*means war.*" Ministers Adams in Britain and Dayton in France agreed, as did northern champions in Britain, Bright and Cobden, whose letters Sumner shared with Seward.[73]

Seward's advocacy for Mason and Slidell's release was particularly significant given President Lincoln's expressed preference as late as December 21 for international arbitration. Worried about the potential public backlash against freeing the southerners, and influenced by Sumner and Bright, the president had drafted a Union position paper to be sent over Seward's signature. In this memorandum the president emphasized that Wilkes had acted without authorization from the administration, that an arbiter's decision would be accepted, and that the United States was prepared to pay proper reparations. Although Lincoln most certainly discussed this policy option with Seward, he did not present it during the cabinet's deliberations. This was wise. Since virtually all important European countries agreed with Britain's position, it would have been difficult to secure an arbiter. Even more important, proposing arbitration and quibbling over a settlement would have occasioned the very delay Russell had rejected in advance and would have imperiled Anglo-American peace and the viability of the US war against the South.[74]

Faced with these dire possible outcomes, the Union's very survival was at stake as Lincoln gathered his cabinet for what became a four-hour meeting on Christmas Day. Only Seward came with a coherent plan to surrender Mason and Slidell, and he had composed a draft dispatch that explained this decision. The secretary based his plan and dispatch on the determination he shared with Lincoln to avoid two wars and on the conviction that the United States could not "be diverted from the cares of the Union into controversies with other powers, even if just cause for them could be found." In the dispatch addressed to Lord Lyons, Seward declared that Wilkes had acted on his own authority and without instructions from the administration. The captain, Seward contended, had lawfully stopped the *Trent,* since the British steamer was transporting Confederate diplomats and their diplomatic correspondence, all of which the secretary termed "contraband of war for the use and benefit of the insurgents." Wilkes had erred when he failed to take the *Trent* and its alleged contraband persons and diplomatic correspondence to a US prize court for a ruling on the legality of the ship's capture.[75]

Given this inadvertent, but illegal, misstep, the United States was prepared to "cheerfully" turn over Mason and Slidell, although Seward had artfully avoided Russell's demand for an apology. To the contrary, the secretary adopted Minister Adams's contention that in relinquishing the Confederates the United States was adhering to an "old, honored and cherished American cause" proclaimed by Secretary of State James Madison in 1804. In the years prior to the War of 1812 Madison had advocated the need for a prize court's decision to determine the fate of sailors seized or impressed by the British from American neutral ships and forced into service in Her Majesty's navy. Therefore, Great Britain had in the *Trent* affair allegedly affirmed the US position on the contentious issue of impressment.[76]

Seward's realistic determination to avoid war and his adroit, face-saving defense of national honor helped sway a majority of the cabinet to his position. Lincoln's other advisers and the president were also impressed by the letters from Adams, Dayton, Weed, Bright, and Cobden, all of which emphasized British belligerence and the necessity for compromise. And, in the midst of the meeting, French foreign minister Thouvenel's anticipated dispatch declaring French agreement with the British position arrived. Anglo-French solidarity eliminated any US hope of acquiring a meaningful European backer in the crisis and excluded France as a potential arbiter.

Even though the secretary of state seemed to be carrying the argument, the meeting ended with one cabinet member's advice that the group not decide hastily but rather ponder the matter and "consider about it tomorrow." As the gathering adjourned, Lincoln instructed Seward to continue work on his "answer, which . . . will state the reasons why they ought to be given up." The president planned to muster an argument why Mason and Slidell should not be surrendered, and they would "compare the points on each side." Seward complied, and, according to Lincoln, came to the December 26 meeting "loaded to the muzzle" for the debate. No one else, including the president, presented a rejoinder to the secretary's arguments, and the cabinet "unanimously concurred to Mr. Seward's letter to Lord Lyons after some verbal and formal amendments."[77]

Following this second and decisive meeting, Seward asked Lincoln why he had not stated the counter case. The president smiled and replied, "I found I could not make an argument that would satisfy my own mind, and that proved to me your ground was the right one." Not all students of this exchange and the accompanying cabinet decision have taken Lincoln's explanation at face value. They have suggested that Lincoln simply allowed his "self-important secretary of state to believe that conciliation was his own idea" or that the president "wanted to go on record" opposing the Confederate envoys' surrender "while knowing" the United States would have to accede to British demands.[78]

Given the president's overall policy of caution, discretion, and determination to avoid two simultaneous wars, both of these speculations are plausible. Still, given the time Lincoln and Seward spent conferring on both domestic and foreign policy issues during 1861; their steadily evolving relationship of trust and respect; and the reality that Seward agreed completely with Lincoln's basic foreign policy parameters and, like the president, was willing to do whatever was necessary to preserve the Union, it is more likely that the shrewd chief executive directed the meeting dynamics toward his other department heads—none of whom entered the Christmas Day meeting completely in favor of releasing Mason and Slidell. Significantly, the final unanimous decision embodied the essential facets of the shared Lincoln-Seward policy. Lincoln had discarded arbitration in favor of Seward's prescription for navigation between national humiliation and war. Seward's son Frederick's subsequent evaluation of Lincoln's actions was telling: "Presidents and Kings are not apt to see flaws in their own arguments, but fortunately for the Union, it had a President, at this critical juncture, who combined a logical intellect with an unselfish heart." The final decision was an example of the productive Lincoln-Seward foreign policy partnership, and it fell to the secretary of state to sell that decision to the American Congress and public.[79]

Seward initiated this effort in characteristic fashion by hosting a dinner party on December 27 for key members of the Senate, including Sumner, who had not attended the previous day's cabinet meeting. After dinner, the secretary invited the legislators into his library, lit a cigar, and announced to his surprised guests that Mason and Slidell were to be surrendered. The senators expressed regret, but after Seward read them all of the relevant diplomatic correspondence, including his twenty-six-page response to Lyons, all endorsed the administration's decision. With several conspicuous exceptions, the rest of Congress also fell into line. The Senate's chaplain summarized congressional opinion: In the face of "domestic treason," "foreign arrogance," and "the remorseless sweep of physical and armed force," the "high principle of human equity . . . must for the moment succumb under the plastic forms of soft diplomacy." In short, the minister's prayer constituted a flowery restatement and acceptance of the Seward rationale for nation-saving compromise.[80]

To make the case for the administration's decision to the nation more broadly, Seward consciously practiced "public diplomacy." As Lincoln's public framing of the war's international significance and his communication with at least one editor during the *Trent* crisis demonstrated, the president understood the significance of stating the Union case publicly; but Seward shouldered the bulk of this task. Over the course of his first year in office, the secretary had selectively fed information to major, pro-administration newspapers such as the *New York Times,* had published diplomatic correspondence with Britain and France to bolster the administration's standing at home, had sent special agents such as Weed abroad to promote northern perspectives, and had used secret service allocations to fund Europeans who served the same purpose. Therefore, it was hardly surprising when the Washington *Daily National Intelligencer* published all the relevant *Trent* documents on December 28, together with laudatory editorial commentary, and the most important New York dailies did the same the following day. These papers praised the administration for acting on its "best judgments," even if that assessment conflicted with "popular desires." Lincoln and his secretary had avoided a war with Britain, which "would have given a certain triumph to the Southern rebellion," and Seward had composed a "masterly" note in support of the "great principles of maritime law to which the United States have always adhered."[81]

Many commentators, both at the time and since, have been far less positive regarding Seward's treatment of the relevant international legal issues. One historian termed his lengthy note "a monument to illogic," and Senator Sumner devoted a three-and-one-half-hour speech on January 9 to endorsing the administration's actions even as he excoriated Seward's knowledge of international law. Both of Sumner's objectives were realized, but the latter was beside the point. Rather than a legal brief, Seward had composed a "*political* paper" meant to win over Lincoln, the cabinet, and the American public, and a "*diplomatic* document" crafted to satisfy the British demands and avoid a catastrophic second war. The secretary acknowledged his expedient goals when he declared, "If the safety of this Union required the detention of the captured persons it would be the right and duty of this Government to detain them." His monument to illogic had met all of its goals, to the delight of George Francis Train, an administration supporter, who declared with some hyperbole, "Seward . . . is, without exception, the cleverist Secretary of State that America has ever possessed. . . . He can talk diplomacy with Lyons, war with Palmerston, Latin with Russell, Greek with Gladstone, or Hebrew with Rothschild."[82]

British officials and their public received Lincoln and Seward's decision with great relief, for they too recognized the calamitous consequences of an Anglo-American war. Russell and his legal advisers dismissed Seward's legal arguments but were quite willing to accept the president and secretary's clear preference for compromise and peace. Palmerston remained "wary of the Yankees" but agreed with Russell's determination to sustain British neutrality. Significantly, Russell emerged from the *Trent* affair convinced that Seward harbored no "animosity to this country." The foreign secretary had come to believe that the anti-Seward reports had been "all buncom[be]." Turning to more general US-British relations, Russell no longer discerned "any excitement here upon the question of America." John Bright concurred and wrote Sumner, "All has changed, and it is difficult to find a noisy advocate of the secession theory." Realizing that a potential turning point in the Civil War had passed, dispirited Confederates reached similar conclusions. A Richmond editor later declared that the incident yielded "a sharp check to the long cherished" hope of English interference "in the war," and a southern War Department clerk added, "Now we must depend upon our own strong arms."[83]

With this peaceful settlement of the *Trent* affair, one of the most serious threats of foreign intervention in the Civil War, Lincoln and Seward had successfully navigated the foreign policy shoals of their first year in office. They had also solidified their friendship, mutual trust and respect, and foreign policy partnership. Over the course of 1861, Lincoln had established and maintained his position as the senior partner. He had set overall policy parameters, such as the strict avoidance of a second war while fighting the Confederacy; had begun to articulate the war's connection to the promotion of democracy and republican government internationally; had recognized the essential connection between Union success on the battlefield and a viable foreign policy; had become a more assertive commander in chief; had intervened at crucial junctures, such as the May 21 instructions to Minister Adams; and had retained ultimate decision-making authority, as demonstrated in the US response to the *Trent* crisis.

Seward, in turn, had overseen the daily operations of the State Department and less consequential, but potentially dangerous, matters such as the Bunch affair and the Union's arrest of foreign nationals. The secretary of state had provided correct and critical policy guidance in the formulation and application of the Union blockade and had been the principal voice for and public defender of the administration's compromise resolution of the *Trent* affair. Perhaps even more vital, Seward's calculated policy of brinkmanship and threat of the use of force against any European nation that intervened in the American war had created crucial uncertainty and caution among British and French policymakers. This caution was evident as those leaders responded to the Union blockade, considered diplomatic recognition of Confederate independence, and grappled with the *Trent* crisis. The latter raised questions about whether the United States could have actually delivered on Seward's threatened use of force in 1861 and demonstrated the possibility of miscalculation by all parties that accompanied the secretary's bluster. The crisis also confirmed Seward's willingness to modify his belligerent posture when the occasion demanded, a change that he had begun in midsummer. Like Lincoln, Seward directed all his flexible foreign policies toward the Union's goals of forestalling European recognition of the Confederacy, avoiding outside military intervention, and hindering the South's search for military equipment and supplies. As the war's first year ended, the two unlikely partners had been remarkably successful.

3

THE RECOGNITION AND CABINET CRISES, 1862

I.

On December 13, 1862, the North suffered a devastating defeat at Fredericksburg, Virginia. This ghastly battle resulted in thirteen thousand Union casualties versus five thousand for the Confederacy. It also helped provoke a revolt by Republicans in the Senate. After all thirty of the Republicans in the US Senate caucused on December 16 and 17, 1862, they dispatched a nine-member delegation to the White House on the evening of the eighteenth to demand that Secretary of State Seward be dismissed from President Lincoln's cabinet. In so doing, this group, led by Senators Charles Sumner and William Pitt Fessenden, precipitated "the most serious governmental crisis" of Lincoln's presidency. Republicans of all stripes were deeply frustrated at the North's lack of military progress, and some even suggested that Lincoln should resign. While most rejected that extreme option and were reluctant to attack Lincoln directly, the overwhelming majority of Senate Republicans agreed that Seward had to go.[1]

Prompted openly by leading Republican legislators, such as Sumner and Fessenden, and more covertly by Secretary of the Treasury Salmon P. Chase, disgruntled Republicans made Seward the target of their multiple discontents. They claimed the New Yorker had opposed and delayed Lincoln's decision to make emancipation of the slaves, rather than preservation of the Union, the war's primary focus and goal; had been responsible for the president's tardy firing of General George B. McClellan; had meddled in the work of the other secretaries and undermined the cabinet's effectiveness; and had exercised a "paralizing [*sic*] influence on the army and the President." All

3. *The First Reading of the Emancipation Proclamation to the Cabinet,* from a painting by F. B. Carpenter. Seward is seated to Lincoln's left, facing him. Courtesy of the Library of Congress.

of these transgressions, the critics asserted, had facilitated Democratic Party gains in the 1862 elections. According to Seward's assailants, he was a "low, vulgar, vain demagogue who had insulted every foreign power since coming into office" while holding "a sponge saturated with chloroform to Uncle Abe's nose."[2]

President Lincoln recognized that much of this animosity was actually directed at him and his performance as president. He understood that the political coherence and operational viability of his cabinet and his powers as the nation's chief executive and commander in chief hung in the balance. That said, his response clearly reflected his great personal and professional regard for the secretary of state, and the feeling was mutual. Upon learning of the senators' demands, Seward immediately submitted his resignation, explaining, "They may do as they please about me, but they shall not put the President in a false position on my account." Lincoln appreciated this concern since the secretary was the "one man in the cabinet" he "trusted completely, . . . and the only one he could call an intimate friend." Even Seward's critics, such as Fessenden and Secretary of the Navy Gideon Welles, admitted that "Lincoln thinks he cannot get along without Seward," since "our foreign affairs are too complicated for a fresh hand," and that the president was "fond of Seward who is affable" and "comforts him." Tellingly, Lord Lyons, the British minister to the United States with whom Seward had sparred through much of 1861, decidedly favored the secretary's retention. His relations with Seward had become "friendly and cordial," and he feared that a new secretary would be "less disposed to keep the peace."[3]

While acting deftly to preserve their unlikely and crucial foreign policy partnership, Lincoln demonstrated his friendship and respect for Seward. The president informed the Republican senators that their denunciation of the secretary "shocked and grieved him," and he exhibited an obvious "air of satisfaction" after resolving the crisis. The president achieved this resolution by inviting the Senate delegation to meet on December 19 with all of his cabinet secretaries except Seward. Lincoln began this meeting by defending Seward and asserting that the cabinet had properly considered and agreed upon all major decisions. He then invited comments from the cabinet members. When Attorney General Edward Bates and Secretary of the Navy Welles generally endorsed the president's contentions, Chase was forced to agree and, in so doing, contradict the information he had conveyed to Fessenden and others. Severely compromised, the treasury secretary submitted his own letter of resignation, which offset Seward's and afforded Lincoln the leverage he sought to resolve the crisis while retaining both the secretaries of state and treasury as cabinet members. When two prominent New York political figures came to the White House soon thereafter and reiterated the call for Seward's ouster, an infuriated Lincoln threw them out. "For once in my life," he confided to his personal secretary, "I rather gave my temper the rein and I talked to those men pretty damned plainly."[4]

These end-of-the-year attacks on Seward were the culmination of more than eighteen months of Sumner-led abuse, including unfounded rumors that the secretary was an ineffectual drunk. From London, Charles Francis Adams could recall no "parallel instance" of such "public abuse and private slander of a statesman." As 1862 began, Seward's red hair had turned "snow white," and he exhibited "deep sunk" eyes and skin of "parchment texture." Usually sanguine and cheerful, the secretary was fatigued and downcast and groused privately that he was ready "to leave public life" and be "free from the suspicions and jealousies of enemies and the reproofs of friends." While momentarily exhausted and personally wounded, Seward never truly considered leaving public life and soon regained his jaunty persona, infectious optimism, and zest for life and society. In truth, he knew no other way of public or private life.[5]

Lincoln's personal burdens in early 1862 were not so transitory or so easily overcome. The tragic death of his eleven-year-old son Willie on February 20 heightened the president's depressive tendencies and often-somber moods. Grief-stricken, "choking with emotion," and "bursting into tears" at the death of a second young son, Lincoln declared, "My boy is gone—actually gone!" Confronted with diverse political, military, and foreign policy challenges, the president still coped with this latest personal tragedy and his own depression. He did so in part by frequently spending evenings at Seward's home on Lafayette Square. The secretary often joined the president on carriage rides around Washington and regularly visited Lincoln at the Soldiers Home, an official residence to which Lincoln and his wife moved in July to escape the summer heat. Lincoln's need for sympathetic, upbeat, and broadly intelligent company strengthened the two men's personal friendship and professional partnership. Seward's company was especially welcome since Mary Lincoln, who was devastated by Willie's death and never fully recovered her emotional equilibrium, could not provide her husband solace during this trying time.[6]

In addition to such personal cares, Lincoln and Seward faced multiple pressing public matters. As the Union entered the new year still devoid of significant battlefield successes, President Lincoln endured mounting criticism. Obstructionist, proslavery northern Democrats opposed him on all antislavery measures and challenged his assertive executive actions, such as the suspension of habeas corpus, from a rigid states' rights perspective. These Democrats, often called Copperheads, also championed General McClellan, an opponent of emancipation who repeatedly refused to prosecute the war aggressively. Radical Republicans and a growing number of the party's moderates decried the North's lack of military success, excoriated McClellan's inaction, and pressured Lincoln to fire the general and to make emancipation the Union's foremost goal. Republican dissatisfaction was evident in the establishment in December 1861 of the Joint Committee on the Conduct of the War, a body through which disgruntled party members asserted that Congress, rather than the president, should be primarily responsible for both the management of the war and the process of emancipation. As he was attacked from all sides politically, the embattled Lincoln worried that the "bottom" was "out of the [national] tub."[7]

Fully cognizant that national morale, political calm, and foreign policy success ultimately depended on Union military victories, the resilient Lincoln continued to develop his mastery of military strategy and to evolve as commander in chief. As his prior proclamation of the blockade and suspension of habeas corpus demonstrated, he flatly rejected the contention of Sumner and others that Congress should assume a greater, perhaps primary, role in the direction of the Union military effort. Lincoln jealously defended his executive authority and continued to take actions that he expected Congress to approve after, rather than before, the fact.[8]

The president also continued his study of military strategy. By early 1862, Lincoln had rejected the prevailing limited war approach advocated by General McClellan. This strategy emphasized military maneuver to avoid pitched battles and the control of enemy territory, and it sought to minimize the war's impact on civilians. When this method of warfare yielded no significant victories, Lincoln felt compelled to "take . . . army matters into his own hands" and moved steadily toward the prosecution of a "hard war" that focused on the aggressive destruction of Confederate military capacity by attacks on its soldiers and the civilian property and resources that supported them. From the hard war perspective, Confederate armies, rather than geographic locations, became the principal military objectives. Lincoln explained his thinking to Senator Orville Browning on January 12: Union armies "should threaten all [Confederate] positions at the same time with superior force, and if they weakened one to strengthen another seize and hold the weakened one." Two weeks later, the president expressed this more overtly aggressive posture in his "President's General Order Number One," which directed the Union military to confront "insurgent forces" by February 22.[9]

Ulysses S. Grant, who fought in the western theater, had reached similar strategic conclusions and shared Lincoln's propensity for aggressive action. In early February Grant oversaw victories at Fort Henry and Fort Donelson in Tennessee and followed with the capture of Nashville and Memphis. Six weeks later, Grant, aided by General Don Carlos Buell, implemented the hard war strategy in spades while defeating the Confederates at Shiloh. Nearly eleven thousand southerners and more than thirteen thousand Yankees were killed, wounded, or captured, and more Americans perished than in the Revolution, the War of 1812, and the Mexican-American War combined. On April 25 Admiral David Farragut complemented these land victories by capturing New Orleans; and by May, Union forces in the western theater had overrun fifty thousand square miles of Confederate territory, secured control of one thousand miles of important rivers, and seized the South's largest city.[10]

Much to Lincoln and Seward's distress, these first clear Union military successes in the West were offset by McClellan's maddening inertia in the eastern theater. A proslavery Democrat, McClellan held both Lincoln and Seward in contempt. He had dismissed the president as "nothing more than a well meaning baboon" and "the original gorilla" and had characterized the secretary as the "meanest of . . . all" the "wretched politicians" who obstructed his military duties. Increasingly concerned that his general in chief did "not intend to do anything," Lincoln summoned McClellan to the White House on March 7, 1862, and prodded him to move against Confederate forces in Virginia. The president's exhortations accomplished little. Only when he personally traveled to Norfolk on May 7 and ordered US gunboats forward did Lincoln and the Union gain tangible results from McClellan's stalled Peninsular Campaign. Four days later, the president removed McClellan from his general in chief post but left him in command of the Army of the Potomac. Lincoln's very public demonstration of executive displeasure was no more effective than his private admonishment or personal intervention at Norfolk. This became clear during the Seven Days Battles in late June. Although he suffered only one tactical defeat in six battles and lost half as many dead and wounded as the Confederates, McClellan repeatedly retreated. The Union campaign ended ignominiously as General Robert E. Lee and the Army of Northern Virginia successfully defended Richmond. This outcome reinforced Lincoln's determination to wage a hard war.[11]

By the end of June, the North was still in search of the decisive military successes Lincoln rightly deemed essential. The stalemated and ever more lethal conflict exposed the administration to continued domestic political attacks and left the nation vulnerable to European intervention. Following resolution of the *Trent* affair, Seward warned that "the next" foreign policy crisis would involve European pressure for "recognition [of the Confederacy] on account of the rigors of the blockade." The secretary's apprehension was prescient. In both London and Paris, Confederate representatives James Mason and John Slidell had lobbied the British and French governments in early 1862 to challenge what they contended was an ineffective or illegitimate paper blockade. These southern diplomats asserted correctly that the great majority of blockade runners attempting to enter and leave Confederate ports had succeeded during 1861. The Union had not sealed off the 3,500 miles of coastline or 189 viable harbors from Virginia to Texas. Subsequent historians have estimated that 90 percent of these cargo ships evaded capture during the war's first year. Thereafter, the blockade became increasingly effective; but, even in the war's last year, half of the blockade runners were successful.[12]

These numbers do not tell the whole story. First, the overwhelming majority of the vessels were small, with limited cargo capacity. Second, southerners who endured the blockade testified to its impact. For example, a Confederate naval officer reported that the blockade "shut the Confederacy out from the world, deprived it of supplies, weakened its military and naval strength." Third, and even more telling, the blockade reduced the South's maritime trade by two-thirds during a time when the Confederacy's needs far exceeded prewar levels.[13]

Although the blockade was effective and thereby conformed to contemporary standards of international law, that reality would have been irrelevant had British and French leaders decided otherwise. Fortunately for the North, they did not. After acknowledging the blockade's legitimacy as the war began, Lord Russell and French foreign minister Thouvenel would have had to reverse the legal precedents they had initially acted upon. Moreover, as leaders of the world's foremost naval power, Russell and Palmerston hesitated to set overly restrictive parameters for an effective blockade—parameters that might interfere with Britain's navy in the future.[14]

On March 7 pro-Union members of the British Parliament, drawing on materials furnished by Seward via Minister Adams, proclaimed the blockade's effectiveness. Far more significant, Russell had already emphasized the refusal of ships to challenge the blockade. On February 2, he informed Parliament that if Union ships stationed before a port presented "*an evident danger*" to blockade runners, "the fact that various ships may have successfully escaped . . . will not of itself prevent the blockade from being an effective one by international law." Soon thereafter, Auguste Billault, a French senator and spokesman for Emperor Napoleon, confirmed France's agreement with this British interpretation and prompted Minister Dayton to report that southern hopes that France would challenge the blockade had been at least temporarily dashed.[15]

Renewed British and French recognition of the Union blockade did not eliminate US-British friction over wartime issues. Although the blockade was legally viable and practically effective, the ships that reached southern ports garnered astonishingly high profits ranging from 300 to 1,000 percent. Since the South essentially had no navy, blockade running existed as a private enterprise carried out primarily by British companies and sailors. These ships, largely British owned and operated, also carried huge quantities of British arms, ammunition, and other materiel. Over the course of the war, some six hundred thousand pieces of equipment worth $200 million were transported from Great Britain to the South. Without these materials, the South could not have sustained the war for four years.[16]

The bulk of this pro-Confederate commercial activity was centered in Liverpool, which has been described aptly as "the most pro-Confederate place in the world outside the Confederacy itself." The world's foremost cotton port, Liverpool was home to Fraser, Trenholm and Company, which served as the South's banker, and Laird Brothers, the principal Confederate shipbuilder. In addition, the indispensable war supplies arrived at southern ports after stops at St. George's in British Bermuda, Nassau in the British Bahamas, and the Spanish colonies of Puerto Rico and Cuba. In these West Indian ports, the material was transferred from larger, oceangoing ships to the smaller blockade runners, which slipped into southern ports. Even Lord Russell, who did not feel he could curb this trade legally, acknowledged its injurious effect on Anglo-American relations. It was "contrary to the spirit of Her Majesty's Proclamation" of neutrality; exposed the British to accusations of "bad faith"; prompted "vexatious detention and search by American cruisers"; and caused "irritation and ill will" in the North.[17]

In addition to active collusion in blockade running, British subjects, again primarily in Liverpool, aided Confederate efforts to build a navy in English shipyards. These efforts yielded two conspicuous successes. The first gunboat, a ship initially called the *Oreto* and ostensibly built for an Italian customer, sailed from England in March 1862. After it went to Nassau rather than Italy and was outfitted with guns, the vessel was rechristened the CSS *Florida* and commenced its attacks on Union merchant ships. Four months later, in late July, No. 290, a larger, more powerful ship reportedly built for the Spanish government, departed Liverpool for the Azores, where it took on armaments and a full crew. On August 24 the 290 officially became the CSS *Alabama*. Together, the *Florida* and *Alabama* captured or destroyed more than one hundred northern merchant ships and laid the bases for extended legal and financial wrangling after the war.[18]

Both of these ships had been built and sailed in the face of strenuous US objections by Consul Thomas H. Dudley in Liverpool and Minister Adams in London. Aided by local detectives, Dudley energetically gathered information that linked James Bullock, the primary Confederate agent for naval construction, to the *Florida* and *Alabama* and challenged the ships' alleged Italian and Spanish ownership and destinations. These efforts failed to convince Lord Russell and the British legal authorities that the vessels' construction had violated the Foreign Enlistment Act (FEA). This measure forbade British citizens from "equipping, furnishing, fitting out, or arming" a ship with the "intent" of the vessel being "employed" in war. Since both ships had been fitted out and armed after departing England, which obscured the intent of their use by the Confederacy, Russell and his legal advisers did not believe the FEA's prohibitions applied. Although the foreign secretary had revised this opinion on the eve of the *Alabama*'s escape, bureaucratic missteps prevented the ship's detention. Dudley, Adams, and Seward were indignant that a second British-built warship and privateer had found its way into Confederate service, and all three feared that the Palmerston government was implementing a purposefully pro-Confederate policy. Seward declared bluntly, "The British Government either sympathizes, or allows itself to seem to sympathize" with the South.[19]

Napoleon III had not yet invited the Confederacy to build ships in France, as he would do in 1863; and, other than periodically aiding blockade runners in Puerto Rico and Cuba, French citizens' role in illicit commerce with the South was negligible. Still, US relations with France were hardly tranquil. Both Napoleon and Foreign Minister Thouvenel were deeply concerned about the potential economic and political impact of a scarcity of raw cotton, and this consideration prompted both to contemplate possible French intervention in the war. Thouvenel expressed his apprehensions to Minister Dayton, and the mercurial emperor did so most blatantly with William S. Lindsay, an aggressive backer of the South in the British Parliament. Lurking in the background of all US-French relations was Napoleon's ongoing imperial intervention in Mexico. By early April 1862, Britain and Spain had abandoned the tripartite intervention, which eliminated France's diplomatic cover. Since Seward had informed France that the United States could not "look with indifference upon an armed European intervention for political ends in a country situated so near and connected with us so closely as Mexico," it was clear the project's success hinged on a Confederate victory.[20]

II.

It was against this background of northern apprehensions and growing hostility toward both major European powers that Seward directed US foreign policies during the spring of 1862. His approach embodied a delicate balance between the more conciliatory posture adopted after mid-1861 and his ongoing, often blunt warnings that any European intervention in the American conflict meant war with the United States. With no apparent sense of irony, the secretary voiced the softer tone to Minister Adams on April 1, 1862, exactly one year after he had submitted his bellicose "Thoughts" to President Lincoln: "Let it be our endeavor," he instructed, "to extirpate the seeds of animosity and cultivate relations of friendship with a nation [Great Britain], that however perversely it may seem to act for a time, can really have no interest or ambition permanently conflicting with our own." Sustaining this attitude in the face of ongoing domestic and foreign crises demanded studied serenity. "In this confusion of nations and men," Seward wrote his daughter, "I must be calm, undisturbed, hopeful of all things, and gracious in every way." And, as he noted on another occasion, were crises to occur, his calm would "be in requisition."[21]

Try as he might, Seward could not always maintain this serenity and optimism. His more somber, more frustrated moods derived in part from his sense by June that no Union military victories, no northern attempts to ease European cotton shortages, and no movement toward a greater focus on freeing southern slaves seemed to elicit more sympathetic policies in London or Paris. He complained that victories did "not satisfy our enemies abroad," and "defeats in their eyes prove our national incapacity." Initially criticized for being "unfaithful to humanity" for failing to proclaim "emancipation," the North by late July was being castigated for making the "war . . . an intolerable propagandism of emancipation by the sword." The secretary unburdened himself to Adams: "Ah, well! Skepticism must be expected in this world" regarding "new political systems, insomuch as even Divine revelation needs the aid of miracles to make converts to a new religious faith."[22]

At other times, Seward consciously returned to his pointed threats that European intervention would be met with war. Britain and France remained on notice that they could not expect to carry out a peaceful intervention. While emphasizing that continued recognition of the Confederates as belligerents and public debates over the possibility of mediation or recognition of the South raised southern hopes and thereby prolonged the war, the secretary asserted that European interference could provoke slave revolts. If a slave insurrection were a possibility, European intervention, he reiterated, rendered war with the Union a certainty. In July Seward directed Adams to inform the British that if "respect of our sovereignty" were challenged, "this civil war will . . . become a war of continents—a war of the world." The following month, Adams was instructed that if Russell attempted to "dictate, or to mediate, or to advise, or even to solicit or persuade," the US minister was "forbidden to debate, to hear, or . . . entertain" any such "communication." The secretary conveyed a similar admonition to French minister Mercier. Napoleon could "commit no graver error than to mix himself in our affairs. At the rumor of intervention all the [northern] factions" would "reunite themselves against you and even in the border states you will meet resistance unanimous and desperate."[23]

As had been the case during 1861, these threats inspired caution among European leaders. In February 1862 Henry Hotze, the Confederacy's principal propagandist in Great Britain, complained bitterly of the British "cowardly dread of war" with the United States. By spring, both Lord Lyons and Henri Mercier, the British and French ministers in Washington, advised their governments that intervention would incite an armed Union response. Mercier voiced this caution in early May when he advised Thouvenel, "Whatever we do, let us be tactful with the North. I have great respect for them since I have seen what they can do [militarily]. . . . We must be friends with this people . . . because we do not know where their bellicose mood might push them." In London, Russell and Palmerston continued to worry about Canada's strategic vulnerability in the short term and to fear possible postwar military complications with the North. From Paris, Thouvenel sustained the French policy of acting only in conjunction with the British and in mid-May reiterated his nation's ongoing "position of strict neutrality." Two historians of Civil War foreign relations have assessed the implications of Seward's policy of threat: they noted that "any offer to mediate" would have needed "to be backed by a covert threat of force" and that European "intervention meant involvement in the war without assured benefits"—such as greater access to cotton, a more profitable trade with North America, or fewer attacks on maritime commerce.[24]

Without abandoning his purposeful threats, Seward exhibited the more conciliatory aspect of his two-pronged policy by opening New Orleans and the less-important ports of Beaufort and Port Royal, South Carolina, to all trade, save contraband. The secretary had permitted the resumption of mail service to New Orleans, considered by many a French city, on May 2. On May 12 he and Lincoln opened the three ports and their ostensible access to raw cotton as a goodwill gesture toward Great Britain and France, where the scarcity of cotton was causing increasing distress among textile workers and provincial government officials. Seward recognized that there was little realistic prospect of "the South getting much aid" via the permissible trade through these ports or of "France . . . getting much cotton." But he hoped to use this concession as part of his effort to induce Britain and France to withdraw their recognition of Confederate belligerency and to put the onus for any cotton scarcity on the South, which had begun to burn cotton stores rather than have them fall into Union hands. Later in July, when little cotton had reached Europe and as US fears of British and French intervention mounted, Seward proposed allowing even greater access to southern cotton, but Lincoln refused. The president balked at permitting the possible export of $50 million of cotton, a step which could preclude "crippling" the South "much in their resources." Despite Lincoln's limits on federal cotton largesse, Seward's proposal, which he intentionally discussed with British diplomats, contributed to better Anglo-American relations.[25]

Seward's response to British protests over Union enforcement of the blockade were similarly restrained. The British had recognized the blockade's legality, but they still complained vociferously about alleged abuses by the Union navy. Many of their complaints were well founded. Union sailors acted from diverse motives. Patriotism underlay their intense desire to deny badly needed goods to the Confederates, and frustration led to rash actions when they failed to capture blockade runners. Union naval forces also resented the profits that flowed to the British and recognized the potential personal returns that derived from the successful capture of any illicit vessel. The proceeds from a ship and its contraband cargo sold by a US prize court were divided between the US government and the crew that had seized the blockade runner.[26]

So motivated, northern crews hovered just beyond the three-mile limit of British, Spanish, or French sovereignty, particularly in the Caribbean, and essentially blockaded neutral ports. US ships also fired upon, destroyed, and captured suspected blockade runners in neutral waters. They did so most flagrantly off the coast of Mexico, where goods flowed through Matamoros across the border into Texas and on to southern armies. Union officers and boarding parties often insulted and mistreated the apprehended crews, and all of these actions elicited protests from the offended parties and their governments.[27]

Seward sought to minimize these maritime conflicts and to keep British and Spanish complaints safely bottled up in prize court proceedings. This approach was crucial, given the lack of Union victories in the eastern theater, the persistent political carping from Democrats and radical Republicans, and the ongoing threat of European intervention in the war. The secretary's delaying tactic postponed and deferred diplomatic confrontations until legal verdicts had been rendered. To complement his policy of legal "evasion and procrastination," Seward attempted to reduce the offensive US naval actions. Over the objections of Secretary of the Navy Welles, who considered Seward too lenient toward Great Britain and overly meddlesome in naval matters, the secretary of state persuaded Lincoln and the cabinet to instruct US naval commanders to refrain from seizing suspect ships "within the waters of a friendly nation," pursuing and firing on a ship without proper warning, or taking a prize without a "reasonable" belief that the ship was "engaged in carrying contraband of war to the insurgents . . . or otherwise violating the blockade." This August 1862 directive also advised American sailors not to open official diplomatic parcels and dispatches.[28]

Perhaps to sustain his dual policy of conciliation and threat, Seward also expressed support for a midsummer congressional authorization of US privateering, which could only have been aimed at the British, and endorsed Welles's decision in the fall to send a flying squadron to the Caribbean commanded by the notorious Charles Wilkes. Although the privateering bill did not pass Congress until early 1863, and returning Wilkes to the Caribbean was ill-advised, Seward's overall response to these myriad issues proved successful in 1862 and afterward, as the British reciprocated the secretary's efforts to avoid any catastrophic confrontation. Lord Lyons rejected the "risk of getting up an excitement on doubtful or small cases," and Russell subsequently observed that his government had been "far from pressing hard on the United States and, in spite of remonstrances from many quarters, put no impediment in the way of the capture of British merchants ships."[29]

In still another arguably conciliatory, but, nevertheless, curious move, Seward suggested that Henri Mercier, the French minister to Washington, visit the Confederate capital in Richmond. Seward extended this most unexpected invitation during a meeting with Mercier in late April following the Union victories in Tennessee. In response to the secretary's overly optimistic prediction that the Union was about to prevail militarily, Mercier declared, "I wish I could be as sure of it as you are," and continued, "It's just too bad I can't go down to Richmond and find out for myself . . . the conditions of things" there. Much to the French minister's surprise, Seward readily endorsed the trip and agreed to provide a diplomatic pass through the military lines.[30]

Seward may have believed that Mercier could convey a sobering assessment of northern strength and determination to the Confederate government. The secretary knew of the French diplomat's friendship with Confederate Secretary of State Judah P. Benjamin and understood that Mercier would be welcome in Richmond. Indeed, the *Mobile Advertiser and Register* applauded Mercier's "friendly sentiments to the Southern Confederacy, and his contempt for Lincolnism and Sewardism." Seward empowered Mercier to assure any chastened and potentially cooperative Confederates that he harbored "no spirit of vengeance" and was "willing to risk" his "political station and reputation in pursuing a conciliatory course towards the South." Other Seward motives were less straightforward. He neither liked nor trusted Mercier, whom he subsequently described as "one of the most impudent men in history." Therefore, he would not have been overly distressed if this bizarre undertaking had embarrassed the French intermediary or weakened the Anglo-French cooperative policy toward the American war.[31]

Mercier, who went to Richmond alone, against the advice of Lord Lyons and without first consulting the disapproving French foreign minister Thouvenel, was personally embarrassed by the venture; but Anglo-French cooperation survived and Seward's conciliatory overture to Benjamin was roundly rejected. Mercier met with the Confederate secretary of state on April 16. Benjamin declared that the South was "determined to win" its "independence no matter what the cost." The North and South were "two distinct peoples," and the North had either to "exterminate us or agree to our separation." Mercier returned to Washington convinced that European mediation was futile since neither American side was willing to compromise its objectives or stop fighting. Therefore, France needed to remain neutral and await military developments. In a characteristic act of public diplomacy, Seward preempted the narrative of Mercier's mission by publishing his own version of the episode in the May 6 *New York Times*. The secretary portrayed the French diplomat as a US agent who sought to convince the South to concede defeat. Seward's hopes for Confederate concessions did not bear fruit, but he had gained additional information at Mercier's expense, neutralized the Frenchman's hopes to promote mediation, and secured assurances of continued French abstention.[32]

Any such foreign policy gains, no matter how small, were welcome, given the downturn in Union military fortunes following the northern victories in Tennessee. Most distressing to Lincoln, McClellan had displayed his usual tactical hesitancy by retreating before Lee in the Seven Days Battles from June 25 to July 1. In his search for decisive Union leadership, Lincoln placed General John Pope in charge of the newly designated Army of Virginia on June 26 and two weeks later appointed General Henry W. Halleck general in chief of the US forces. McClellan, still in command of the Army of the Potomac, and Pope were to report to Halleck, to whom Lincoln sought to refer all military questions. To the president's intense frustration, these changes produced no victories. Instead, as Pope committed tactical blunders and McClellan refused to provide reinforcements, the North lost the Second Battle of Bull Run in late August.

The president was convinced that McClellan had "wanted Pope defeated"; but, as wounded and disorganized Union soldiers again staggered back into Washington and Confederates advanced within fifty miles of the capital, the president restored the still inert and disrespectful Democratic general to effective command of Union forces in the East. Lincoln did so despite the heated opposition of cabinet members, especially Chase and Secretary of War Edwin M. Stanton. Although Lincoln turned again to "Little Mac" because he deemed him best able to rally northern soldiers and defend Washington, the dejected president was described as "greatly distressed," exhibiting the "bitterest anguish," and fretting that "he felt almost ready to hang himself."[33]

The hostile response of the majority of his cabinet, with the conspicuous exception of Seward, was symptomatic of the North's fractured political environment in the summer of 1862. Democrats, many of whom were hostile to any thought of emancipating the slaves and were champions of states' rights, denounced the administration on both partisan and ideological grounds as the president exercised strong executive powers and moved toward a more aggressive antislavery position. Simultaneously, the Republican Party, led by Sumner, Henry Wilson, Benjamin F. Wade, Lyman Trumbull, and Thaddeus Stevens, grew increasingly caustic in their criticism of the administration. These Republicans derided Lincoln for moving too slowly toward emancipation and for not sacking McClellan, whom they considered incompetent, disloyal, and a friend of black bondage.

Sumner was particularly persistent and often intemperate in his efforts to pressure Lincoln to issue a general proclamation freeing the slaves. He made repeated trips to the White House to prod the president, whom he described as "slow, with an immense *vis inertiae.*" When Lincoln did not promptly follow the senator's advice, Sumner contended that Congress should assume control of the war and emancipation. Previous interactions with the rigid and self-righteous Sumner had led Lincoln to observe, "I have never had much to do with bishops . . . , but . . . Sumner is my idea of a bishop." Still, the president avoided a personal break with the annoying but important chair of the Senate Foreign Relations Committee. This fit the chief executive's preference for "short statutes of limitation in politics" and demonstrated his ability to manage those around him. Seward undoubtedly voiced his and Lincoln's frustration with the endless political skirmishes and carping when he complained that, anytime he sent a document to Congress, "they fall into altercation about letting slaves fight and work. Every day is a day lost, and every day lost is a hazard to the whole country." In an ill-advised July 5 dispatch to Minister Adams, the secretary vented further by asserting that the "extreme advocates of African slavery and its most vehement opponents were acting in concert to precipitate a servile war"—"the former by seeking to overthrow the federal Union, the latter by demanding an edict of universal emancipation as . . . the only legitimate, way of saving the Union."[34]

In addition to the grim military situation and noxious politics, Lincoln and Seward faced an acute foreign policy crisis as both Britain and France again pondered intervention in the American war. A host of factors prompted Palmerston and Russell in London and Napoleon and Thouvenel in Paris to contemplate actions that would likely have led to Union defeat and Confederate victory. Napoleon spoke for all four of these key leaders when he declared in mid-July that he "considered the re-establishment of the Union impossible." The assumption that the North could not prevail, that, as Thouvenel added, "a definitive separation of the South from the North" was inevitable, led to several corollary considerations. One, put forward primarily by Russell, was humanitarian and argued for ending the ostensibly needless suffering. The *London Morning Herald* voiced this sentiment: "Let us do something, as we are Christian men." Whether "arbitration, intervention, diplomatic action, recognition of the South . . . or forcible pressure of some sort . . . let us do something to stop this carnage."[35]

Other European calculations were much more self-interested. Napoleon recognized that an independent South augured well for his Mexican imperial project and the enhancement of French influence in the Western Hemisphere. Although Palmerston and Russell were more discreet regarding Britain's potential strategic gains from Confederate independence, they understood the advantages of confronting a militarily and economically weaker United States. Two competing North American nations would be more manageable than one emerging world power. They also worried that the raging war endangered Canada and threatened to spread beyond North America and that northern losses could lead Lincoln and Seward to incite a slave rebellion to defeat the South. A so-called "servile war" would further disrupt the Atlantic economy and spur racial strife that might spread to the West Indies.

Looming over and reinforcing all of these concerns was Europe's reduced access to raw cotton and the potential impact on the British and French textile industries, broader economies, and domestic politics. The South had left the Union convinced that depriving Britain and France of raw cotton would be a decisive diplomatic weapon. Senator James H. Hammond of South Carolina proclaimed the power of the South and its principal crop in 1858: "Without firing a gun, without drawing a sword," the South "could bring the whole world to our feet." Should southerners withhold cotton from international commerce, "England . . . and . . . the whole civilized world" would be devastated. "No," Hammond thundered, "you dare not make war on cotton. . . . Cotton is king!" Following secession, the *Charleston Mercury* agreed, "The cards are in our hands and we intend to play them out to the bankruptcy of every cotton factory in Great Britain and France or the acknowledgement of our independence." Hammond and the *Mercury*'s editors were correct that British and French manufacturers obtained the great bulk of their raw cotton from the South as the war began; but these southerners, like most of their contemporaries in North America and Europe, greatly overestimated cotton's diplomatic influence.[36]

As the Civil War began, larger British and French cotton manufacturers had amassed an oversupply of both raw cotton and finished goods. Therefore, during most of the war's first year, the North's blockade and the South's embargo on cotton exports actually helped these manufacturers to adjust their inventories and mitigated any serious pressure on European foreign policymakers. By early 1862, conditions had changed. Economic distress deepened more quickly in France, where textile workers' hours had been reduced by one-sixth during fall 1861. French manufacturers of coarse cotton cloth were hardest hit, and by 1863 an estimated 250,000 textile workers were unemployed. As layoffs in French mills mounted, chambers of commerce petitioned the government for relief, and Napoleon and Thouvenel grew increasingly vocal in their complaints to Minister Dayton and Secretary Seward. Despite these concerns, neither French leader was prepared to act independently of Great Britain.[37]

Economic dislocation also ravaged Great Britain. Over the war's first year, British raw cotton imports plunged by 50 percent overall and by 96 percent from the United States. By midsummer 1862, the nation's store of cotton had fallen from 1.2 million bales in 1861 to a paltry two hundred thousand. Only 497 of Manchester's 1,678 textile mills were operating full-time. Some eighty thousand British textile workers had been laid off and another three hundred thousand were working part-time. In November, the unemployed numbered three hundred thousand, with only about two hundred thousand working full-time. The following year, desperate workers rioted in several deeply depressed cotton towns. Both Union supporters, such as Richard Cobden, and normally hostile papers, such as the *Economist,* warned that the hardships attributed to the cotton scarcity might force British intervention. This suffering among British workers and their families and the possible political implications prompted Palmerston and Russell to anxiously monitor the situation.[38]

Despite the anxiety of the European leaders, King Cotton's ultimate power was vastly overrated. Before the war began, Lord Lyons provided an acute appraisal: "It is true that cotton is almost a necessity to us, but it is still more necessary for them to sell it than it is for us to buy it." With far stronger, more diverse economies than the Confederacy, both Britain and France were much better equipped to endure the dislocation of the international cotton trade. To mitigate this dislocation, both nations drew on alternative sources of raw cotton from India, Egypt, and Brazil. Although British textile workers suffered badly, cotton manufacturers, shipbuilders, and linen and woolen producers profited from the war. Moreover, the North had long been a valued consumer of British steel and metal goods, liquor, pottery, and investment capital; and Britain imported massive quantities of corn and wheat from the United States during the 1850s. In short, the cotton crisis and the influence of textile interests never carried sufficient influence to persuade Palmerston and Russell to risk war with the North—a better customer, a principal provider of foodstuffs, and a potentially formidable military adversary. The London *Times,* no friend of the North, noted correctly "that it would be cheaper to keep all Lancashire [textile workers] on turtle and venison than to plunge into a desperate war with the Northern States of America."[39]

Similarly, the influence of France's watchmaking, gold, glass, lace, chinaware, wine, and shipbuilding businesses far outweighed the influence of the cotton textile producers and their allies. Deeming peace essential to their prosperity, these other French business interests may have supported mediation with Union approval, but they did not favor risking conflict with the North. And, as in Britain, the linen, wool, and hemp industries did well during the American war, and the French economy was much too varied to be forced to bow before King Cotton.[40]

Still, none of the American or European foreign policy makers fully grasped these economic and associated geopolitical realities in mid-1862. Based on contemporary economic anxieties, humanitarian concerns, and strategic considerations, leaders in both Britain and France explored the possibility of intervention. As the summer began, restraint seemed dominant in both London and Paris. In May Napoleon had asserted, there was "nothing to be done for the moment but to watch events," and Thouvenel had agreed that, given "the . . . [military] uncertainty," France should not "abandon a position of strict neutrality." In July Palmerston flatly rejected a parliamentary motion urging British diplomatic recognition of the South. The prime minister reiterated his fundamental position that recognition should be extended only after the South had "firmly and permanently" secured its independence. Since the Confederacy had not yet done so, British intervention "meant war" with the North and "greater sufferings" for English textile workers.[41]

British and French commitment to strict neutrality and abstention wavered after McClellan dithered before Richmond, Pope was badly defeated at Second Bull Run, and the war seemed to settle into a horrifyingly lethal stalemate. In a July 16 interview with Confederate diplomat John Slidell, Napoleon declared "my sympathies have always been with the South," and over the summer, the French emperor first sought to enlist Britain in joint recognition of the Confederacy and subsequently floated a potential tripartite Anglo-French-Russian mediation proposal. Both schemes failed. Russia, the most consistently pro-North nation in Europe, wanted no part of what was, in essence, an effort to aid the South, and Foreign Minister Thouvenel quashed the overture to Britain. Thouvenel opposed Napoleon's Mexican project, and he recognized that "an adventure" leading to war with the United States would be "even more serious than the Mexican one." Thouvenel's opposition to premature intervention was reinforced by his concern over contemporary developments in Italy and Germany and his commitment, which Napoleon shared, to act only in conjunction with Britain regarding the American war. Still, the foreign minister revealed the tenuous nature of French policy and its threat to US survival when he admitted that the ideal American outcome would have been "the formation of two *federated confederations.*"[42]

As Napoleon and Thouvenel refused to act independently of Great Britain, Palmerston and Russell pondered whether and how to intervene. Even before they received details of Second Bull Run, the two British leaders had agreed in early August that some form of neutral mediation should be considered. After news of the stunning Union defeat and General Lee's preparation to invade Maryland reached London a month later, Palmerston anticipated that "still greater disasters" awaited the northern army, and Russell endorsed a prospective plan calling for an Anglo-French-Russian "offer of mediation." The plan specified that the United States end the blockade and accept southern independence. If the North rejected the terms, diplomatic "recognition of the South" would follow.[43]

Ever the realist, Palmerston refused to act before learning the outcome of the "great conflict" about to take "place to the north-west of Washington." The prime minister was correct to await the outcome of what became known as the Battle of Antietam; however, he and Russell were badly mistaken to think that Lincoln and Seward were willing to accept any form of European intervention. As Palmerston and Russell perfected their proposal, Seward reminded French minister Mercier on September 8 of his country's "trouble" in Mexico and Italy and bluntly warned him, "Do not for a moment believe that either the President, Congress, myself or any person connected with this Government, will in any case entertain any proposition or suggestion or arrangement . . . from within or without" that included "a surrender of the Federal Union." Potential European intruders, Seward emphatically cautioned, should understand, "We shall prosecute this war to its end."[44]

IV.

Lincoln and Seward formulated a two-pronged response to the disastrous military developments, the savage political attacks from both Democrats and Republicans, and the unnerving rumors of imminent European intervention. The first response was immediate and designed to bolster the nation's military and diplomatic fortunes. The second also addressed these crucial issues and the administration's domestic political standing; but, even more significantly, it defined the North's stated war goals on a much more elevated, timeless level.

First, the immediate response. As McClellan faltered in Virginia, Lincoln recognized that the Union needed thousands more troops to fight the war, which had no clear end in sight. Seward agreed and believed that a larger force would also help deter British and French intervention. In early April Secretary of War Stanton had closed recruiting offices in response to bipartisan political pressure to reduce war expenses by limiting the size of the northern army. Therefore, a renewed recruiting campaign was mandatory. The president correctly feared that the call for these volunteers amid the military defeats in Virginia could spark panic from the northern public. In what one of his biographers has termed Seward's "greatest service" to the Union in 1862, "outside of his diplomatic role," the secretary conceived of and implemented the plan to supply the needed soldiers. Working from the Astor Hotel in New York City, he drafted a letter in early July and persuaded northern governors to send it to Lincoln. The governors requested the president to solidify "recent successes of the federal arms" by recruiting additional soldiers. In accordance with Seward's scheme, Lincoln responded with a call for three hundred thousand volunteers. When Governor John Andrew of Massachusetts doubted that his state could comply unless recruits received a signing bonus, Seward convinced a reluctant Stanton to provide a $25 enlistment bounty. By late September, Seward reported that two hundred thousand northern men had answered the call, and he anticipated another one hundred thousand would do so within a month.[45]

After the indispensable reinforcements had been inducted, the secretary emphasized the foreign policy implications of this deft recruiting effort. American ministers abroad were instructed to accentuate this evidence of the Union's determination to fight "with greater vigor and certainty of success than before." Europeans who contemplated intervention needed to understand the implications not just for prosecution of the American war but also the imposing challenges that confronted any nation that dared to intervene in the conflict. To bolster and clarify the latter, Seward sustained his threat of war against any country that acted to aid the South.[46]

The secretary sought to augment this domestic recruiting by attracting European immigrants who might join the US forces. Seward utilized the Homestead Act, which had been passed by the Republican Congress in May, as the vehicle for appealing to potential immigrants and recruits. The act granted 160 acres to any settler who built a home and improved the land. In Circular 19, sent to American diplomats abroad on August 8, Seward instructed them to publicize this generous incentive and stress that "Nowhere else can the industrious laboring man and artisan expect so liberal a recompense for his services." These "truths" were to be made "known in any quarter and in any way which may lead to the migration of such persons to this country." As he launched this obvious recruiting campaign, Seward met the letter of international law by cautioning that the US government had "no legal authority to offer any pecuniary inducements," or, as he had confided to Consul John Bigelow in Paris, "Nobody is [formally] authorized to do anything or pay anything." Official recruitment may have been illegal, but, he noted, the war was "a trial between the two parties to exhaust each other" and the "immigration of a large mass from Europe would . . . decide it."[47]

President Lincoln was responsible for the second, more significant, response to the nation's midsummer crises. At the war's beginning, Lincoln, with Seward's complete agreement, had emphasized that the North fought to preserve the Union, rather than to abolish slavery. Both northern leaders deemed this emphasis essential to prevent the secession of the strategically crucial border states of Maryland, Missouri, Kentucky, and Tennessee. Lincoln's doubts that he had the constitutional authority to abolish slavery where it was lawfully in place in 1861 reinforced the decision to make emancipation of the slaves a secondary objective. Finally, both he and Seward assumed, incorrectly, that European observers would understand that the Republican Party and the North, having gone to war to prevent the spread of slavery, were opposed to the institution that the South revered and defended. When the South also deemphasized the role of slavery in 1861 and contended that its defense of self-determination and free trade had led to secession, British and French leaders did not reach the conclusions the two principal US foreign policymakers considered so obvious. In May 1861 the London *Times* declared, "The real motives of the belligerents" were identical to those that incited all wars—"national power, territorial aggrandizement, political advantage and commercial gain. Neither side can claim any superiority of principle." The following October, Lord Russell agreed that the antagonists were "contending . . . not upon the slavery issue," but instead "as many States in the Old World have contended, the one side for empire, and the other for independence." As these representative statements demonstrated, the South had successfully established the parameters for interpreting the war's first eighteen months.[48]

On July 13 Lincoln announced to Seward and Welles, while they shared a carriage ride, that he was about to transform those debate terms and to clarify the war's essence by issuing a proclamation emancipating the slaves: "We must," he declared, "free the slaves or be ourselves subdued." As Lincoln explained over the next several weeks, he believed that "things had gone from bad to worse." Teetering on the edge of collapse, the Union had to "change our tactics, or lose the game." Lincoln retained his "paramount objective . . . to save the Union" and was determined to leave no "available card unplayed" in pursuit of that end. His decision for emancipation had come after numerous other less-sweeping antislavery measures had failed to clarify slavery's centrality to the American war and the essential connection of Union victory to the institution's demise.[49]

Working from Lincoln's assumption that no "European power would dare to recognize and aid the Southern Confederacy if it became clear that the Confederacy stands for slavery and the Union for freedom," the administration had adopted or promoted a series of measures after December 1861 that distinguished the North from the South on the issues of race and slavery: Lincoln and Seward issued passports to blacks, to whom the Buchanan administration had denied this right of citizenship based on the *Dred Scott* decision; extended diplomatic recognition to Haiti and Liberia, whose populations were largely composed of former black slaves and their descendants; ended slavery in the District of Columbia while compensating DC slaveholders; and negotiated an anti–slave trade treaty with Great Britain.[50]

Signed on April 7, the Seward-Lyons Treaty allowed for the mutual search of suspected slave traders sailing under the US and British flags. The authorization of British naval ships to board and search American vessels reversed the previous nationalistic and proslavery position that had been in place throughout the nineteenth century. This joint Anglo-American policy administered a death blow over the ensuing three years to the transport of slaves to Cuba, the most important New World destination. Seward was especially proud of this treaty, which he helped convince the Senate to approve by posing as the originator of the idea and the winner of key points of negotiation, all with Lyons's covert approval and cooperation. The British minister agreed to be "guided" in this subterfuge by "Seward's long experience" with the Senate, where Sumner also added important support. The outcome was a treaty of substantive impact that the secretary of state hoped would also bolster the North's antislavery credentials and demonstrate his conciliatory inclinations to British leaders.[51]

The administration's final antislavery effort during the spring of 1862 received much harsher treatment in Congress, particularly from targeted border state representatives. In March Lincoln submitted to Congress a bill that envisioned gradual emancipation, with federal compensation for slaveholders who agreed to free their bondsmen and bondswomen. This method of voluntary emancipation and federal compensation reflected the president's conviction that the Constitution precluded federal interference with slavery within those states where the institution was legal. He hoped this approach would appeal to slaveholders in the border states and add pressure on those in the Deep South. To this moderate proposal for gradual emancipation, Lincoln affixed a warning that he reserved the right to employ any alternate measures that "may seem indispensable, or may obviously promise greater efficiency towards ending the struggle." When border state representatives rejected this overture and Lincoln's bill died in committee, he moved on the option revealed to Seward and Welles on July 13. All of the administration's more restrained antislavery actions had failed to resolve the political, military, and foreign policy crises.[52]

The president announced his decision for emancipation to the cabinet on July 22. Before reading his proposed draft of the Emancipation Proclamation, Lincoln informed his department heads that he was "resolved" to take this momentous step. He was interested in their responses to the draft but did not seek their "advice" on the decision itself. Lincoln then read the document, which designated January 1, 1863, as the date on which the slaves in those states still in rebellion against the United States would be freed "thenceforward, and forever." If issued, the proclamation promised to liberate the South's 3.5 million slaves, but it did not apply to the approximately 425,000 slaves held in the border states. The delicate politics of keeping those states from siding with the South remained in play.[53]

Lincoln justified this notable shift in personal and public policy as a "military necessity." As he told Seward and Welles during their carriage ride, slavery was at "the heart of the rebellion." The loss of this vast source of labor would severely weaken the Confederacy. Hard war was now imperative. "Having made war on the Government," the rebels had to be made to suffer, to "be subject to the incidents and calamities of war." Fully aware that escaped slaves sought safety behind advancing Union lines, Lincoln also recognized that the Militia Act and Second Confiscation Act, both passed in July 1862, authorized the seizure of slave property and the service of "persons of African descent" in the US military. Emancipation, he discerned, would encourage the slaves' flight from bondage and their potential military service. Subsequent developments confirmed this perception. By 1865, 180,000 freedmen (12 percent of the Union army) fought for the North. Of this number, 135,000 were freed slaves who chose to confront their former masters in battle rather than labor for the Confederate cause. The president also grasped the potential political benefits associated with adopting the policy Sumner and the majority of the Republicans advocated. Democrats might be further alienated, but Republicans would be more united as the 1862 midterm elections approached. Finally, Lincoln envisioned significant foreign policy implications: Emancipation of the slaves, he later declared, "would help us in Europe, and convince them that we are incited by something more than ambition."[54]

By invoking his authority as "Commander-in-chief . . . in time of actual armed rebellion against the authority and government of the United States," Lincoln derived the constitutional justification for the proclamation. This justification, on which he had acted when instituting the blockade and suspending habeas corpus, was essential for a president "devoted . . . to the order of law." According to Lincoln's constitutional rationale, the unprecedented national emergency of secession and war justified these extraordinary executive actions. His thinking agreed with the contemporary international legal analysis of William Whiting in his 1862 volume, *War Powers of the President.* Whiting, whom Lincoln appointed special counsel to the War Department, contended that the war's existence permitted the suspension of certain constitutional guarantees, such as the sanctity of private property. It was, wrote Whiting, "in accordance with the law of nations and with the practice of civilized belligerents in modern times, to liberate enemy's slaves in time of war by military power." Based on these arguments, Lincoln reversed the declarations in his inaugural address. In March 1861, he had claimed "no lawful right" and "no inclination" to "interfere with . . . slavery in the States where it exists."[55]

According to Noah Brooks, a well-informed reporter, Seward's "concurrence" with Lincoln's "emancipation measures" was "tardy and reluctant." Although Seward had long condemned slavery and its malevolent humanitarian, economic, and political impacts, he preferred that the institution be destroyed gradually by the North's advancing armies without any announced proclamation. Unable to foresee how truly transformative Lincoln's action would be, the secretary worried that proclamations were merely ineffectual announcements that could not substitute for necessary military force. He also feared that the proclamation could provoke a backlash among antiblack groups in the North, incite a slave rebellion in the South, and even induce European intervention to secure cotton. Given Lincoln's notice to the cabinet that he was determined to issue the proclamation, Seward expressed these reservations and then fell into line. His loyalty to Lincoln, concern for their personal relationship, and the force of the argument for military necessity left the secretary no real choice, and he grudgingly admitted that the proclamation would "reach a weakness in every nook and cranny of the insurrectionary region."[56]

In a critically important contribution to the July cabinet discussion, Seward questioned the "expediency" of the proclamation's "issue at this juncture." In the wake of the Union's "repeated [military] reverses," the secretary feared the proclamation would be "viewed as the last measure of an exhausted government, a cry for help . . . our last *shriek,* on the retreat." He suggested delaying the announcement until the North had achieved "military success." Lincoln agreed and later recalled, "The wisdom" of Seward's suggestion "struck me with very great force" as "an aspect of the case . . . I had entirely overlooked." The president "put the draft proclamation aside" and awaited a northern "victory."[57]

While Lincoln, Seward, and key European observers watched for instructive battlefield developments, the president prepared the American public for his impending proclamation. He first met with a group of freedmen at the

White House on August 14 and made the case for the colonization of free blacks in Central America. The president characterized slavery as "the greatest wrong inflicted on any people," but asserted that blacks and whites were separated "by a broader difference than exists between almost any other two races." This difference and white prejudice would prevent African Americans from achieving "equality with the white race." Therefore, Lincoln continued, free blacks could advance much more rapidly by moving to a colony outside of the United States. The delegation with whom he met; other black leaders, including Frederick Douglass; and prominent abolitionists decisively rejected the president's overture. Lincoln may still have held out hope for colonization as a viable solution for the nation's racial woes since he assigned the project to Secretary of the Interior Caleb Smith and signed a related $500,000 appropriation bill during the summer of 1862. But, as a precursor to the Emancipation Proclamation, he was also using potential colonization as a vehicle to make emancipation more palatable for northern whites who rejected the prospect of numerous free blacks living among them.[58]

Given the lack of adequate funding and transportation and the strong opposition of African Americans to leaving the United States, colonization of blacks from the United States to other countries did not gain traction in the 1860s. Significantly, Central American countries, which became the most plausible destination for potential black emigrants during the decade, decisively rejected US overtures. Historian Robert May has observed that diplomats and officials in Mexico, Nicaragua, Honduras, and Costa Rica feared that African American immigrants "represented a new iteration of Manifest Destiny," filibustering, and US imperial expansion. Lincoln did not think primarily in these terms, but other members of his administration did. Secretary of the Interior Smith predicted that significant migration of "Colored Americans" to the Chiriquí region of Costa Rica "would most probably secure to us the absolute control" of that territory. Secretary Chase agreed that colonization could yield a US "foothold in Central America." Since Lincoln accepted Seward's September 1862 recommendation that any colonization effort should require consent, preferably by a treaty, from the country to which American blacks moved, Latin American opposition provided the final nail in the colonization coffin. As was true of westward expansion across the North American continent, Lincoln may not have thought of colonization in expressly imperial terms, but others envisioned and feared the actual and potential effects of US power.[59]

In a far more public action than his meeting with the African American delegation, Lincoln responded to an August 20 editorial by Horace Greeley in the *New York Tribune* demanding that the president make the abolition of slavery the primary focus of the Union war effort. Without revealing that he was about to shift in that direction, Lincoln did suggest a possible policy change, and he again moved beyond his inaugural pledge not to interfere with slavery in the southern states. The president reiterated that his "paramount objective" was "to save the Union" rather than "to save or destroy slavery." "If I could save the Union," he wrote, "without freeing *any* slave I would do it, and if I could save it by freeing *all* the slaves I would do it; and if I could save it by freeing" some and not others "I would also do that." Southern slavery was clearly no longer off limits.[60]

Three weeks later, Lincoln completed his preparatory campaign for the release of the Emancipation Proclamation by meeting with two Chicago ministers who conveyed a pro-emancipation resolution that had been passed by a meeting of "Christians of All Denominations." The president used the occasion to discuss and ponder a range of religious and strategic issues. He gently prodded the clergymen to explain why, if God's position on abolition was so obvious, would the Supreme Being "reveal his will to others on a point so connected with my duty" and not "reveal it directly to me"? He also queried, in the absence of sufficient Union military force, "What *good* would a proclamation of emancipation from me do?" In a nod to Seward's advice, he continued, "I do not want to issue a document that the whole world" would deem "inoperative, like the Pope's bull against the comet!" The president reiterated his concern over a proclamation's impact in the border states but also repeated his confidence that a clearly stated northern war goal ending slavery would command backing in Britain and France. Concluding with what was perhaps his principal reason for the meeting, Lincoln queried his visitors on the state of public opinion, and they responded that a clear fight for "Liberty and Union" would "rouse the people and rally them to his support beyond anything yet witnessed."[61]

Although Seward had fallen in line behind Lincoln's decision for an emancipation proclamation, the secretary of state retained his basic reservations. Nor was the secretary in uniform agreement with the president's attempts to prepare the public for this transformative action. Seward endorsed Lincoln's letter to Greeley, with its stated priority of preserving the Union over the destruction of slavery. "Salvation of the nation," he subsequently noted, was "of vastly more consequence than the destruction of slavery." Lincoln certainly concurred; but, unlike his friend, the president had come to recognize that national salvation and emancipation were inseparable. Seward may have also misunderstood that Lincoln's argument for colonization was meant as a palliative for antiblack northerners. But the secretary rejected the idea on more substantive grounds. Colonization would cause foreign relations problems; free blacks did not want to leave "the country of their birth"; and dispatching African Americans to the tropics contradicted Seward's career-long advocacy of immigration to bolster the nation's numbers and economy. He was "always for bringing men and states *into* the Union" and "never for taking any *out*." Based on these reservations, Seward neither endorsed nor actively promoted this response to the nation's racial ills. It was, he later claimed inaccurately, the only issue over which he and Lincoln disagreed.[62]

The "military success" that Lincoln and Seward sought came on September 17, the war's bloodiest single day, when northern forces stopped Lee's invasion at the Battle of Antietam near Sharpsburg, Maryland, and forced the Confederates to retreat into Virginia. The battle, which left six thousand dead and another seventeen thousand wounded, yielded no decisive strategic outcome, but the South's first attempt to invade the North had been repulsed. Characteristically, McClellan, much to Lincoln's disappointment, failed to capitalize on the opportunity to pursue Lee's retreating forces. Although he waited until one day after the midterm elections, Lincoln removed the Democratic, proslavery McClellan from command of the Army of the Potomac on November 5—a decision consistent with the president's more aggressive antislavery posture.

Although the virtual military draw at Antietam was not the decisive outcome Lincoln would have preferred, the battle afforded him the occasion to announce the Emancipation Proclamation—a document eventually indispensable to the Union's central foreign policy objective of blocking European intervention in the war. On September 22 the president informed the cabinet of his intentions, and the following day he issued essentially the same document he had read to his advisers in July. The provisional September 22 version, which was to become official on January 1, 1863, if the South were still in rebellion, declared slaves in the Confederacy free but did not alter the status of slaves in the border states. The provisional proclamation was altered only by the incorporation of several changes Seward had suggested:

the United States pledged to both "recognize" and "maintain" the slaves' freedom; addressed European and domestic fears of a servile rebellion by exhorting freedmen "to abstain from all violence unless in necessary self-defense"; and made any colonization projects contingent upon the consent of participating free blacks and any country to which they might emigrate.[63]

Despite his persistent ambivalence regarding the wisdom of the proclamation, Seward promptly employed it for the Union's diplomatic advantage. Indeed, the "interests of humanity" had "now become identified with the cause of our country." He instructed US diplomatic representatives to emphasize that the northern cause had been converted from the "Union and not abolition" to the "Union and abolition." Therefore, by intervening in the American struggle, "the enlightened and humane nations of Great Britain and France" would interfere in a "war between freedom and bondage" and cast "their protection over the insurgents" and the hated institution of slavery. In a final ideological flourish, Seward, now armed with Lincoln's pledge to end slavery, acknowledged Lord Russell's charge that the North fought to defend its empire. "But the empire," he retorted, was "not only our own already, . . . it was lawfully acquired, and is lawfully held." It was empire that equated with republicanism, that stood for freedom and against bondage. Secession and war had not extinguished Seward's vision of American imperial growth and pursuit of international power.[64]

Although Lincoln and Seward's hopes for the proclamation's ideological and foreign relations impact in Europe were eventually fulfilled, neither Antietam nor the Union's clear stand on the side of emancipation served as immediately decisive impediments to European intervention. At best, they prompted ongoing caution and watchful waiting in London and Paris; at worst, they induced Lord Russell and Emperor Napoleon to promote intervention more aggressively. These latter responses reflected the generally negative reception accorded the proclamation in Europe. Both Mercier, the French minister to Washington, and William Stuart, Lord Lyons's temporary replacement, denounced Lincoln's pronouncement as transparently expedient and hypocritical. The president, Stuart declared, had only addressed slaves in the South where the Union exercised no authority in an attempt to "render intervention impossible." His proclamation embodied no "pretext of humanity"; it was "cold, vindictive, and entirely political" and was likely to incite a slave revolt. Mercier dismissed the decree as "an act of desperation, atrocious in the intent it reveals and consequences it might entail." The European diplomats agreed that the proclamation enhanced, rather than reduced, the justification and necessity of British and French intervention.[65]

Majority opinion in the British and French press agreed with Stuart's caustic assessment. The *Times* of London decried Lincoln's proclamation as a hypocritical step that freed slaves "where he has no power" but left them in bondage "where he retains power." His decree was more akin to "a Chinaman beating his two swords together to frighten his enemy than like an earnest man pressing on his cause." *Punch* belittled "Abe Lincoln's Last Card; or Rouge-et-Noir." From Paris, Napoleon's imperial press agreed and emphasized that the contrast in the proclamation's treatment of slavery in the border and southern states demonstrated the edict's failure to free the mass of slaves and its actual goal of inciting a slave rebellion.[66]

These press assessments, though worrisome, distressed Lincoln and Seward far less than the October 7 assertion by British chancellor of the exchequer William E. Gladstone that there was "no doubt that Jefferson Davis and other leaders of the South have made an army; they are making it appears a navy; and they . . . have made a nation." The London *Economist* promptly added that Gladstone's speech "echoes the general sentiment of the country, and probably the real opinion of most members of the government." Even this seeming harbinger of British diplomatic recognition of the Confederacy would have paled, had US foreign policy leaders known of Lord Russell's private efforts to realize Gladstone's public advocacy to acknowledge southern independence. Following Antietam and Lincoln's proclamation, the foreign secretary renewed his late-summer campaign for European mediation of the conflict. Whether through lack of comprehension or willful disregard of Lincoln and Seward's unwavering rejection of intervention in any form, Russell called mediation necessary to avoid unleashing "the passions of the slave" and the "protraction of so calamitous a war." During October and early November, he pressed for an Anglo-French-Russian intervention that would force an armistice on the American belligerents and responded favorably to a similar French proposal proffered by Napoleon on October 27.[67]

Fortunately for the Union, Prime Minister Palmerston and the British cabinet rebuffed Russell and Napoleon's armistice proposals. Despite the war's deleterious economic impact on textile workers, an intervention that jeopardized British trade with the North and overall British economic prosperity seemed dubious. Geopolitical considerations also played a key role.

Russia, which viewed a strong United States as an essential geopolitical counterweight against Great Britain and France, promptly refused all overtures for joint mediation. In addition, internal struggles on the Italian peninsula, the prospect of war between Austria and Prussia, international rivalries in Greece, and rebellious rumblings in Poland prevented Britain and France from devoting undivided, or even priority, attention to the American war.[68]

Other British leaders objected cogently to Russell's proposals. Secretary of War George Cornewall Lewis, with the aid of his stepson-in-law William Vernon Harcourt, an expert in international law, devastated the rationale for mediation. Lewis emphasized a central Palmerston perspective that the South had not established clear, unchallenged independence from the North and warranted diplomatic recognition only as the "acknowledgement of a fact" rather than an aspiration. Turning from legal and political to practical, policy objections, Lewis doubted that European mediators could specify acceptable postwar boundaries, terms for use of the Mississippi River, or the status of slavery. And, tellingly, he warned that attempted intervention in any form would lead to war with the United States: "If the Great European Powers are not contented to wait until the American conflagration has burned itself out, they must not expect to extinguish the flames with rose-water."[69]

Always more cognizant of the threat of war with the United States, more realistic, and more opposed to slavery than Russell, Palmerston shared Lewis's fear of a military clash with the North. Following Antietam, Palmerston, who had contemplated mediation, remained wary. He rightly considered the "whole matter . . . full of difficulty" and looked to the "contending armies" for a clear resolution. Therefore, Britain should remain "lookers on till the war shall have taken a more decided turn." Although willing to discuss an armistice proposal, he doubted that mediation could succeed "without some agreement as to a Bases of negotiation" and understood the North would not accept southern secession until it had experienced "a good deal more pummeling by the South." Like Lewis, the prime minister could envision no slavery-related proposal that would be acceptable to the North, the South, and the antislavery British public, "especially after Lincoln's Emancipation Decree." The Union would not agree "to sanction Slavery and . . . to give back Runaways," while the Confederacy would "insist upon" both of those outcomes. Based on these reservations, his consistent distrust of Napoleon, and the primacy of European geopolitical concerns, Lord Palmerston decided against intervention, and his decision effectively quashed Russell and

Napoleon's proposals. The United States had survived what Minister Adams termed the "very crisis of our fate" and historian Howard Jones considered the Union's "most severe" foreign relations trial.[70]

Palmerston and Britain's fateful decision reflected a broad range of personal, economic, moral, and geopolitical considerations, but Lincoln and Seward's foreign policy strategies also played a central, if not decisive, role. Seward's consistent, forceful warnings that intervention in any form meant war with the United States had been heard clearly in London since April 1861, and the secretary remained verbally belligerent in the wake of the recognition crisis. In late November 1862 he instructed Minister Dayton to "warn foreign powers of the injurious effect of any apprehended interference on their part." Following the war, "the whole American people" would "be asking" which "foreign nations were most just" and "most forbearing" during the North's "hour of trial." Fear of war with the North was a key component of Lewis's compelling brief against intervention and had been in the forefront of Palmerston's cautious and noninterventionist response to the war. Lincoln's decision to equate emancipation with restoration of the Union complemented and reinforced Seward's admonitions. Palmerston's refusal to place Britain in a position to "sanction Slavery, and to give back Runaways" fulfilled the president's January 1862 prediction that major European nations could not align themselves with the proslavery South after the North made emancipation an explicit objective.[71]

If the Emancipation Proclamation's immediate foreign policy impact was mixed, Lincoln's decision to make freeing the slaves central to the Union's stated war objectives assumed ever greater importance during late 1862 and early 1863. Relieved that no bloody slave revolts occurred, Europeans gradually realized what the London *Morning Star* recognized in early October—that Lincoln's decree was "a gigantic stride in the paths of Christian and civilized progress . . . the great fact of the war—the turning point in the history of the American Commonwealth." Beginning in November 1862 and running well into late spring 1863, antislavery activists, Quakers, other dissenting clergymen, and British workingmen participated in numerous meetings and demonstrations to endorse the proclamation and the North's stand on behalf of emancipation. Two quite different groups of Americans augmented the impact of these gatherings. White American expatriates, especially in London and Liverpool, aided unemployed workers and circulated pro–United States propaganda. They also helped organize pro-Union meetings at which some forty African Americans, many of them former slaves, spoke. Cumulatively, these pro-Union actions confirmed Palmerston's realization that intervention in the war would effectively aid the South and defy majority antislavery sentiment in Britain. Although less free to hold public meetings, French backers of the Union also devised ways to support the antislavery North. For example, in March 1863, almost seven hundred French Protestant ministers released a petition addressed to British counterparts that denounced the "revolting spectacle" of the South making slavery "the cornerstone of its constitution." This dissent in France, combined with the anti-interventionist predilections of the new foreign minister Edouard Drouyn de Lhuys, engendered caution from Emperor Napoleon akin to that of Prime Minister Palmerston in Britain.[72]

Through acts of public and private diplomacy, President Lincoln sought to reinforce these pro-northern European actions. In response to sympathetic petitions from workingmen who met in Manchester and London in January 1863, he wrote public letters that were widely published in British newspapers. Lincoln, having acknowledged and commiserated with the workers' suffering, emphasized that the United States was advancing international "human rights" by fighting to ensure that "a government, established on the principles of human freedom, can be maintained against an effort to build one upon the exclusive foundation of human bondage." Later in April 1863, the president sent John Bright a model petition for possible use by northern supporters. He again focused on slavery and asserted that no "new Nation" whose "fundamental object" was "to maintain, enlarge, and perpetuate human slavery" should "ever be recognized by, or admitted into, the family of Christian and civilized nations."[73]

Lincoln sounded similar themes in his December message to Congress and in the final Emancipation Proclamation, signed on January 1, 1863. On December 1 the president continued to situate the American war in timeless and inspiring terms. He reemphasized that slaves liberated by northern armies would remain "forever free." "Fellow citizens," Lincoln continued, "we cannot escape history." Congress and the administration would "be remembered in spite of ourselves. . . . The fiery trial through which we pass, will light us down, in honor or dishonor. In *giving* freedom to the *slave,* we *assure* freedom to the *free. . . . We shall nobly save, or meanly lose, the last best hope of earth.*" Although Lincoln displayed no such eloquence on January 1, he decisively responded to those doubters at home and abroad who feared he might fail to fulfill his promise to issue the final version of the historic proclamation. By so doing, the president sealed the linkage of emancipation and salvation of the Union and solidified the foreign policy implications of that powerful combination.[74]

Those implications, together with Seward's sustained policy of threat, were apparent by early 1863, especially in Great Britain—the decisive European nation. Confederate diplomat James Mason spoke to Seward's warnings when he offered the dispirited assessment that "both parties are guided . . . by the fixed English purpose to run no risk of a broil, even far less, a war with the United States." Charles Francis Adams and his son Henry accentuated emancipation's influence as they lauded Lincoln's historic pronouncement. The elder Adams reported that the proclamation would "annihilate all agitation for recognition," and the younger concluded that the document had "done more for us here than all our former victories and all our diplomacy. It is creating an almost convulsive reaction in our favor." By February 1863, Russell admitted that he preferred any course "to being obliged to take the part of the Confederates," and Seward could declare that his and Lincoln's foreign policy strategies had succeeded: "There was no prospect of foreign interference now—that France and England were jealous of each other and neither had any intention of interfering with us."[75]

Seward's appraisal was accurate. Eighteen sixty-two proved to be the pivotal year for US Civil War foreign relations and for the Lincoln-Seward partnership that directed successful Union policies abroad. Although significant points of irritation and potential conflict arose from 1863 through 1865, with Confederate shipbuilding in Great Britain and France, the French imperial presence in Mexico, and Confederate activities in Canada, no European nation would again come so close to intervention. As had been the case during 1861, Lincoln had retained ultimate control over Union policies, but Seward continued to play an indispensable role. Together they had melded timely strategies of threat and conciliation and had avoided the repetition of potential *Trent*-like maritime crises. Most significantly, Lincoln, with the secretary's reluctant but useful assistance, had brought emancipation and its powerful international message to the forefront of northern diplomacy. The president had recognized the necessity of doing so and had skillfully made the case to the cabinet, the American public, the international community, and posterity. The secretary had rendered crucial advice on timing and wording and had deftly exploited the Emancipation Proclamation in Anglo-American and Franco-American relations.

Despite their differences over this critical foreign relations decision and instrument, Lincoln and Seward ended the year with their friendship and foreign policy partnership not only intact but strengthened. This outcome was hardly inevitable. While the decisive impact of the year's foreign policies was not yet evident, the lack of decisive Union military progress, so clearly demonstrated at Fredericksburg, was all too apparent. This military frustration, political and personal hostility toward Seward, and impatience with Lincoln's cautious movement on emancipation combined to produce a revolt among Republican senators, who demanded the secretary of state's dismissal. When Lincoln rejected the demands of Sumner and his Republican allies, the president retained the services and counsel of his friend and secretary of state, and the Union's foreign policy leaders continued to manage US foreign relations over the final two years of the war.

4

VICTORY AND THE DEATH OF THE PARTNERSHIP, 1863–1865

I.

As the war neared its end in the spring of 1865, the conflict's burdens had taken their toll on both President Lincoln and Secretary Seward. Visitors to the White House described Lincoln as "worn down in health and spirits" and noted "the lines . . . of vast responsibilities, intricate questions, the demands of life and death cut deeper than ever upon his dark brown face." At times in mid-March, the president's ill health required that cabinet meetings be held in his bedroom.[1]

For Seward, who had been described as "thin and worn and much aged" even as the war began four years earlier, a similar state of exhaustion and impaired health was compounded by the severe injuries he suffered in a carriage accident on April 5. After he jumped from the carriage in a vain attempt to stop the runaway horses, Seward suffered a badly broken jaw and fracture of his right arm near the shoulder. His face was so badly cut and bruised that Frances, his wife of nearly forty-one years, found him almost unrecognizable. At the time of Seward's mishap, Lincoln had traveled to Virginia to meet with General Grant and continued on to Richmond following the Confederate government's evacuation on April 3. After assurance from Secretary of War Stanton on April 6 that Seward had survived and was in "good spirits" and "complete control of his faculties," the president extended his trip until April 9, when he returned to Washington and went directly to his dear friend's home. Since the secretary could hardly speak above a whisper, the president lay down beside Seward in his bed and conveyed the best possible news: "I think we are near the end [of the war], at last."[2]

4. Charles Sumner, the most significant Republican critic of Lincoln and Seward's foreign policies. Courtesy of the Library of Congress.

Five days after this meeting with Seward, Lincoln attended a play at Ford's Theater on Friday evening, April 14. A regular at both Ford's and Grover's theaters, Lincoln turned to the theater as an effective outlet for coping with the war's stress. Seward, ordinarily the president's most frequent companion for these theatrical diversions, was still confined to his bedroom on Lafayette Square. Mrs. Lincoln had accompanied her husband, and both seemed to be enjoying the comedy when John Wilkes Booth, an actor and southern sympathizer, entered the box behind them and shot and mortally wounded the president.[3]

Lincoln's assassination tragically realized one of Seward's greatest fears. Following the Union capture of Richmond, the secretary had warned that the "Southern people would feel as though the world" had ended, and "the President, being the most marked man on the Federal side, was the most liable to attack." Although not oblivious to the danger, Lincoln had long resisted an overly prominent security detail. He was acutely aware of the ridicule that had accompanied his first, surreptitious entry into Washington in February 1861 and was "determined henceforth not to show any fear." From a less personal and more ideological perspective, Lincoln worried that "guards with drawn sabers" would create the impression of an "emperor" rather than the leader of a democratic republic. In a fatalistic moment, he doubted any "precautions" would deter a resolute attacker. Seward's apprehensions were warranted; and, perhaps, Lincoln's fatalism was as well. Unlike so many correct Seward observations over the previous four years, the secretary took no satisfaction in this one.[4]

The well-planned plot to assassinate Lincoln was the pivotal act in a broader conspiracy that was also aimed at Seward and Vice President Andrew Johnson. The attack on Johnson went awry; but, at almost the same time that Booth shot the president, Lewis Powell, a former Confederate soldier, called at Seward's home purporting to deliver medicine for the secretary. Confronted by Seward's son Frederick and Sergeant George Robinson, a male nurse, Powell fractured the younger Seward's skull and slashed Robinson with a knife. He then repeatedly stabbed the secretary in the face and neck. Before Powell could kill the secretary, he was pulled away by Robinson and Seward's younger son Augustus and fled from the house. The doctor, summoned to the Sewards' home, found his "feet . . . deep in blood" and thought the secretary "looked like an exsanguinated corpse." Miraculously, Powell had narrowly missed Seward's jugular vein but left the secretary's cheek terribly gashed.[5]

A few days after the attack, Seward had his bed moved close to a window, where he noticed that the American flag flying over the War Department was at half-mast. He turned to his attendant and said, "The President is dead." When the attendant demurred, Seward declared, "If he had been alive he would have been the first to call on me; but he has not been here, nor has he sent to know how I am." The secretary cried openly as he came to grips with the death of his dear friend and foreign policy partner. While contemplating his professional and personal identification with the senior partner, Seward subsequently declared, "I have always felt that Providence dealt hardly with me in not letting me die with Mr. Lincoln. My work was done, and I think I deserved some of the reward of dying there."[6]

In fact, his work was far from completed; and, fortunately for the nation, Lincoln and Seward had maintained their foreign policy partnership long enough to steer the nation to victory over the final two years of the war. Their association had remained grounded in mutual respect and enjoyment of one another's company. According to John Hay, one of Lincoln's private secretaries and a close observer of the president and secretary of state, there were "few instances of an official connection hallowed by a friendship so absolute and sincere." Secretary of the Navy Welles agreed, noting unhappily that Seward "spends more or less of every day with the President," and on matters "of the gravest importance," the New Yorker was Lincoln's "only confidant and adviser."[7]

Critics of the administration and Seward's rivals in the cabinet continued to charge that the secretary of state exercised far too much influence and was responsible for many of the administration's failures. Lincoln did leave much of the nation's foreign policy to Seward and consulted him on a wide range of other public issues, but the ultimate authority in their relationship had long since been established. As Seward readily noted, "There is but one vote in the Cabinet, and that is cast by the President." This understanding, coupled with their mutual respect and genuine fondness for one another, was evident in their willingness to poke fun. As the two spoke with a British journalist, Seward declared his surprise that "any man could ever get to be President of the United States with so few vices. The President, . . . I regret to say, neither drinks nor smokes." Lincoln, of course, was never without a humorous response, such as, "Mr. Seward is limited to a couple of stories which from repeating he believes are true."[8]

Neither Lincoln nor Seward found the military, political, or foreign policy landscapes they confronted in early 1863 nearly so amusing. The war was far from won militarily. The North's defeat at Fredericksburg helped precipitate the late-1862 cabinet crisis. Some four months later, but only nine miles west of Fredericksburg, General Robert E. Lee brilliantly outmaneuvered Joseph Hooker and the Union forces at Chancellorsville and cast a pall over northern spirits. Not until midsummer did the North win the crucial battles at Gettysburg and Vicksburg, and Lincoln went through several more ineffectual generals before he gave Ulysses S. Grant overall command in March 1864.[9]

The political challenges were equally troublesome. The most aggressively antislavery elements in the Republican Party, often led by Senator Charles Sumner, continued to criticize the Union's lack of military success and to demand more overt, aggressive steps to abolish the peculiar institution. Some elements of the party suggested that both Lincoln and Seward should be replaced and the squabbling within the cabinet continued. Democratic obstructionism complicated these Republican divisions. In the wake of the Emancipation Proclamation, the Democratic Party grew more strident in its opposition to Lincoln's linking the end of slavery to northern victory. Democrats also condemned the Union's military draft, denounced Lincoln's suspension of habeas corpus, and contended that a negotiated peace should take precedence over the destructive war on behalf of blacks and against fellow white Americans and states' rights. As 1863 began, Lincoln characterized this Democratic "'fire in the rear'" as a greater threat than the Confederate military.[10]

Lincoln and Seward found no respite when they turned their attention to foreign affairs. The United States had weathered the most serious threat of European recognition of the Confederacy during the fall of 1862, but Napoleon III continued to contemplate intervention in the American conflict, to sponsor Confederate shipbuilding in France, and to move ever more aggressively into Mexico. US-British relations were no less complicated and were also fraught with danger. Anglo-American friction over US infringements on neutral trade with the Confederacy, ongoing Confederate shipbuilding in Great Britain, and southern military operations launched against the United States from Canada all demanded the administration's attention during 1863 and 1864.

While Lincoln and Seward grappled with these myriad issues, the president remained aware that the North's successful military performance was indispensable to a viable foreign policy. As he searched for a commander committed to and capable of executing his strategic concept of hard war, Lincoln emphasized that destroying the Confederate army and punishing its civilian supporters took precedence over conquering territory. He instructed General Joseph Hooker, who replaced Ambrose E. Burnside as commander of the Army of the Potomac following Fredericksburg, "*Lee's* army and not *Richmond* is your true objective point." When Hooker lost badly at Chancellorsville and began to demonstrate a McClellan-like reluctance to tangle with Lee again, Lincoln turned to George G. Meade. Meade commanded the Union forces in the brutal and victorious battle at Gettysburg. From July 1 to 3, 161,000 young Americans slaughtered one another—at a cost of one-fourth of the northern army and one-third of the southern forces.[11]

Lee's second attempt to invade the North was repulsed, and the Union had finally scored a major military victory in the eastern theater. This victory proved to be a decisive turning point and carried significant foreign policy implications when both British and French leaders recognized that the military tide was turning against the South. But Lincoln was not satisfied since Meade had failed to pursue Lee back into Virginia. The president railed to John Hay, "We had them within our grasp. . . . We had only to stretch forth our hands & they were ours." Although Lincoln overestimated the North's military advantage and its ability to destroy Lee's army, he dismissed Meade's performance as "a dreadful reminiscence of McClellan."[12]

Fortunately for Lincoln and the nation, Grant, the very general the president had been seeking, scored an equally strategic victory on July 4 when the Confederates surrendered at Vicksburg. The seizure of Vicksburg afforded the North control of the entire Mississippi River and divided the South into geographic regions east and west of the great river. The Union victory also solidified Grant as the general most attuned to Lincoln's hard war strategy. Recognizing Grant's tenacity; aggressive, rather than defensive proclivities; and willingness to repress both southern civilians and armies, Lincoln declared, "Grant is my man and I am his the rest of the war."[13]

Thereafter, Lincoln made Grant commander of all US forces from the Appalachian Mountains to the Mississippi in October 1863 and effectively promoted him to commander of all Union forces in March 1864. At last comfortable that he had found a general who shared his strategic vision, Lincoln gradually stopped interfering in day-to-day military matters. Grant, like Seward, understood that the commander in chief exercised ultimate authority, and the general's primary interest was to fight rather than engage in politics or court public opinion. As Lincoln stated approvingly, "General Grant is a copious worker and fighter but a very meager writer or telegrapher." When rumors of Grant's alleged drunkenness circulated, the general's military accomplishments trumped any exaggerated charges regarding his sobriety.

Lincoln left no room for misunderstanding when he advised a startled group of accusers that perhaps other Union generals should start drinking Grant's brand of whiskey.[14]

II.

These military successes after mid-1863 and the steady expansion of Union manufacturing and military capacity provided the North with crucial foreign policy leverage during the war's final two years. Augmented strength in both areas made more credible Seward's ongoing threat of war against any power that dared to intervene in the American conflict. Since this leverage did not become fully apparent until summer, Lincoln and Seward experienced no respite from foreign relations challenges in the interim. The first of these came in January 1863 with a renewed French offer of mediation, reinforced by a bizarre endorsement of Napoleon III's proposal by Horace Greeley, the influential editor of the *New York Tribune.* French foreign minister Drouyn de Lhuys made the proposal on January 9. In his note and subsequent discussions with US minister William Dayton, Drouyn professed only the most benign intention to help end the war and its suffering and denied that the offer of mediation involved "interference of any kind by a foreign power." Instead, France was simply urging Union and Confederate representatives to meet without any immediate "cessation of hostilities" and to explore the possibilities of reconciliation or definitive separation.[15]

Before Drouyn's note arrived in Washington, Clement Vallandigham from Ohio and other Peace Democrats openly advocated French mediation to help "Stop fighting. Make an armistice. . . . Withdraw your [US] army from the seceded states" and "Let slavery alone." William Cornell Jewett, a globetrotting, self-important American businessman recently returned from France, also endorsed French mediation. Jewett met with Horace Greeley and persuaded the editor to go to Washington. Greeley conferred with French minister Mercier, who continued to believe that the North was incapable of thwarting ultimate southern independence. Having embraced the idea of French mediation, the mercurial Greeley lobbied Lincoln and other important Republicans and promoted the proposal in the *Tribune.*[16]

None of this lobbying or public pressure convinced Lincoln or Seward to accept French mediation. Neither was prepared to discuss the permanent division of the country; and, despite French denials, a meeting with Confederates at Napoleon's behest would have constituted foreign intervention and also lent credence to the South's claim to have achieved international standing as an independent nation. Seward deftly disposed of the entire "Jewett-Greeley affair" with the help of Henry Raymond, the editor of the *New York Times.* On January 29, Raymond published an account of the Jewett-Greeley-Mercier interactions and suggested that Greeley's "*personal negotiations*" with the French minister violated the Logan Act of 1799, which forbade private US citizens from engaging in diplomatic negotiations with a foreign power. Both Greeley and Mercier were publicly shamed and domestic pressure for French mediation was repulsed.[17]

Soon after Raymond's January article, Seward sent an equally decisive message to Paris. In his response to Drouyn's January 9 note, Seward acknowledged Napoleon's allegedly "benevolent desire for the immediate restoration of peace," despite the secretary's correct suspicion that the emperor was attempting to curry favor among French workers or to further his project of installing a European monarch in Mexico. Conveniently ignoring Greeley's lobbying and the Peace Democrats' demands, Seward asserted that no one other than the secessionists had argued "in favor of foreign intervention, of mediation, of arbitration, or of compromise" involving the "relinquishment of one acre of national domain." While "engaged in suppressing an armed insurrection," "maintaining constitutional national authority and preserving the integrity of the country," the Lincoln government rejected "any diplomatic discussions with the insurgents" that addressed these core issues. To accentuate the administration's refusal to compromise on the emancipation of slaves, southern independence, or European interference and to bolster the administration's public standing, Seward promptly published his exchange of notes with Drouyn. His success on all fronts was evident when the normally hostile *New York Herald* praised his "masterly diplomacy" and Lincoln's "sagacity, consistency and steadiness of purpose" in retaining the New Yorker as a member of the cabinet.[18]

In characteristic fashion, Senator Sumner attempted to use this most recent Napoleonic attempt at intervention to discredit Seward and perhaps succeed him as secretary of state. Unsurprisingly, relations between the two powerful men were severely strained following the late 1862 cabinet crisis. The two rivals did not see one another socially for the first three months of the new year, and Sumner's visits to the State Department frequently ended in caustic, sometimes boisterous exchanges. Consistent with his hope to replace Seward, Sumner maintained a functional relationship with the president but could not resist another assault on the secretary.[19]

The senator's fear that Seward would provoke French intervention by an overly incendiary response to Drouyn's overture reinforced Sumner's ambition and personal rancor toward the secretary. Sumner sought to mollify potential French grievances. He immediately consulted Mercier and then took several members of the Senate Foreign Relations Committee to meet with the French minister and "protest" Seward's "attitude." To this unsolicited intrusion into the conduct of US-French diplomacy, Sumner added his cooperation with James W. White, a New York Supreme Court judge and bitter Seward enemy, who claimed in the *New York Tribune* that the secretary of state had sent harmful diplomatic dispatches without Lincoln's prior approval. Sumner had previously leaked the cabinet crisis proceedings to White and readily provided information meant to confirm the judge's accusations.[20]

Sumner was especially disturbed by a dispatch Seward had sent to Charles Francis Adams in July 1862 and later unwisely published. In this note the secretary asserted, "the extreme advocates of African slavery and its most vehement opponents" appeared to be "acting in concert to precipitate a servile war." Seward cited the former's "desperate attempts to overthrow the Union" and the latter's "demanding an edict of universal emancipation" as the "only legitimate way, of saving the Union." Since this sentiment ran counter to Lincoln's simultaneous, if hesitant, movement toward issuing the Emancipation Proclamation and conflicted with the president's efforts not to alienate the Radical Republicans, Seward could not have cleared the dispatch in advance. But the note was more an expression of Seward's conservatism and fear of a possible race war than a substantive foreign policy position or directive and did not contradict his practice of close consultation with Lincoln on the substance and implementation of US foreign relations.[21]

Seward artfully countered the White-Sumner assault by providing Raymond and the *New York Times* an irrefutable rebuttal: "Every dispatch that was not merely and technically formal" had been "fully submitted, in words and substance, to the President, and read by him or to him before it was sent." White was left to appear a blatant liar without contrary evidence from Lincoln or Sumner. The president was not about to contradict his valued friend and partner, and Sumner refused to go public, despite gleeful prodding from Raymond in the *Times* that Seward's adversaries in the Senate should "put the case before the world" rather than plot privately. An experienced and skilled political infighter, Seward had foiled Sumner's last serious covert ambush.[22]

Drouyn's note and the Jewett-Greeley episode marked Sumner's last serious threat to Seward's tenure as secretary of state, but the incident was not Napoleon's final attempt at intervention in the American war. That came with what the emperor later termed the "awkward Roebuck affair." This foreign policy misstep originated with William S. Lindsay and John A. Roebuck, two pro-Confederate members of the British Parliament. After Roebuck announced in late May his intention to present Parliament with a motion calling for diplomatic recognition of the South, he and Lindsay traveled to France and met personally with Napoleon on June 22. They came away from this meeting convinced that the emperor had committed to join Great Britain in recognizing the South, and Napoleon did sound out Drouyn on whether to "state unofficially to Lord Palmerston that I am resolved on recognizing the independence of the Southern Provinces."[23]

Drouyn, who, together with the French cabinet, opposed risking US wrath and the accompanying demise of the French monarchial project in Mexico, conveyed a far less direct overture to Great Britain. Palmerston and Russell, always suspicious of Napoleon and much more concerned with European developments, turned a decidedly cold shoulder, and Roebuck blundered badly by divulging much of his private conversation with the emperor during the Parliamentary debate over his motion on June 30. With the motion's decisive rejection, French efforts to intervene in the Civil War ended.[24]

Much of the Roebuck-Napoleon project, aptly "described as a fiasco and an anticlimax," had played out in the British, French, and American press. Because it occurred before the news of the Union victories at Gettysburg and Vicksburg could be conveyed to Europe, it caused Seward and Lincoln great concern. Indeed, since Seward knew little about the British-French private machinations and deliberations over possible recognition of the Confederacy the previous fall, the secretary of state may have mistakenly considered this event "the most serious diplomatic threat to arise from Paris during the course of the Civil War." His uncompromising warnings to Napoleon and the French government were certainly consistent with that level of apprehension.[25]

On July 8, before he had learned of the Roebuck motion's failure, Seward sent Dayton dispatches by special messenger. The US minister was directed to remind Drouyn "that any new demonstration of activity" by Napoleon "prejudicial to the unity of the American people, will be necessarily regarded as unfriendly." Should the emperor "by any official act violate" US "sovereignty," Dayton was to request "an explanation" of French policy and to consider his "*functions* . . . suspended." Although Seward's latest stern threats had not caused this final serious recognition effort to fail, both the British and French governments had long understood his warning that recognition of the Confederacy could mean war with the Union. In an interesting contrast to the secretary's consistent and fundamental axiom, Drouyn responded to the demand for an explanation of Napoleon's policy by admitting, "He has none; he awaits events."[26]

The Roebuck affair, combined with the Union victories at Gettysburg and Vicksburg, dashed any lingering Confederate hopes for European recognition, but these key developments did not eliminate persistent, potentially dangerous, US diplomatic difficulties. Union efforts to enforce the blockade and the accompanying interference with neutral trade, especially British commerce, remained a major irritant in Anglo-American relations. Similar to the war's first two years, British merchants, crews, and ships were responsible for most of the crucial material reaching the West Indies and Matamoros, Mexico, where it was transshipped and carried by blockade runners bound for the Confederacy. US attempts to stop the Confederacy from exporting cotton and importing contraband war materials via Matamoros, which lay just across the Rio Grande from Brownsville, Texas, proved particularly troublesome. Technically neutral, Matamoros was by "early 1862 the great commercial thoroughfare of the Southern states." More than 180 merchant ships were anchored near the mouth of the Rio Grande in early 1863, and the number was estimated at between 200 and 300 by the end of 1864.[27]

Over the war's first year and one-half, Seward, aided by Lord Lyons in Washington and Palmerston and Russell in London, had prevented Anglo-American frictions over blockade enforcement from escalating into dangerous threats to peace between the two countries. Although they objected to US ships hovering just outside British ports in the Caribbean, often seizing neutral British vessels on scanty evidence, and imprisoning British subjects accused of unlawful actions, Russell and Palmerston appreciated the North's frustrations and the greedy, frequently dubious actions of British subjects. They shared Seward's commitment to prevent blockade and trade issues from rupturing diplomatic relations between the United States and England.

The secretary had listened carefully to Lyons's protests, had sought to delay matters by referring objectionable ship seizures to US prize courts, and had paid the specified compensation when the courts ruled in favor of British citizens. He and Lincoln, over the objections of Secretary of the Navy Welles, had issued an August 1862 directive designed to restrain overly aggressive US sailors. Although Seward had partially offset these conciliatory policies when he agreed to Admiral Charles Wilkes's reassignment to the Caribbean in September 1862 and endorsed a midyear bill authorizing Lincoln to commission US privateers, his overall policy of restraint had worked well.[28]

This changed abruptly in early 1863. On February 25 Wilkes confirmed the worst British fears by ordering the seizure of the *Peterhoff* just as the vessel departed St. Thomas en route to Matamoros. Combined with the capture of several other British ships under similar circumstances, the seizure of the *Peterhoff,* which, in fact, carried a large cargo of war materiel bound for the Confederacy, infuriated the British public and alarmed the Palmerston government. The British were particularly angered that Wilkes, who had overseen the capture of the *Trent* in November 1861, was again the offending US naval officer. William H. Aspinwall and John Murray Forbes, American businessmen in London, reported correctly that "everything" Wilkes did "hits twice as hard in irritating John Bull as the same thing done by anybody else." Voicing this irritation, the *London Times* declared, "There are limits to the forbearance which even a great nation can exercise towards a struggling but still petulant and presuming Government." With the seizure of the *Peterhoff,* those "limits have been passed."[29]

While compelled to protest Wilkes's depredations and more general US policies in the Caribbean, Russell and Palmerston were far more restrained than the British public and press. The two British leaders were preoccupied with potentially explosive events in Europe, determined not to adopt positions that might constrain future English naval policies, and wary of any possible armed conflict with the United States, where Lyons reported the situation "more alarming than it has been since the 'Trent' affair." Before Russell sent his obligatory protest to Seward, he reminded Parliament that the secretary of state had consistently made "proper reparation" for unlawful US interference with neutral trade and that there was no reason to expect "that Mr. Seward will deny just compensation and apology for any proved illegal acts of American vessels." After he recommended the "addition of two or three ships" to the British North American squadron, the foreign secretary directed Lyons to inform Seward that Britain could not tolerate US policy or actions that subjected legitimate neutral trade "to vexatious capture and arbitrary interference."[30]

Lincoln and Seward exercised equal forbearance. On these maritime issues, they worked from the president's inclination "to give up all the splits" if the US position were in doubt. Just as Russell took the precaution of augmenting the British fleet, Seward worked with Senator James Grimes, the chairman of the Naval Affairs Committee, to revive and pass the bill authorizing President Lincoln to sign letters of marque and thereby create the threat of unleashing privateers on British trade. Lyons initially worried that Seward had resorted to his "old bluster"; Senator Sumner was aghast at the secretary's provocative posture; and Russell envisioned US privateers harassing British commerce. Upon greater reflection, Lyons concluded correctly that Seward sought the option of employing privateers as "a means of negotiation with Europe," rather than as a violent weapon against neutral trade with the Confederacy.[31]

Lincoln and Seward's other responses to the *Peterhoff* crisis substantiated the British minister's conclusion. Seward rejected the British demand that the United States release the ship and compensate its owners for their losses. Instead, and consistent with previous US practice, he referred the case to a New York prize court. His prior policy of delay and evasion remained intact. In an even more conciliatory step, Seward and Secretary of the Navy Welles transferred Wilkes from the West Caribbean command on June 23 in deference to British angst and protests and thereby eliminated a potential flashpoint with London. Consistent with their directives in August 1862, Lincoln and Seward also reiterated that US naval officers should exercise caution and adhere strictly to international law when they stopped and searched neutral vessels. In July the president advised Welles that US commanders should "avoid the reality, and as far as possible, the appearance of using any neutral port to watch neutral vessels and then to dart out to seize them on their departure."[32]

Finally, the two foreign policy partners, over the protests of both Welles and Sumner, returned the *Peterhoff* mail pouches unopened to British authorities. Welles asserted that returning the mail was a fawning "concession" to the British and would surrender evidence that confirmed the *Peterhoff* had carried contraband bound for the Confederacy. After he assessed Seward's arguments for surrendering the mail pouches and Welles's opposition, Lincoln sided with the secretary of state. His ongoing rationale "was to 'keep the peace,' for we could not afford to take upon ourselves a war with England and France, which was threatened if we stopped their mails." A disgusted Welles complained that Seward had "humbugged" the president by "daily . . . wailing in his ears the calamities of a war with England"—an interpretation that ignored Lincoln's persistent determination to avoid war with any other nation while the United States fought the South. Although Seward and Lincoln agreed that the *Peterhoff* affair and the larger neutral trade did not warrant the risk of war with Great Britain, the president had long since recognized the wisdom of one war at a time.[33]

Resolution of the *Peterhoff* affair had turned primarily on British and US diplomatic policies, but the legal dimension was important. Seward and Union lawyers contended that the ship had been legally seized. Even though the *Peterhoff* was en route between two neutral ports, St. Thomas and Matamoros, the ultimate destination of its contraband cargo via "continuous voyage" was Brownsville, Texas, and the Confederacy. Lawyers for owners of the vessel countered that there was insufficient evidence to support this contention. Britain had cited the continuous voyage argument when it seized US ships bound for French possessions during the Napoleonic Wars, and the Palmerston government concluded that a pro-US court decision would help diminish the problematic Matamoros trade and accompanying injury to Anglo-American relations. When the prize court upheld the seizure of *Peterhoff* and its cargo, Russell offered no objection and Seward's policy of delay prevailed, even though the US Supreme Court overturned this decision in 1867—well after the threat of a US-British war had receded.[34]

The decisions of the prize court in the *Peterhoff* case and the British response were vital contributions to pacific Anglo-American relations, but in March 1863 the US Supreme Court had rendered an even more significant decision related to the blockade and neutral trade. The *Prize Cases* centered on President Lincoln's proclamation of the blockade on April 11, 1861, and the subsequent delay until August 6 when Congress endorsed his executive order as if it had "been issued . . . under the previous express authority and direction of Congress." In the interim between April and August, the US navy seized numerous suspected blockade runners and referred them to local US prize courts. The owners of four of these ships, which, along with their contents, had been condemned by the prize and appeals courts, appealed to the Supreme Court. The shipowners argued that without a congressional declaration or authorization, the blockade, allowable by international law only in time of war, was illegal. Therefore, the seizure and condemnation of the ships were also illegal.[35]

A majority of the Court agreed with the US government's contention that the South's secession, raising of an army, and hostile acts constituted an obvious state of war—a reality that foreign nations had acknowledged by recognizing the Confederates as belligerents. No congressional action had been needed to establish that a war was in progress. The Court majority asserted that President Lincoln, as commander in chief, could install a blockade, as a necessary step to defend the nation. Significantly, the Court rendered its decision without acknowledging the South's existence as an independent sovereign country. This sustained Lincoln and Seward's position that the United States was acting to suppress a domestic insurrection rather than fighting a war against a foreign adversary. The decision further upheld Lincoln's exercise of his emergency powers as commander in chief when he suspended habeas corpus and instituted a military draft. As historian Stuart Bernath concluded, the *Prize Cases* decision "likely" discouraged "sustained assaults on the validity of the Legal Tender Act of 1862, the Conscription Act of 1863, the Emancipation Proclamation, and the various suspensions of free speech and press." The Court had solidified "the theory . . . that Lincoln, as Chief Executive and Commander in Chief, wielded plenary powers."[36]

III.

While British domination of the neutral trade with the South caused serious problems with the Union, those issues were less inflammatory than the ongoing construction of Confederate vessels in English shipyards. The *Alabama* and *Florida,* both built in Liverpool, had sailed in 1862 despite Minister Adams's protests and had inflicted extensive damage on US commercial shipping over the ensuing year. The South had contracted for five additional vessels, two of which were dubbed the "Laird rams." These two armored ships were named for their six-foot iron rams designed to destroy wooden ships and decimate the Union blockade. Scholars have concluded that the rams could not have sailed successfully across the Atlantic to confront the US naval blockade, but contemporary northerners feared these ships would provide the South a decisive advantage.[37]

US Secretary of the Navy Welles voiced the Union perspective. He complained that "a devastating and villainous war" was being "waged on our commerce by English capital and English men under the Rebel flag with the connivance of the English Government"; and Minister Adams advised the British Foreign Office on July 11, 1863, that the American public and Lincoln administration considered shipbuilding for the Confederacy "tantamount" to Britain's "participation in the war" on the side of the South. British officials recognized the mounting northern outrage and the dangerous implications for Anglo-American relations. Lord Lyons warned Foreign Minister Russell of US "exasperation against England" and observed, "Everybody is furious with England and with everybody and everything English." Prime Minister Palmerston worried that British policy was becoming one of "neutral hostility" toward the Union, and Lord Russell lamented that the *Alabama* and *Florida* were "roaming the ocean with English guns and English sailors to burn, sink and destroy the ships of a friendly nation." Their actions, he concluded, were a "scandal and a reproach" to the British legal system.[38]

With the able support of Minister Adams and US Consul Thomas H. Dudley in Liverpool, Seward relentlessly pressured Great Britain to halt the Confederate shipbuilding and to block additional ships from joining the South's navy. Dudley continued his tireless and effective collection of evidence linking Confederate operatives to the ships under construction. He and his hired spies also secured design and equipment specifications that demonstrated the vessels' intended use as warships. Adams presented this evidence to Russell along with Seward's and his own blunt warnings that, if left uninterrupted, this form of British intervention could lead to war with the Union.

Seward and Adams began to articulate this perspective in late March. The US minister read Seward's rather blunt dispatch to Russell. It equated the British government's response to southern shipbuilding to an alliance with the Confederacy and the source of "strong" anti-British "feelings" in the United States. Later in the interview, Adams asserted that British policies and actions rendered the maintenance of peaceful relations "a most difficult task." In July, Adams admonished Russell that allowing the rams to join the Confederate navy would "endanger the peace and welfare" of both the United States and Great Britain. With the fate of the rams still in doubt in September, Seward and Adams were even more direct. An attack on the United States by the rams, Seward emphasized, would render "a retaliatory war inevitable." In a September 5 note to Russell, Adams was uncharacteristically belligerent. Were the rams not detained, he lectured, "It would be superfluous . . . to point out to your lordship that this is war."[39]

Seward's threat of war sustained one facet of his ongoing strategy to avert all forms of European intervention in the American conflict, a posture that became increasingly viable following Gettysburg and Vicksburg. The steadily increasing strength of the US military prompted caution in both Britain and France. Lyons and Russell fretted that the North might retaliate against Britain following a victorious war. Other considerations also argued for a fundamental shift in British policy toward Confederate shipbuilding. Concern over European disputes in Poland and Schleswig-Holstein and the persistent British distrust of Napoleon III reinforced the British leaders' determination to avoid any military conflict with the North. In addition, lucrative trade with the United States had returned to prewar levels by the first quarter of 1863, and the cotton crisis had eased appreciably. Conflict with the United States threatened injurious economic consequences, and neither British leader wanted to imperil national prosperity. Finally, Russell and Palmerston recognized that allowing the Confederates to build a navy in their neutral nation could set a frightening precedent for Great Britain, the world's greatest maritime power. One member of Palmerston's cabinet summarized this perspective: If this practice were continued, "'Alabamas' will certainly be fitted out against us from neutral ports," most likely from the United States, during the next British war.[40]

Acting on these considerations, Russell reversed British policy and halted Confederate shipbuilding. The British government's interpretation of the Foreign Enlistment Act (FEA) had inhibited its prior action. According to the FEA, ships could be built in Great Britain as long as they were not clearly intended for use by a belligerent or equipped for war within British jurisdiction. Only equipment or other clear evidence that confirmed belligerent intent sufficed to block a ship from leaving Great Britain and joining the Confederate navy. On April 5 Russell ordered the seizure of the *Alexandra,* a small wooden steamer, on the grounds that the ship was "*apparently*" being constructed for the Confederacy, rather than on the basis of conclusive evidence. The foreign minister thereafter worked cooperatively with Adams, Dudley, and William M. Evarts, an American attorney Seward had sent to London to bolster the US legal efforts; but a British jury upheld the traditional interpretation of the FEA and ruled that the *Alexandra* should not be retained. Russell then promptly appealed the verdict and subsequent court proceedings stretched into 1864, well past the time the ship could have affected the course of the war.[41]

Although the Palmerston government had lost in court, the *Alexandra* incident marked a decisive turning point. Confederate operatives in Britain recognized this shift in British policy. James R. Hamilton predicted "every vessel now building in England will be seized and subjected to the same injurious delay," and James Bulloch complained of constant harassment "by Yankee spies" and "British officials" and agreed that no ships could depart "without inquiry, interruption, and delay."[42]

Stalemated by the courts, Russell based his subsequent actions to stymie unneutral Confederate shipbuilding on "policy" rather than "law." His most important application of this revised approach focused on the detention of the Laird rams. Convinced that it was "clear to commonsense" that the rams were battleships destined for the South, Russell ordered their retention on September 8. Government law officers sustained this decision in October, and, after vain attempts by the Confederates to obtain the vessels through a French intermediary, the British admiralty purchased them in May 1864. By forestalling the rams' escape Russell had eliminated the threat of Confederate shipbuilding dragging Britain into the war and had resolved what historian Warren Spencer has termed the "most dangerous moment" in Anglo-American maritime "relations since the *Trent* affair."[43]

Two days after Russell's September 8 decision to retain the rams, Charles Sumner delivered a blistering four-hour indictment of Great Britain before an audience of three thousand at the Cooper Institute in New York City. He later justified his tirade by claiming that he hoped to convince England to "reconsider her course" and avoid a potential war. Only by putting the "truth . . . before" the British "plainly" could this pacific outcome be achieved. The senator's objective was not so selfless or benign. He once again sought to outshine and perhaps replace Seward by either appearing to force British concessions on the rams or by being in the forefront of US national outrage if Russell and Palmerston allowed the Confederates to obtain the ships. Sumner failed miserably on all counts when news arrived from London that Seward and Adams's more circumspect pressure had helped influence Russell's announcement *two days* before the Cooper Institute speech. The British press denounced Sumner's arguments as "sadly childish"; Russell was indignant at the senator's "misrepresentations"; and Seward took ill-disguised pleasure as he congratulated Sumner on his "very important public service" and applauded him for seeking to "rouse the nationality of the American People." The secretary of state's irony was obvious: Sumner, the Anglophile, who had consistently criticized Seward for being overly harsh toward the British, had adopted a needlessly caustic and Anglophobic tone at a most inopportune time.[44]

Just as the threat of Confederate shipbuilding in Great Britain receded, US Minister Dayton and Consul John Bigelow in Paris heard rumors that southerners had undertaken similar efforts in France. The rumors were alarmingly true. In October 1862 Napoleon had suggested to Confederate diplomat John Slidell that the South should expand its naval construction to France. The emperor may have envisioned French ironclads breaking the blockade and affording his nation access to much-needed raw cotton; or, he could have foreseen the ships contributing to a Confederate victory, which would have hindered potential US interference with his Mexican venture. Reassured by members of the French cabinet and by Napoleon personally in June 1863, Slidell and Bulloch acted on this remarkable invitation. In April 1863 they contracted with Lucien Arman, Napoleon's close associate and France's largest shipbuilder, to purchase four armed clipper ships, and in July they added an agreement for two ironclads. Arman alleged that the clippers were destined for use in the Pacific Ocean and were being armed to combat pirates. The two ironclads were reportedly being built for the viceroy of Egypt. By claiming these ships were intended for use by another government or beyond the Atlantic war, Arman and the Confederates followed Napoleon's instructions on how to circumvent French neutrality guidelines. By midsummer 1863, as Confederate naval construction floundered in Britain, the South, with government assistance, seemed to have four cruisers and two ironclads well on the way to completion in France.[45]

In contrast to Consul Dudley's elaborate intelligence network in Great Britain, Dayton and Bigelow lacked even a rudimentary system to track the rumored Confederate naval construction in France. The absence of Union spy operations made the events of September 9 particularly fortunate for the United States. Arman had farmed out the construction of two of the Confederate cruisers to J. Voruz, a businessman in Nantes. On the ninth a clerk from Voruz's office called unannounced on Dayton and presented him with ten original documents that conclusively proved Bulloch had contracted for the six ships and that they were meant for use by the Confederacy—not in the Pacific or by Egyptian rulers. Armed with copies of these documents, Dayton voiced strong protests to Foreign Minister Drouyn on September 22 and repeated these objections over the ensuing three months. Dayton demanded that the French government prevent the cruisers from being armed and block their transfer to the South.[46]

Seward endorsed his minister's actions, as he had done with those of Adams in London. The secretary also applied stern but not overly provocative pressure, consistent with his prodding of Palmerston and Russell. In late December he emphasized that were France to allow the Confederates to obtain the ships it would be equivalent to France making war on the United States. Six months later, Seward recognized that the ships could not reach the Confederacy in time to impact the war, and he responded to Bigelow's criticism of his handling of France as "too conciliatory and courteous." With an eye ever on Napoleon's Mexican intervention and the war at home, the secretary cited President Lincoln's emphasis on US military success: "If our armies succeed . . ., we shall have no conflict with France or with any other foreign Power. . . . If we escape war with all, my courtesy to France will have done no harm." Were "the calamity of a foreign war" to befall the United States, "we shall be none the less able to meet it for all the prudence we practiced in trying to delay and if possible, to avert it."[47]

Foreign Minister Drouyn was no more interested than Seward in a US-French confrontation. Convinced that Napoleon was badly overextended in Mexico and worried about the same European conflicts in Poland and Schleswig-Holstein that troubled Lord Russell, Drouyn responded deftly to Dayton and Seward's pressure. The foreign minister employed the Voruz documents to outmaneuver Napoleon and other cabinet members less inclined toward true neutrality. In October 1863 the government revoked Arman's permission to arm the cruisers; in February 1864, the Marine Department detained the ironclads and, in May, the cruisers; and, also in May, Arman was directed to sell all of the ships to neutral countries. Bulloch did acquire one ironclad, the *Stonewall,* in December 1864, but rough seas forced the ship into a Spanish port in February 1865 as it attempted a transatlantic crossing. In a fate typical of overall Confederate shipbuilding efforts, the *Stonewall* remained docked in El Ferrol in March 1865 when Seward instructed US diplomats in Europe to ignore the ship and any responsibility for its origins or subsequent use. Its fate had become irrelevant to the American war and Franco-American relations.[48]

IV.

Four other 1863 events provided additional insight into the Lincoln-Seward foreign policy and the reasons for its success. As Seward echoed his severe strictures against outside interventions in the Civil War, he simultaneously exhibited his more conciliatory posture by inviting the European ministers in Washington on a tour of upstate New York. Over the last two weeks of August, the secretary of state led all the important European ministers on a trek that included stops in Albany, Schenectady, and his hometown of Auburn. While in Auburn, he hosted half of the group in his home and boarded the others in a house next door. Seward undoubtedly enjoyed the escape from the steamy Washington summer and was in his element as the gracious host, but he also had more practical objectives—both of which were realized. He wanted these important observers of the war to see the evolving US industrial might and the Union's prosperous economy in the midst of the conflict.

The secretary also sought to solidify his personal relations with the European diplomatic corps, especially Lord Lyons. Since the tour had conflicted with Lyons's plans for a trip to Canada, the British minister reluctantly agreed to join the caravan. But after being transported via a special train, regaled with ice cream on hot days, and provided a carriage if walking became too onerous, the often-prickly Englishman confessed to Russell that the trip had proved quite enjoyable. He also acknowledged, "When one comes to really know [Seward] one is surprised to find much to esteem and even to like in him." Russell was similarly positive, if more guarded. In September the foreign minister declared that Seward and the American government had discussed tough foreign policy issues "very fairly with the English Government. Sometimes we think them quite in the wrong; sometimes they say we are quite in the wrong; but we discuss them fairly, and with regard to the Secretary of State I see no complaint to make." And, as the year ended, French minister Mercier, with whom Seward had even rockier personal relations, asserted, "Il est très sage. [He is very clever.]" Seward, however, had not won over Palmerston, whose assessment of the secretary remained unchanged. When Seward floated the idea of visiting Britain, the prime minister was aghast. In a display of his haughty elitist pretensions, Palmerston was convinced the "vulgar and ungentlemanlike" Seward would not "be very well received in Society" and would only worsen Anglo-American relations.[49]

Lincoln and Seward extended hospitality akin to that of the secretary's New York tour to more than three thousand officers and sailors who entered New York harbor unexpectedly aboard six Russian naval vessels on September 24, 1863. Although Lincoln had characterized Russia as despotic and decried the nation's oppression of Hungary in the 1850s, he and Seward had been most appreciative of Russian friendship over the first two years of the war. Russia, which had long viewed the United States as a strategic counterbalance to Britain and France, had conspicuously expressed its support for the Union in July 1861, and had decisively rejected overtures for joint European intervention in the Civil War during the fall of 1862. At the president's suggestion and with Russia's consent, Seward had published the two nations' 1861 diplomatic correspondence in another revealing example of public diplomacy, and Lincoln had been described as "extremely grateful" for Russian refusal to join European mediation efforts in 1862.[50]

Still, the ships' arrival in New York, and that of another four vessels at San Francisco the next month, was not primarily intended to bolster the North's cause. Rather, the Russian admiralty had dispatched their ships across the Atlantic, and to a lesser extent, to the US northwest coast, to exhibit the nation's modernizing navy, to execute a valuable training exercise, and to position the fleet strategically in case of a potential European war over the crisis in Poland. Unaware of these Russian calculations, residents of both New York and San Francisco greeted the sailors warmly as allies and boosters of the United States. They feted the visitors with parades and banquets, and European leaders worried about a possible US-Russian military alliance.[51]

Although Seward gained no official clarity on the reasons for the ships' presence, he and the president did nothing to alter northern perceptions or European apprehensions. When the sailors who had docked in New York traveled to Washington, the president and secretary of state welcomed them at the White House and at Seward's home. At another event hosted by Secretary of the Navy Welles, John Hay marveled at the guests' "vast absorbent powers" when served alcoholic drinks but dismissed them as "fiendishly ugly." When the Russians departed New York and San Francisco in April 1864, the rationale for their visit was still obscure, but their presence had buoyed northern spirits and puzzled European diplomats. The latter provided a telling example of how European political and military developments diverted attention from and discouraged meddling in the American war—a dynamic Lincoln and Seward fully understood and consistently sought to exploit.[52]

Six weeks after the Russian fleet arrived, Seward accompanied Lincoln to Gettysburg, where the president delivered his timeless address dedicating the northern military cemetery on the site of the North's decisive victory the previous July. The two friends met alone for an hour the night before the November 19 speech and very likely discussed the president's final draft. The next day, before an audience of approximately fifteen thousand, Lincoln brilliantly situated the war, its costs, and its stakes in an inspiring and internationally relevant context. In only 272 words, he pointedly reminded his fellow countrymen and international observers that in 1776 the United States had been "conceived in Liberty, and dedicated to the proposition that all men are created equal." Eighty-seven years later, the Civil War "was testing whether that nation, or any nation so conceived" could survive. While honoring those who had died on the Gettysburg battlefield, it fell to Lincoln, his audience, and the Union to ensure that the valiant soldiers "shall not have died in vain—that this nation, under God, shall have a new birth of freedom—and that government of the people, by the people, for the people, shall not perish from the earth." Edward Everett, the occasion's featured orator who had spoken for two hours, appropriately congratulated Lincoln on his "eloquent simplicity & appropriateness" and admitted, "I should be glad, if I . . . came as near to the central idea of the occasion in two hours, as you did in two minutes." Everett's assessment was correct. Lincoln's timely and inspiring depiction of the conflict's significance complemented his strategic vision and leadership as commander in chief as central components of the successful US foreign policy. Military victories and the prominent defense of republican government were both crucial to fending off European intervention in the American conflict.[53]

President Lincoln's sense of US national destiny was also fundamental to his policies regarding Native Americans. The president's approach to US-Indian interactions, a dynamic that should be viewed as foreign relations, reflected several basic assumptions. Like virtually all of his Caucasian contemporaries, Lincoln considered Native Americans and their cultures inferior to whites. When he met with a group of Indian leaders in March 1863, he lectured that whites were "numerous and prosperous because they cultivate the earth, produce bread, and depend upon the products of the earth rather than wild game for subsistence." Failing to recognize the irony of his assertion in the midst of the Civil War, he added that whites "as a race," were not "so much disposed to fight and kill one another as our red brethren." In addition to the adoption of settled agriculture and rejection of warfare, Native American progress required the "moral training" provided by the "Christian faith." The president agreed with his Commissioner of Indian Affairs William P. Dole that "concentrating Indians and confining them to reservations" was the proper policy for instructing them in the "arts of civilization," and he later touted his administration's success in "extinguishing" their claims "to large and valuable tracts of land." Eradicating these claims and promoting US westward expansion through legislation and military might helped make the West "secure for the advancing [white] settler."[54]

Lincoln was neither as insensitive nor as hostile toward Native Americans as these statements might suggest, and he repeatedly cited the need to reform the corrupt Bureau of Indian Affairs; but winning the Civil War and the related development of the trans-Mississippi West took precedence over reform or Indian welfare. Control of Indian Territory in what would become Oklahoma was important to prevent Confederate attacks on Kansas, apply pressure against the southern states of Arkansas and Texas, and ensure that the North maintained control of New Mexico and Arizona. Similarly, the Sioux could not be allowed to impede the westward movement of free-soil northerners, obstruct the Union's connection to a non-slave Oregon and California, or imperil US continental coherence.[55]

By promoting westward development and its strengthening of the Union, the president subscribed to and voiced the spirit of Manifest Destiny, even if he employed little of the Democrats' or his secretary of state's more flamboyant language. Westward expansion was a primary US goal, as long as it could be accomplished without extending slavery. Lincoln endorsed the adoption of key legislation that was designed to facilitate westward development and northern political control of these valuable territories. In 1862 Republicans passed the Homestead Act and the Morrill Land-Grant College Act and created the Department of Agriculture, all meant to encourage white migration to the West and the practice of settled agriculture. Two years later, Lincoln backed the Transcontinental Railroad Act, which he and his fellow Republicans intended to provide access to the West's mineral wealth, assist western farmers in marketing their crops, aid in the movement of the US military, and forge strong transportation and political links to the west coast. The Republican Congress, with the president's blessing, added the political dimension by creating the Colorado, Dakota, Nevada, Arizona, Idaho, and Montana territories between 1861 and 1864 and admitting Nevada as a state in 1864. All of these new political entities were staffed by Republican officials; and, tragically, the cumulative strategic, political, and economic objectives came at the expense of Native Americans, as did the Civil War's primary trans-Mississippi military campaigns.[56]

Faced with dire military threats east of the Mississippi as the war began, Lincoln and the US government had essentially abdicated control over Indian Territory in Oklahoma to the South. In the absence of any Union military and diplomatic presence, the Confederacy filled the vacuum. Between July and October 1861, the South negotiated treaties with the Cherokee, Creek, Seminoles, Chickasaw, and Choctaw. In return for military and political alliances, Richmond guaranteed the Indians territorial and political integrity, representation in the Confederate Congress, the opportunity for statehood, and the legal right to own slaves. In November 1861 the South designated Indian Territory as a distinct military department.[57]

Northern responses were disorganized and ineffectual. The president authorized military campaigns in December 1861, March 1862, and June 1862 to retake Indian Territory. All three campaigns failed badly. Inadequate numbers of Union soldiers, conflicts and confusion over and among the designated Union commanders, and the refusal of white settlers to accept Indians as allies fatally undermined the North's efforts. Fortunately for the Union, the Confederacy's military presence was even weaker, which led to northern victories at Pea Ridge, Arkansas, in March 1862 and Honey Spring, Oklahoma, in July 1863. Although the Union victories came largely by default, US dominance of Indian Territory was strategically important to controlling Kansas and allowed the Lincoln administration to force some five thousand Indian refugees, who had fled the fighting, to return from Kansas. After 1862, the North's Indian policy from Colorado into the Southwest had become militarized and would remain so during the Civil War and after, as US troops battled Mescalero Apache, Navajo, Cheyenne, Arapaho, Kiowa, Comanche, and Sioux across Colorado, New Mexico, and Arizona.[58]

The other principal Union military confrontation that involved Native Americans came in response to a mid-August 1862 attack by the Santee Sioux on white settlers in Minnesota. As in Indian Territory, Lincoln viewed this incident primarily as a distressing diversion from the principal task of vanquishing the South—especially given the Union's nearly simultaneous defeat at the Second Battle of Bull Run and the looming threat of European diplomatic recognition of the Confederacy. But reports from the frontier were too unsettling to ignore. One assessment held that "Indians, from Minnesota to Pikes Peak, from Salt Lake to near Fort Kearney, [were] committing many depredations." After Lincoln transferred John Pope, the losing US commander at Second Bull Run, to Minnesota, the general excitedly predicted in mid-September that "the whole of Minnesota west of the Mississippi and the Territories of Dakota and Nebraska" could be "entirely depopulated" as whites fled the region. The fear of Confederate machinations with the Indians compounded northern anxiety and prompted Lincoln to warn Congress of his "suspicions" and "information . . . that a simultaneous attack was to be made upon white settlers by all tribes between the Mississippi River and the Rocky Mountains."[59]

All of these reports and suspicions were greatly exaggerated. By early October 1862, Pope reported that the war had ended, with nearly 1,500 Indian men, women, and children being held as prisoners. On November 8, General Henry Sibley, the other Union commander in the region, sent Lincoln a list of 303 Sioux, who had been given death sentences for the alleged murder or sexual assault of white settlers. The president requested the trial records for all of these condemned prisoners. He and government lawyers scrutinized these materials, and, despite intense pressure and vocal protests from Minnesotans and their political leaders, Lincoln reduced to 39 the number of Indians to be executed. Although he had challenged and defied majority white opinion in Minnesota by granting clemency to 264 Native Americans, the president's subsequent policies were decidedly injurious to the Indians. During the remainder of the Civil War, none of the other Indian prisoners were released, and in 1863 the military forced the Sioux and Winnebago, who had no role in the fighting, to move from Minnesota to land on the Upper Missouri River. The US military estimated that eight to ten thousand Indians had been banished from their upper midwestern homelands, and twenty thousand US troops were stationed in the West when the Civil War ended.[60]

Lincoln's military policies and the long-term impact of the Republican Party's comprehensive legislative program designed to develop the West for white Americans displaced Indians from their land and devastated their cultures. According to one careful analysis, the president had assessed immediate US-Indian relations primarily in "the context of larger military concerns" and their "impact on the War for the Union." Therefore, his conduct of this aspect of US foreign relations was consistent with his and Seward's overall foreign policies and interactions with Europeans during the course of the war. Lincoln, Seward, and their party were equally dismissive of Indian welfare when they enacted the Homestead Act, Transcontinental Railroad Act, and Morrill Land-Grant College Act, and created territorial governments across the intermountain West. Indeed, the military, political, economic, and cultural aspects of US-Indian relations during the Lincoln years were representative of white America's nineteenth-century expansion across the continent—an expansion that embodied "U.S. empire."[61]

As 1863 and the much-exaggerated Sioux threat ended, Lincoln and Seward could look back on a most successful, even decisive, foreign policy year. Together with the crucial military victories at Gettysburg and Vicksburg, the president had maintained and extended his powers as commander in chief; had sustained his strategic military vision and identified General Grant as the commander who was willing and able to implement that vision; and had continued to oversee the building of the massive Union war machine. Against the backdrop of US victories and rising military power, no troublesome maritime issue with Britain or France had led to diplomatic disputes or armed clashes that might have resulted in a two-front war and Confederate victory. Similarly, the British and French governments had settled the most threatening diplomatic confrontations when they quashed Confederate shipbuilding in their countries. Finally, Napoleon's last, futile, but dangerous, attempts to instigate European mediation or diplomatic recognition of the Confederacy had failed conclusively.

V.

When Lincoln and Seward embarked on 1864, the president's reelection was already much discussed. Democrats continued to criticize his leadership, and he faced significant opposition within his own party. Fellow Republican David Davis, who had managed Lincoln's 1860 campaign and been rewarded with a seat on the US Supreme Court, opined, "The politicians in and out of Congress . . . would put Mr. Lincoln aside if they dared." Secretary of the Treasury Salmon P. Chase was the Republican politician who most wanted to cast Lincoln aside and replace him as president. Backed by many from the radical wing of the party, Chase wrote widely to Republicans nationally and covertly cooperated in the publication of a laudatory campaign biography and the foundation in February of a "Chase for President" committee headed by Senator Samuel Pomeroy from Kansas. Chase, who privately censured Lincoln's "want of energy and force," particularly in the prosecution of the war and elimination of slavery, asserted that the nation required "a man of different qualities" as its leader.[62]

Lincoln, aware of and irritated by Chase's actions, attributed them to a case of "'the White House fever'" and compared the Treasury secretary to "the bluebottle fly which [lays] his eggs in every rotten spot he can find." Lincoln supporters urged him to challenge his disloyal cabinet member publicly; but, reflecting his appreciation of Chase's excellent work at the Treasury Department and his own keen sense of political timing, the president held back. His patience was rewarded when the Pomeroy committee circulated two pamphlets: a public one, titled "The New Presidential Election," and a covert one calling for Chase's nomination. Strategically prodded by Lincoln men, Republicans soundly rejected this Chase presidential boomlet. Numerous state legislatures, most importantly in Chase's home state of Ohio, passed resolutions endorsing Lincoln, and the *New York Times* praised "the universality of public sentiment in favor of Mr. Lincoln's reelection." Chase was left to claim lamely that he had no "knowledge" of the Pomeroy circular prior to its publication, and, when the treasury secretary offered to resign for the fourth time in June, Lincoln accepted. The president informed the surprised Chase that their relations had reached the point of "intolerable mutual embarrassment."[63]

Lincoln had cleared his path to the Republican nomination, which came officially from the National Union Party after the Republicans changed their name in an effort to attract broader support in the North and border states. But the *Times*' claim for universal public support for his reelection badly missed the mark. Grant and the Union army were stalled before Petersburg, Virginia; Confederate General Jubal Early and his fifteen thousand soldiers maneuvered near Silver Spring, Maryland, where they had burned the home of US Postmaster General Montgomery Blair. These developments led numerous observers, including Lincoln, to doubt whether the president could be reelected. *New York Times* editor Henry Raymond, who had chaired the National Union Party convention, lamented in August, "The tide is setting strongly against us," and in late August Lincoln declared, "I am a beaten man unless we can have some great victory." The Democratic platform, which called for an end to the war by accepting the South and slavery back into the Union, appealed to the nation's war fatigue and appeared to be a political winner. To balance their peace platform, the Democrats nominated General George McClellan, a pro-war figure, as their standard bearer.[64]

In the midst of the near-pervasive gloom within the Lincoln camp, Seward was conspicuously optimistic. He agreed that "the signs of discontent and faction are very numerous and very painful," but predicted correctly that "any considerable [military] success would cause them all to disappear." That very considerable success came in early September when Admiral David Farragut captured Mobile, Alabama, and General William T. Sherman overran Atlanta. With the hybrid Democratic campaign discredited, Lincoln outdistanced McClellan by 212 to 21 electoral votes and carried all the states except New Jersey, Delaware, and Kentucky.[65]

While reiterating the Civil War's significance, President Lincoln cited the "grave question whether any government, not too strong for the liberties of its people, can be strong enough to maintain its own existence, in great emergencies." His answer: The election had clearly "demonstrated that a people's government can sustain a national election, in the midst of a great civil war," a possibility previously not "known to the world." The peaceful election signaled to international observers "how sound and how strong we still are." General Grant elaborated on the foreign policy implications of US strength. He asserted, "The election having passed off quietly, no bloodshed or riot throughout the land, is a victory worth more to the country than a battle won. Rebeldom and Europe will so construe it."[66]

Even as Lincoln achieved political survival and reelection in 1864, he and Seward managed two serious international issues—one with Great Britain over Confederate actions in Canada, the other with France over Napoleon III's imperial intervention in Mexico. As Confederate prospects for a military victory and a diplomatic breakthrough faded, the South sought to provoke an Anglo-American crisis by mounting attacks on the United States from British North America. These efforts began in November 1863 with a plot to commandeer the USS *Michigan* and use the vessel to attack the Union prisoner of war camp on Johnson's Island in Lake Erie near Sandusky, Ohio. The Confederate operatives intended to free the two thousand prisoners and then attack Ohio and Indiana. The raid was postponed after Governor General of British North America Lord Charles S. Monck and Michigan governor Austin Blair drew on their respective surveillance systems and warned Seward and Secretary of War Stanton of the planned raid. The following month, Confederates stowed away on and seized the *Chesapeake,* a commercial ship sailing from New York to Portland, Maine. Two US naval vessels located and captured the *Chesapeake* off the coast of Nova Scotia in British waters. When Lord Lyons protested, Seward promptly expressed "profound regret" for the US Navy's violation of British sovereignty but also used the occasion to highlight the Confederate plots and attacks from British territory. Lyons was equally cautious, and the matter faded, as neither Seward nor the British minister wanted another *Trent* affair.[67]

In late 1863 Confederate Secretary of State Judah Benjamin sought to move beyond these uncoordinated, haphazard southern efforts. The secretary appointed Jacob Thompson and Clement C. Clay, former US senators from Mississippi and Alabama, respectively, and J. P. Holcombe, a law professor at the University of Virginia, as commissioners to Canada and provided $1 million for their use. Under these commissioners, the Confederates conducted two additional, significant raids during the fall of 1864. In September southern operatives seized two lake steamers, the *Philo Parsons* and *Island Queen,* as part of a second scheme to take control of the USS *Michigan,* free southern prisoners on Johnson Island, and use the *Michigan* to attack Great Lakes shipping and US coastal areas. When a key southern plotter got drunk and revealed aspects of the plan to his dinner companion, "variously described as a prostitute, a French spy, and an innocent maid of chaste and patriotic" practices, this second Lake Erie operation ended as disastrously as the first. It served only to inflame further northern outrage at Britain's seeming inability or unwillingness to prevent attacks on the United States from Canadian territory.[68]

A final incident, though potentially more inflammatory, proved no more beneficial to the South's attempt to provoke a war between the United States and Great Britain. On October 19, 1864, Confederate Lieutenant Bennett H. Young led an attack on St. Albans, Vermont. Young and his fellow Kentuckians robbed three banks, killed one person, wounded two others, and absconded with several horses and $200,000, but they failed in an attempt to burn the town. An enraged American posse pursued the attackers across the border into Canada, where they captured Young and four others. After a tense standoff, the prisoners were turned over to Canadian authorities, who later apprehended another ten of the raiders. Had the raid not been sufficiently shocking, a Montreal magistrate released the Confederates in mid-December.[69]

US politicians and much of the press demanded a belligerent response.

The *Chicago Tribune* declared the United States should throttle Canada, "as a St. Bernard would throttle a poodle pup," and the *New York Times* asserted that Canadian territory should be treated like that of the Confederacy. If this action should yield "war with England . . . let it come" since the United States had "never" been "in better condition" for such a fight. General Joseph Hooker relished this fight. He complained of the "conscious weakness" of the Lincoln government's "foreign policy" and advocated invading Canada.[70]

Lincoln and Seward's response was far less extreme. Acting on the president's directive to "pursue . . . the habitual policy of . . . a friendly and even fraternal disposition toward Great Britain," the two US foreign policy leaders applied measured pressure on British and Canadian officials. Seward agreed with Senator Sumner's accurate warning that the raid "was a trap in which to catch the government of our country" and "gain the powerful British intervention" on behalf of the Confederacy. Neither Seward nor Lincoln took the bait. The president and secretary refused to countermand the order of General John A. Dix, US commander of the Military District of the East, that authorized US forces to pursue the southern raiders "into Canada if necessary and destroy them." Seward temporarily risked the possibility of a border war in order to gain diplomatic leverage, but he also dispatched former US senator Preston King, a close political ally, to confer with and smooth relations with Governor General Monck. When Dix issued a similar second order following the raiders' release, Lincoln and Seward revoked it and required prior permission from Washington before US forces crossed the Canadian border. With Canadian officials left to wonder for three months, the American leaders were unwilling to further risk a military misstep.[71]

While working behind the scenes with Lord Lyons to preserve the US reciprocity trade treaty with Canada, Seward cited congressional hostility to this agreement as additional evidence that Canadian officials needed to police Confederate actions more effectively. He and Lincoln applied more direct pressure by requiring passports for persons who entered the United States from Canada and by threatening to end the 1817 Rush-Bagot Treaty, in which the United States and Britain had agreed not to arm naval ships on the Great Lakes. Soon after the raid, Seward gave Britain the required six-month notice for abrogation of Rush-Bagot and declared his intention to increase naval "armaments upon the lakes" if "the condition of affairs" warranted. He further chastised the British for granting "asylum . . . to active agents of the enemies of the United States" and for allowing the "use of British ports and British borders" for attacks upon the United States. Lincoln reinforced Seward's warning in his December 4 Annual Message to Congress when he echoed Seward's threat to augment US naval forces on the Great Lakes. On December 17 the president issued a proclamation that required any person entering the United States from Canada to have a passport. Both the threat to end Rush-Bagot and the passport regulation remained in effect until March 1865 when the Confederate defeat was imminent. With northern victory assured, Seward backed away from abrogating Rush-Bagot and rescinded the passport requirement.[72]

These Lincoln-Seward actions succeeded admirably. They induced British-Canadian restraint of southern attacks and avoided any military or diplomatic confrontations that might have salvaged the fast-fading Confederate hopes of winning the war. Seward was "especially desirous to avoid writing or doing any thing that might . . . embarrass the Ministry of Lord Palmerston." Administration actions helped convince Governor General Monck, with the approval of the Palmerston government, to aggressively pursue Confederate operatives, to share intelligence with Washington, to increase the number of militias dedicated to enforcing Canadian neutrality, to re-arrest the raiders freed by the Montreal judge, and to pass a strong neutrality law. The 1865 Alien Act provided that foreign nationals who acted from Canada against a friendly nation were to be fined and expelled. In a fitting end to the Confederate plots and a telling commentary on Lincoln's innate diplomatic savvy, the president allowed Jacob Thompson to escape as he traveled secretly from Canada to England via Portland, Maine. On April 14, the president declined to have Thompson arrested and explained, "When you have got an elephant by the hind leg, and he's trying to run away, it's best to let him run."[73]

The second major 1864 foreign policy issue, the ongoing French intervention in Mexico, was potentially much more explosive. The European intervention had begun in 1861 as a joint British-French-Spanish campaign to collect their citizens' claims and debts owed them by Mexico, but Britain and Spain had withdrawn from the coalition in April 1862 when it became apparent that Napoleon's objectives stretched well beyond monetary claims. His "Grand Design" envisioned the imposition of a European monarchy in Mexico that would work closely with Paris to restore Mexican domestic order and prosperity. Napoleon hoped that, as a close French ally, a rejuvenated Mexico would help empower the Latin race in Europe and the Americas, become a lucrative commercial partner for France, safeguard French possessions in the West Indies, block further US territorial expansion, and eventually draw Texas and Louisiana into the French orbit. With these ambitious ends in view, France declared war on Mexico in April 1862; invaded Mexico the following month; and, with thirty thousand soldiers, captured Mexico City in June 1863.[74]

Since it took a year for the expeditionary forces to capture Mexico's capital, Napoleon's project was in trouble from the beginning. Fierce Mexican resistance and disease took their toll on the French military. The expedition became a heavy drain on the French treasury, and the war left France strategically vulnerable to contemporary European crises in Poland, Prussia, Italy, and Schleswig-Holstein and in its relations with Britain. Ironically, although Napoleon's Mexican adventure hinged on positive Confederate fortunes, his imperial project precluded aiding the South to achieve victory. This need for an independent Confederacy prompted his repeated attempts to organize a joint European mediation of the conflict or recognition of the Richmond government. But, just as the French army occupied Mexico City in midsummer 1863, the United States triumphed at Gettysburg and Vicksburg, and the march toward a Union victory and the ever-greater US military strength began. France and its leader were mired in a failing intervention and increasingly threatened by a powerful North. Napoleon was unwilling to risk a conflict with the United States, which would guarantee failure in Mexico. This dynamic helped convince the French emperor to give up his inclination to intervene in the American war and to curb Confederate shipbuilding in 1863. The Mexican intervention, which initially appeared so menacing to Lincoln and Seward, had ultimately redounded to US foreign policy advantage.[75]

This advantage did not materialize automatically; rather, the two principal US foreign policymakers had "exploited" these shifting power realities "with high competence." Both Lincoln and Seward were appropriately anxious about the tripartite European intervention in the Western Hemisphere and, by early 1863, had a full understanding of Napoleon's Grand Design, which had been published in France and translated in New York papers. Potential French attempts to acquire Texas especially disturbed President Lincoln and led him to favor military expeditions to ensure a countervailing US presence there. These expeditions during the fall of 1863 and early 1864 accomplished little. Amphibious attacks on the Sabine River in September 1863 and the Red River in early 1864 failed miserably, and General Nathaniel P. Banks's occupation in November 1863 of Brownsville neither blocked the flow of goods to the Confederacy via Matamoros nor shifted the balance of power in the region.[76]

All of these actions fell far short of the ones advocated by more aggressive northerners, such as General Joseph Hooker, who lobbied for a US military invasion of Mexico. These unsuccessful military ventures deviated from the more general Lincoln-Seward policy of patience and restraint designed to avoid conflict with France. In 1864 Seward emphasized Lincoln's one-war policy: The United States should not "gasconade about Mexico when we are in a struggle for our own life," and no US military forces should be allowed to compromise "the neutrality of the United States in the war between France and Mexico."[77]

From the beginning of the French-Mexican war in April 1862, Seward had maintained US neutrality while making it clear that his government rejected all efforts to impose a European monarchy in the Western Hemisphere. In March 1862 the secretary predicted that Napoleon's project would fail, and French minister Mercier decided Seward had "become very calm on the question of Mexican monarchy because he is persuaded it is an abortive enterprise." Seward adhered to the same policy of strict neutrality and nonintervention that he demanded of European nations contemplating interference the American Civil War, but he left no doubt that the United States preferred a republican government in Mexico and recognized Benito Juárez as the president of the country. As US military strength increased and the tide turned against the Confederacy, Seward augmented this subtle but unmistakable pressure.[78]

This pressure, the prospect of a formidable postwar United States, the financial drain of the war in Mexico, and various European complications forced Napoleon to reassess his North American intervention. In November 1863 the French emperor admitted, "I have gone to bed in a bad bed, . . . but the affair must be liquidated." He sought to achieve that end by persuading Austrian Archduke Ferdinand Maximilian Joseph to accept the position of emperor of Mexico and, thereby, allow French withdrawal. The long-rumored transaction came to fruition in April 1864, when the hapless Maximilian, known by many in Europe as the "Archdupe," accepted the offer and sailed for Mexico the following month with his wife Charlotte, who would become Empress Carlota. In return for Napoleon's commitment to keep French troops in Mexico until 1867, Maximilian agreed to assume responsibility for France's monetary claims against Mexico and the

French war costs. Neither party fulfilled these obligations, but Napoleon had secured a cover to exit Mexico without publicly admitting his strategic error since, as he admitted, "in France," he was not "allowed to make mistakes."[79]

During the year from Maximilian's ascent to the throne in Mexico until the end of the American Civil War and Lincoln's death, the president and Secretary Seward sustained their cautious Mexican policy. They did so in the face of French overtures to recognize Maximilian's government and domestic US demands to drive him from Mexico militarily. In response to the recognition overture, Seward declared that he was "quite as likely" to recognize Jefferson Davis as the "King of Richmond" as to acknowledge Maximilian's legitimacy as Mexico's emperor. Given the secretary's longstanding and increasingly viable threat of war against any nation that recognized the Confederacy, Napoleon blocked Maximilian from recognizing the Confederacy and forging an alliance that seemed essential to the survival of both failing governments by 1864 and 1865. The French ruler refused to run the risk of a US attack in response to actions by his handpicked Mexican emperor.[80]

Even as Seward and Lincoln maintained this threat of war against any European nation that intervened in the American conflict, they steadfastly rejected calls for the use of force in Mexico. This domestic pressure increased in early 1864 as Maximilian assumed the throne. The *New York Herald* decried the administration's "namby-pamby, wishy-washy foreign policy." In January, Senator James McDougall of California unsuccessfully sponsored a resolution asserting that unless France withdrew from Mexico by March 15, it would "become the duty" of Congress "to declare war" on Napoleon's government. In April the House of Representatives unanimously denounced the "deplorable events now transpiring" in Mexico; and in June the National Union presidential convention that renominated Lincoln included a plank in its platform that characterized Maximilian's regime "as menacing" to US "peace and independence."[81]

While deploying the domestic US demands for military intervention as diplomatic leverage with Napoleon and France, Seward and Lincoln carefully avoided a Franco-American confrontation. The president reiterated his determination to "attend to only one trouble at a time" and predicted correctly that once the French army withdrew, "the Mexicans will take care of Maximilian." Seward, consistent with his conception of American destiny, adopted a complementary perspective. In May 1864 he forecast that "the ever-increasing expansion of the American people westward and southward" would prevail. When Mexico opened itself to Americans, no "European power" could "maintain an army in Mexico capable of resisting the martial and moral influence" of this American "emigration." The secretary also feared that England and France could unite as allies were the United States to go to war with the latter. Finally, in a perceptive observation that countless subsequent US foreign policymakers should have noted when contemplating US military interventions abroad, Seward warned, "If we got into a war and drove out the French, we could not get out ourselves."[82]

Although France was not directly involved, Napoleon's imperial project played an interesting role in the Civil War's final diplomatic episode. In January 1865, Francis Preston Blair, a newspaper editor and veteran political operative, approached Lincoln and, with the president's permission, traveled to Richmond to meet with Jefferson Davis. Blair sought to arrange the reconciliation of the North and South on the basis of an armistice and a united military campaign to expel France from Mexico. Lincoln agreed to the meeting with the Confederates but carefully specified that he was doing so "with the view of securing peace to the people of our common country." Even though the president had pointedly refused to acknowledge the South's standing as a separate nation, an increasingly desperate Davis also consented to the conference. On February 3, 1865, Lincoln and Seward met with Confederate Vice President Alexander H. Stephens, former US Senator R. M. T. Hunter, and former US Supreme Court Justice John A. Campbell aboard the *River Queen,* a Union warship, at Hampton Roads, Virginia.[83]

As Lincoln and Seward sat down with the Confederate envoys, the president made three issues nonnegotiable: there could be no compromise on "restoration of national authority"; no "receding" on the emancipation of the slaves; and no "cessation of hostilities short of an end of the war." Given these preconditions, there was no possibility of a negotiated settlement based on the mutual attack on a common enemy. This alternative was no more viable in 1865 than it had been when Seward unwisely proffered it four years earlier. When Stephens posed the option of a temporary armistice and joint campaign against the French, Lincoln responded bluntly that "the restoration of the Union" was his "*sine qua non.*" Only Confederate recognition of US "National Authority" and an end to the armed "resistance" would lead to an armistice. Hunter countered that English King Charles I had negotiated temporary compromises in the midst of ongoing hostilities. Lincoln was immovable and characteristically quick. "I do not profess to be posted in history," he replied. "On all such matters I will turn you over to Seward. All I distinctly recollect about the case of Charles I, is, that he lost his head in the end." Lincoln and Seward had ended their successful Civil War diplomacy just as they had begun—by making all considerations secondary to restoration of the Union.[84]

VI.

US foreign policy success over the war's final two years had resulted from most of the same international dynamics and Lincoln-Seward policies that characterized the Union's overall wartime diplomacy. European nations, especially Great Britain and France, remained much more worried about one another and European power politics than the American Civil War. Despite the conflict's impact on the British and French economies and politics, Palmerston, Russell, Napoleon, Thouvenel, and Drouyn never made American developments their first priority. Napoleon III's ill-advised invasion of Mexico and Britain's fear of establishing injurious legal and tactical precedents in the areas of neutral commerce and shipbuilding reinforced British and French reluctance to intervene in the war. Although shortages of raw cotton disrupted Atlantic commerce during the war's first eighteen months, the cotton crisis eased appreciably by late 1862. Access to raw cotton never decisively overshadowed other segments of the British and French economies and their lucrative ties to the United States or tipped the scales toward a prosouthern foreign policy. Augmenting these geopolitical and economic considerations was the crucial ideological one—slavery. Personally opposed to slavery, Palmerston and Russell were decidedly disinclined to side with the South and defy Britain's majority public opposition to the peculiar institution. Although Napoleon displayed no such personal moral qualms, he, too, hesitated to disregard the antislavery elements of the French public.

Union foreign relations also benefited from a much-inferior Confederate effort in this realm. Waging a war to preserve slavery imposed a heavy burden on southern attempts to garner support in Western Europe. Jefferson Davis and the Confederacy failed to devise and implement a foreign policy that compensated for this burden. Davis and his government vastly overestimated the economic and political influence of King Cotton and the institution of slavery and greatly undervalued the importance of diplomacy and the necessity of securing substantial and sustained foreign assistance. Save Judah

P. Benjamin and James Bulloch, Davis appointed far too many substandard diplomatic representatives; he and his government failed to leverage cotton for critical loans and credits early in the war; the Richmond administration never developed a centrally directed and well-coordinated program for blockade running and purchasing abroad; and its efforts at public diplomacy and the dissemination of propaganda in Europe were equally deficient. Lincoln and Seward had been correct to fear that the South's prewar proclivity for territorial expansion was not solely defensive. The war had forced Dixie not only to give up its imperial agenda but also to discard the Monroe Doctrine, invite European intervention in the American War, and endorse the imposition of a European colonial regime in Mexico.[85]

In decided contrast to deficient Confederate diplomacy, Lincoln and Seward had combined their respective talents to formulate and implement a US foreign policy that took full advantage of the relevant geopolitical, economic, and ideological landscape of the early 1860s. Their unlikely partnership was based on a clear understanding of Lincoln's ultimate authority, an appreciation and respect for one another's abilities, a genuine friendship and mutual affection, and a productive division of labor. Both men made preservation of the Union the touchstone of their shared foreign policy and immediately grasped the indispensable role of successful foreign relations, even if they did not always agree completely on the proper measures to make the nation whole again. The president and secretary recognized that restoration of the Union had a foreign policy dimension: to prevent British and French official recognition of the South as an independent nation and to deny Richmond access to European-produced ships and war materiel. Despite the miscalculation of Seward's initial "Thoughts" for Lincoln's "Consideration" in April 1861, they understood that, even as they entreated and pressured the major powers not to intervene in the American conflict, the United States could not become involved in a second war. As Lincoln pronounced and Seward reiterated, a second war would have doomed the effort to conquer the Confederacy and, thereby, ensured southern independence. Ever practical, Lincoln and Seward practiced the art of compromise as they walked the tightrope of pressuring the Great Powers but avoiding war with them.

From his position as senior partner, Lincoln established the overall foreign policy framework and periodically assumed a primary role. He ruled out a second war, moderated the tone of some Seward dispatches during the spring of 1861, proclaimed the blockade, and issued the Emancipation Proclamation. The latter two measures embodied the president's determination to maintain executive authority over foreign relations and the conduct of the war and demonstrated his dramatic enhancement of the president's powers as commander in chief. Lincoln recognized the connection of military success to the North's viable foreign policy and directed the Union's war effort with that connection in mind, as well as the obvious need to defeat the Confederacy. He also advanced the Union cause both at home and abroad by repeatedly and brilliantly portraying the conflict as a struggle for the survival of the nation's experiment in republican government. He emphasized to fellow citizens and contemporary Europeans that the fate of both US national coherence and republicanism internationally depended on the epic struggle's outcome. The Emancipation Proclamation built on this theme while unmistakably casting the war as one over the survival of slavery and erecting a formidable barrier to European intervention on the side of the South. Both the Emancipation Proclamation and Lincoln's declarations on behalf of republicanism, such as the First Inaugural Address, his July 4, 1861, address to Congress, and the Gettysburg Address, were effective examples of public diplomacy, as were his letters and funds sent to pro-northern groups of workingmen in Great Britain.

Seward made his most significant contribution to the US diplomatic effort by convincing Britain and France that any intervention that went beyond recognition of the South as a belligerent would lead to war with the North. He drove this message home over the war's first crucial seven months through purposefully belligerent rhetoric and unsubtle brinkmanship. Seward's tone had moderated before the *Trent* affair, when he led the administration decision to surrender Mason and Slidell and offered the public rationale for this necessary concession. Thereafter, his overall posture was much more conciliatory toward Britain and France, but he continued to deliver stern reminders of a potential US military response to London and Paris at critical moments, such as the recognition crisis in the fall of 1862 and the Confederate shipbuilding threat the following summer and fall. These warnings became steadily more credible as US military and manufacturing strength increased over the course of the war.

The secretary ably managed day-to-day foreign policy matters, which encompassed a broad array of issues ranging from disputes over US incursions on neutral commerce and the arrest of foreign nationals to military recruitment at home and abroad, Confederate raids against the United States from Canada, and French military and political intrusion into Mexico. As he conducted these diplomatic interactions, Seward earned the respect and trust of key British and French policymakers and diplomats, particularly Lyons, Russell, Mercier, and Drouyn. Their initially negative, even hostile assessments of Seward and his work were transformed, which testified to his performance as secretary of state and was a boon to US foreign relations. The secretary also contributed to the administration's innovations in public diplomacy by working effectively with northern newspaper editors and political allies, such as Henry Raymond and Thurlow Weed, to explain and defend the administration's and his own policies, and by selectively publishing key portions of US diplomatic correspondence in the *Foreign Relations* series, which he initiated in late 1861. Finally, the secretary served President Lincoln as his closest adviser on foreign policy, his primary sounding board and counselor on virtually all domestic matters, and the person with whom the president was most able to relax and gain private comfort and refuge from the burdens and tensions of his office.

The unlikely partners' highly successful foreign policy played an indispensable role in the northern victory. Their efforts had forestalled European intervention in the American Civil War while avoiding armed conflict with Great Britain and France. Just as the US victory and the preservation of the Union were coming to fruition, John Wilkes Booth abruptly ended the partnership. Seward, the surviving member, had made essential contributions to the preservation of the Union. Over the ensuing four years, he would promote his ambitious and prescient vision to expand the reunited nation, both territorially and commercially.

5

SEWARD AND EMPIRE, 1865–1869

I.

In June 1869, following the end of his tenure as secretary of state, William Henry Seward embarked on the first of two remarkable trips. Out of public life for the first time since 1830, Seward had turned sixty-eight in May and suffered from rapidly advancing paralysis in his arms and hands—a condition that required the aid of two personal attendants by 1871. Still, the indomitable New Yorker spent virtually all of the period between June 1869 and October 1872 in continuous and demanding travel. During these two and one-half years, he visited four continents and left behind observations that formed the essence of a 720-page travelogue that sold more than sixty thousand copies.[1]

What prompted this aging, physically handicapped statesman to undertake such challenging and draining odysseys? Seward explained to his neighbors in Auburn, New York, that "at my age, and in my condition of health, 'rest was rust,' and nothing remained, to prevent rust, but to keep in motion." He was also indulging the lifelong intellectual curiosity and love of travel that had prompted extended European tours in 1833 and 1860 and a four-week cruise of the Caribbean in 1867. The second of his valedictory trips, which stretched around the world, also allowed him to spend time with Olive Risley, a twenty-five-year-old family friend of whom he had grown quite fond. Seward was lonely following the death of his wife and daughter in 1866 and unquestionably enjoyed the attention and company of this young woman, but there was nothing untoward about their relationship. Still rumors circulated that his relations with Olive were not just fatherly and platonic and that

5. Napoleon III, the most consistent and deliberate European opponent of Lincoln and Seward's foreign policies. Courtesy of the Library of Congress.

a marriage was imminent. To quell such gossip, he legally adopted the young woman in November 1870 as they traveled across China.[2]

Seward's two trips symbolized key aspects of his global imperial vision and his accomplishments as secretary of state. Both journeys commenced from his home in Auburn and headed west—the direction in which Seward believed the course of world empire had long been moving toward its ultimate location in a powerful United States. On the first trip, he traveled via the recently completed transcontinental railroad, a key component of the national integrity, strength, and commercial growth that Seward considered prerequisites to US standing as a world power. After several stops in the Midwest, Seward, accompanied by his children Anna and Frederick, received a hero's welcome in Sacramento and San Francisco in July 1869. The reception was fitting since the retired statesman had been convinced that California statehood was vital to national cohesion and to acquisition of frontage on the Pacific Ocean. The latter was indispensable to US commercial expansion into East Asia and to dominance over world trade. From California, the Sewards sailed north to visit Alaska, the secretary's most important territorial acquisition, and a stepping-stone toward trade with China and Japan. The former secretary and his companions then headed south to Mexico, where he was applauded as a national benefactor for helping to overturn the French occupation and Napoleon III's attempt to impose a European empire in the Western Hemisphere. After Mexico, the party returned home via Cuba, just the kind of Caribbean strategic and commercial outpost that Seward had coveted after 1865 when slavery no longer burdened US expansion. His Auburn neighbors welcomed the weary travelers home in early March 1870.

Five months later in August, Seward undertook an even more ambitious trip. Seward, Olive Risley, her sister Hattie, and the girls' father, Hanson, again traveled by rail and were feted in San Francisco before they sailed for Japan on September 1. Hanson Risley did not cross the Pacific, but Alexander Randall, a former postmaster general, and his wife did. This group spent five weeks in Japan, where Seward met with the nation's foreign minister and with the Meiji emperor, a distinct and most unusual honor. From Japan, Seward and his entourage moved on to China, the other principal East Asian target in his blueprint for US commercial expansion. By February 1871, with the examination of China, Singapore, and Saigon completed, the Randalls headed home, while Seward and the Risley sisters pressed on to India. They traveled there for three months and then continued to Syria and Egypt, where Seward was especially interested to assess the Suez Canal. Its anticipated completion in November 1869 had helped prompt his attempt to construct a US waterway through Panama to better compete with the Europeans for trade with Asia. From the Middle East, Seward continued on to Europe, where he treated the two Risley sisters to a grand tour, including stops in Turkey, Hungary, Greece, Germany, Italy, Switzerland, France, and England. As had been the case the previous March, a large contingent of Seward's neighbors welcomed him home to Auburn in October 1872 from the journey Seward calculated at some forty-four thousand miles.

Seward's two victory laps carried such historical symbolism because he had remained secretary of state from 1865 to 1869 following Lincoln's death. This tenure required a working relationship with Lincoln's successor, Andrew

Johnson, a relationship that was even more unlikely than the one Seward had forged with the fallen president. Prior to Johnson's ascent to the presidency, he and Seward shared virtually nothing in common personally or politically. Born in 1808 in Raleigh, North Carolina, Johnson received no formal schooling and was apprenticed at the age of ten to a local tailor who probably taught his young charge to read. The teenager subsequently spent time as a journeyman tailor in South Carolina and Alabama before settling in Greenville, Tennessee. In this east Tennessee village at the foot of the Great Smoky Mountains, Johnson built a thriving business as a tailor, married Eliza McCardle in 1827, and acquired several slaves.[3]

"Always impeccably dressed," Johnson demonstrated a "zest for learning" and voraciously consumed books on politics and debating, but he shunned social gatherings. Consistent with his reading preferences, the young tailor soon entered public life, where he emerged as a forceful and caustic public speaker. He was first elected to office as a Greenville alderman in 1829, became mayor in 1834, and advanced to the state legislature the following year. Johnson served in the Tennessee legislature over the next decade, during which he became a staunch Jacksonian Democrat. In 1843 he began another ten-year legislative stint, this time in the US House of Representatives. After Tennessee Whigs redrew his congressional district in 1852, Johnson was forced out of Congress, but not out of public life since he surprisingly won two terms as the state's governor and was elected to the US Senate in 1857.[4]

In true southern Jacksonian fashion, Johnson defended states' rights, slavery, white supremacy, the annexation of Texas, the US war with Mexico, and the common man versus aristocrats. He opposed the Second Bank of the United States, protective tariffs, and federal spending on public works (save for railroads in Tennessee). This record provided a mirror image of Seward's political history. Indeed, Johnson's commitment to strict government economy yielded opposition to not just major federal projects such as the transcontinental railroad, but also the renovation of the White House, funding the Smithsonian Institution, and paving the streets in Washington, D.C. His two conspicuous departures from this political pattern reflected his declared love for the "people" and hatred of the "upstart, swelled headed, iron heeled, bobtailed aristocracy." While governor, he championed the passage of unprecedented funding for public education; and from his positions as a congressman and senator, he relentlessly advocated homestead legislation designed to afford "every poor man in the United States who is the head of a family" the opportunity to acquire land in the New West. His "maverick" tendencies were on full display in the latter campaign since no other southern legislator backed homestead legislation during the 1850s.[5]

The senator's personal and political independence was even more evident in 1860–1861 when Tennessee and ten other southern states seceded from the Union. The only southern senator to remain loyal to the United States, Johnson pronounced secession equivalent to treason and assigned responsibility for the South's actions to Dixie's aristocrats. He was appointed the Union's military governor of Tennessee in March 1862 and, in June 1864, was nominated as Lincoln's vice presidential running mate on the National Union Party ticket. Both the Republican Party's new name and Johnson's nomination were meant to appeal to prewar Democrats and to bolster Lincoln's reelection prospects. Seward endorsed Johnson's nomination primarily to block the selection of New Yorker Daniel S. Dickinson. Had the latter become vice president, Seward might have been forced out of office in deference to the contemporary assumption that only one person per state could hold an office as important as vice president or cabinet member in an administration. Regardless of Seward's motivation, Johnson appreciated and remembered the secretary's support.[6]

Given Johnson's personal and political background, how did Seward, a highly educated, cosmopolitan, Whig-turned-Republican who had been in the forefront of the North's antislavery movement, coexist with this poorly educated, provincial southerner who had owned slaves and been a lifelong Democrat? Upon assuming the presidency, Johnson sought to reassure the nation by retaining all of Lincoln's cabinet. Although Johnson and Seward were never close personally, the new president was grateful for Seward's role in his nomination on the National Union Party's 1864 ticket. Seward also afforded Johnson, who never really joined the Republican Party ideologically or organizationally, a link to more conservative Republicans. This potential political asset diminished rapidly as Johnson's policies and actions alienated all wings of Seward's old party. When this alienation became outrage and led to the Republicans' unsuccessful attempt to impeach Johnson in 1868, Seward helped save the president by raising vital funds and recruiting talented legal counsel for the president's defense. Johnson, who had overseen only disaster on the domestic front, may also have valued the positive record Seward had compiled in foreign policy by directing US responses to the French occupation of Mexico and purchasing Alaska.[7]

Seward's reasons for staying on as secretary of state are more readily discernible. Although he may still have entertained fleeting aspirations of becoming president, the aging statesman was far too politically astute not to realize that his prospects for attaining the highest office had ended by 1865. As head of the State Department, he could remain a significant public figure and enjoy the celebrity and Washington social life he coveted. Seward certainly did not want to go home to the quiet life in Auburn. During the four years of war, he had made fewer than ten trips to the sleepy New York village, and his motivation to make the trek diminished even further in June 1866 when his wife Frances died, followed in October 1866 by his twenty-two-year-old daughter Fanny.[8]

Significant policy considerations reinforced Seward's personal reasons for sustaining a working relationship with Johnson and continuing to direct US foreign policy. Crucial foreign policy issues beckoned, and Johnson left virtually all major decisions in this sphere to the secretary of state. As the war ended, France's occupation of Mexico and attempted installation of a European monarch on the United States' doorstep demanded a stern but cautious response, and Seward was supremely confident that he was most qualified to formulate the delicate American rejoinder. The war's conclusion also afforded the secretary the opportunity to pursue his refined and prescient vision for US commercial expansion—an opportunity he eagerly embraced.

Seward and Johnson's basic agreement on the appropriate policies for Reconstruction, or the South's reincorporation into the Union, reinforced the secretary's desire to remain in office and the president's willingness to retain him. Despite their vastly different pathways to this crucial juncture in the nation's history, they agreed that the prompt reinstatement of national harmony and reincorporation of the southern states should take priority; that the sectional and national welfare of whites should take precedence over that of African Americans, whom they both deemed inferior; and that the states should determine voting rights for both races. Despite these general policy agreements, Seward, who had defended blacks in court, harbored runaway slaves, and endorsed African American social and economic opportunity, was far more liberal on race than Johnson, a former slave owner.[9]

When Johnson acted on these policy priorities, his actions led to southern defiance and political disaster. Various states refused to repudiate their Confederate debts; balked at ratification of the Thirteenth Amendment abolishing slavery or the Fourteenth making African Americans citizens;

condoned widespread violence against newly freed slaves; and elected numerous former Confederates to public office. When these actions caused great apprehension among Republicans that the war's hard-earned results were in danger, Johnson rejected all overtures for compromise and denounced his political foes in vitriolic terms. The president disregarded Seward's advice to seek common ground with the Republicans and to recognize that Congress had a legitimate role in Reconstruction. And, Johnson discarded the secretary's much more moderate and less inflammatory drafts of his principal public addresses. These cumulative, ill-advised decisions elicited intense political hostility among Republicans and led eventually to the unsuccessful Republican attempt to impeach the president.[10]

As Johnson and his policies grew steadily more inflammatory, Seward's general support for the president and continued presence in the cabinet engendered harsh criticism from across the political spectrum. Reminiscent of the Lincoln years, many Johnson critics blamed Seward for the president's actions. After Johnson took a disastrous speaking tour in 1866, a Democrat wondered if the secretary meant "to kill him off by this tour?" Republican senator William Pitt Fessenden, an old Seward adversary, opined that "Seward's evil counsels" had "carried [Johnson] beyond the reach of salvation." Democrats had detested Seward since the 1840s and many Republicans were equally antagonistic and often pressed Johnson to replace the secretary of state. The *Chicago Tribune* charged him with "political apostasy" and declared that Seward had committed "political suicide" by supporting Johnson; the *Nation* concluded correctly that Seward was "a leader without a party"; the more sympathetic Johnson dismissed him as essentially "a dead carcass" politically by 1867; and even Thurlow Weed, his oldest political friend and ally, lamented that same year that the secretary was "one of the most unpopular men in the country" and should retire from office.[11]

The secretary's political stands and choices and his alienation from the moderate and radical elements of the Republican Party have led historian Richard Immerman to pronounce Seward "in fundamental ways his own worst enemy" on the foreign policy front. This judgment is overly harsh. Although political hostility complicated Seward's adept and ultimately successful response to Napoleon III's intervention in Mexico, endangered but did not block the purchase of Alaska, and was a crucial factor in the defeat of his efforts to annex the Danish West Indies, the secretary had very limited options from 1865 to 1869. As demonstrated by the pressure on Lincoln to banish him from the cabinet in December 1862, Seward had run afoul of a broad cross section of the Republican Party and key leaders such as Fessenden and Charles Sumner well before Johnson took office. Moreover, he could not have sided with the radical wing of the party and still remained secretary of state. Seward was indeed a "dead carcass" politically by 1866, but he was still the secretary of state and the principal formulator of US foreign policy—two positions he could not have retained had he broken openly with the president and sided with Republicans in the House and Senate. Had he not remained secretary for those additional four years after 1865, Seward would not have compiled the overall record of achievement which has qualified him to be considered one of the nation's two greatest secretaries of state.[12]

II.

While Seward recovered in the summer of 1865 from the injuries he had suffered in the April carriage accident and Lewis Powell's assassination attempt, the ongoing French occupation of Mexico provided the greatest threat to US national security. In June forty thousand French troops achieved their greatest territorial control; and Emperor Maximilian, whom Napoleon III had installed the previous year, had not yet encountered the devastating difficulties that would lead to his demise two years later. Napoleon's military intervention in Mexico and attempt to impose a European monarchy in the Western Hemisphere blatantly violated the US Monroe Doctrine and its strictures against such actions. With the Confederacy defeated and a powerful Union army still in place, many Americans believed that the time was right to abandon Lincoln and Seward's policy of strict neutrality and to aid President Benito Juárez and his Mexican forces in their war against the French and Maximilian.[13]

General Grant and several other prominent US military leaders were the most influential Americans arguing for this more belligerent US policy. They formed an alliance with Matías Romero, the Mexican minister to the United States, to pressure the Johnson administration to intervene directly on behalf of the Mexican opposition. Grant considered "the French occupation of Mexico as part and parcel of the late rebellion in the United States" and believed it needed "to be suppressed before the entire peace" could be "assured." The general cited alleged Confederate-French wartime cooperation, the potential for the flight of ex-Confederate soldiers to Mexico, the possibility of a hostile military force on the US border, and injurious commercial restrictions as the rationale for US intervention.[14]

On his own authority and without consulting President Johnson, Grant first ordered General Philip H. Sheridan to move his fifty thousand US troops to the Rio Grande River in mid-May 1865. Sheridan, who shared Grant's views on the connection of Maximilian's regime to the Confederacy and the hazards that accompanied the French presence in Mexico, remained in the border region over much of the ensuing two years. His forces posed a visible threat to the French-Maximilian army and facilitated the transfer of war materials to Juárez's soldiers. Grant and Minister Romero also devised a scheme to attract former US soldiers into the service of the Juarez army by offering the American immigrants land grants in Mexico. To ensure the effectiveness of these immigrant forces, Grant and Romero sought to place them under the command of a former US general. After General William Tecumseh Sherman refused to participate in this bizarre project, Grant and Romero approached General John M. Schofield, who expressed greater interest.[15]

Grant then arranged a meeting for Romero to brief President Johnson and solicit the president's endorsement of the evolving plan. Significantly, Grant and Romero did not inform Seward or the State Department of the soldier-immigration scheme or the presidential meeting. Romero, who had represented the Juárez government in Washington since 1861, first as chargé d'affaires and after 1863 as minister, had long deplored Seward's restrained and essentially neutral policy toward Napoleon's intervention in Mexico and had worked assiduously to "keep the phrase 'Monroe Doctrine'" prominent in "public discourse." The Mexican diplomat and lobbyist had regularly denounced Seward's refusal to intervene against the French during the Lincoln presidency. He had cooperated with Radical Republicans who were hostile to Seward and Lincoln, had endorsed the effort to expel Seward from the cabinet in December 1862, and had collaborated with officials such as Senator James A. McDougall and Representative Henry Winter Davis in efforts to embarrass the Lincoln administration and pressure it to aid the Juárez government. After Lincoln's death, Romero had expected a more sympathetic response from Johnson, if "Seward's continuation in the Cabinet" could be blocked.[16]

Much to their disappointment, Romero and Grant failed to bypass Secretary Seward or to force him out of the cabinet. Johnson had proclaimed belligerently in 1864 that once the "Rebellion is put down," the United States should "attend to this Mexican affair"—that "an expedition into Mexico would be a sort of recreation" for Union soldiers. He responded more cautiously in the summer of 1865 by directing Grant to present the cabinet with a written summary of the immigration proposal and the plan to dispatch Schofield. Just back to work after the Powell attack, Seward quashed the project in the cabinet and in a subsequent Johnson-directed meeting with Romero.[17]

The secretary of state pressed successfully for continuation of the restrained, noninterventionist policy that he and Lincoln had implemented over the previous three years. Unlike Grant, Sheridan, and many Radical Republicans, Seward did not consider the French presence in Mexico an extension of the American Civil War. Nor did he deem US military intervention necessary. Rather, he agreed with the US minister to Belgium's observation that Napoleon was "like a man with his fingers between two cogwheels in motion." Given the French emperor's commitments in Algeria, Italy, and East Asia; Bismarck's rise in Prussia; the financial drain of the Mexican occupation; and the domestic French opposition to the intervention, Seward forecast accurately that the French emperor could not sustain Maximilian's regime. US intervention, he wisely asserted, would be no more popular among Mexicans than the French intrusion, and might even extend Maximilian's rule. Secretary of the Navy Gideon Welles, certainly no ally of the secretary of state, noted, "Seward acts from intelligence, Grant from impulse."[18]

Working from these assumptions and never publicly mentioning the Monroe Doctrine, Seward skillfully directed policy until French forces withdrew and Maximilian fell from power and was executed in June 1867. The secretary first issued a circular that instructed foreign diplomats to communicate with the US government through the State Department rather than speak directly to the president. Romero complained correctly that the statement "appears to be directed exclusively at me." Although the Mexican minister continued to talk periodically with Johnson, Seward monitored these meetings and repulsed all attempts to end his domination of US policy.[19]

He also successfully frustrated the Grant-Romero effort to have General Schofield command a contingent of former US soldiers in Mexico. With this proposal on the table, the secretary invited Schofield to visit him and his family at Cape May, New Jersey, where they were on a summer vacation. While ostensibly agreeing to a Schofield inspection trip to the Rio Grande, where he might lead a military operation, Seward proposed that the general first accept a special mission to Paris to meet with the French emperor. Seward's directions seemed clear and flattering: "I want you to get your legs under Napoleon's mahogany, and tell him he must get out of Mexico." Schofield accepted the assignment, but waited nearly three months for Seward's official instructions, which did not mention meeting with Napoleon. The general finally sailed on November 15, spent time in London, and had a pleasant time in Paris and Europe before he returned to Washington in June 1866. He met Napoleon and Empress Eugenie only briefly at a social event in January and arrived home generally supportive of Seward's Mexican policy, but he never went to Mexico.[20]

The secretary of state manipulated another former general, John A. Logan, in equally adept fashion. A twice-wounded Civil War veteran, Logan was serving in Congress, where he had adopted a belligerent, pro-Juárez posture. In mid-November 1865, Seward named Logan the administration's choice to become the US minister to the Juárez government. For all of his tough talk, Logan declined the nomination in favor of a run for the Senate. Still, his deliberations consumed several weeks, and the nomination played well with Grant and Romero and, at least temporarily, muted Radical Republican attacks on Seward and Johnson's cautious opposition to Napoleon and Maximilian. The Logan nomination also set off alarm bells in Paris and Mexico City, where Napoleon and Maximilian's governments worried that Seward and Johnson might abandon the noninterventionist US policy.[21]

Cultivating such apprehensions and uncertainty was precisely Seward's intention as he gradually tightened the screws on Napoleon in the fall of 1865. Two weeks before the Logan nomination, the secretary had conveyed his sterner stance to the US minister in Paris, John Bigelow. Bigelow was to emphasize that the French imposition of Maximilian's monarchy on the Mexican people was "disallowable and impracticable" and "in direct antagonism" to the pro-republican policy of the US "government and the principle on which it was founded." When Marquis Charles de Montholon, the French minister to the United States, formally presented Napoleon's offer to withdraw his troops from Mexico in return for US recognition of Maximilian's government, Seward flatly refused. He informed Montholon, already shaken by the Logan nomination, that US recognition was out of the question and that France needed to jettison its "aggressive attitude in Mexico." Seward's campaign in 1865 to pressure France, deflate the Grant–Romero–Radical Republican bellicosity, and avoid direct US intervention concluded with the foreign policy portion of President Johnson's annual message in December. The president declared that the United States would "regard it as a great calamity to ourselves, to the cause of good government, and to the peace of the world, should any European power challenge the American people" and their "defense of republicanism against foreign interference."[22]

William H. Russell, the British newspaper reporter, offered a perceptive assessment of Seward's Franco-Mexican diplomacy: "My dear friend King Villum's oracular style, bless him, is at times obscure, is very pleasant, but there's a smack of powder in it too." By early 1866, this policy of persistent but restrained pressure began to yield tangible results. In January Napoleon announced publicly that French troops would be withdrawn from Mexico, and in April he provided the United States a timetable. France's soldiers would return home in three groups, with departures from Mexico in November 1866, March 1867, and November 1867. Napoleon's promises satisfied neither Grant nor Sheridan. Grant dismissed Seward as "a powerful practical ally of Louis Napoleon," and Sheridan attributed the secretary's refusal to adopt a more bellicose approach to "butt-headedness or the indifference or vanity of old age."[23]

Neither butt-headed nor indifferent, Seward was no more willing than Grant or Sheridan to trust Napoleon or his promises. The secretary reasserted his position clearly, albeit indirectly, in response to reports that several thousand former Austrian soldiers might volunteer to fight on Maximilian's behalf in Mexico. During February and March 1866, both John Bigelow and John Lothrop Motley, the US ministers to France and Austria, respectively, informed Seward of rumors in Paris and Vienna that as many as ten thousand Austrian troops could be involved. Without substantive confirmation of these rumors, Seward fired off blunt instructions to Motley on April 6 and 16. Were "Austrian subjects, under the command or with the sanction of the government of Vienna" to enter the fight in Mexico, the United States would consider "these hostilities . . . a state of war by Austria against the republic of Mexico," and "*the United States could not . . . remain as silent or neutral spectators.*" To augment this threat that the United States would abandon its neutral, but far from disinterested policy, toward the Mexican conflict, Seward further instructed Motley ten days later that he should break diplomatic relations and "withdraw from Vienna to some convenient place in Europe and await instructions" if Austria intervened militarily in Mexico.[24]

Why had Seward departed so blatantly from his formerly restrained, cautious policy toward the war in Mexico? In reality, he had not. First, Austria was preoccupied with the rapid deterioration of its relations with Prussia, relations that would lead to a war in June. Therefore, threatening Austria carried none of the dangers that would have accompanied a comparable hectoring of France. Second, Seward's stern warning was actually directed at Napoleon and "the continually recurring reports of the departure of new troops from French camps and stations in Europe and Africa to Mexico." Bigelow readily discerned that "it suited his [Seward's] convenience" to communicate with France "by way of Vienna." Finally, Seward most likely hoped to use this more belligerent posture to relieve some of the domestic pressure from Grant and Sheridan and to bolster President Johnson, who was in the midst of his politically destructive confrontation with the congressional Republicans over the Freedmen's Bureau and Civil Rights Bill. Although the diplomatic dustup with Austria did little to aid Johnson, Seward had reasserted his control over foreign policy and reinforced US pressure on Napoleon to fulfill his promises to withdraw French forces from Mexico.[25]

Seward returned to more conventional foreign policy signaling in November 1866 when Napoleon deferred the withdrawal of remaining French troops from Mexico until the following March. Fully aware of the domestic political "embarrassment" Napoleon's announcement would produce for the Johnson administration, Seward declared the decision "in every way inconvenient and exceptionable" and stressed to Bigelow that the United States could not "acquiesce." Still, the secretary was unwilling to go beyond this firm protest. To accentuate this message to France, he selected Lewis D. Campbell, an Ohio editor and politician, as the new US minister to the Juárez government on November 10. Campbell departed for Mexico accompanied by General William Tecumseh Sherman, whose presence suggested that US military intervention remained a possibility. The hack politician and the famous general traveled to Havana, Veracruz, Tampico, and Brownsville, Texas, but never located Juárez, who was ensconced in Chihuahua. Sherman put it bluntly: "I have not the remotest idea of riding on mule back 1,000 miles to find . . . [the] chief executive." This abortive mission had no immediate effect on Napoleon, Juárez, or Maximilian, but it did testify to Seward's political savvy and his ongoing measures to maintain pressure on Paris and to pacify political and military critics of the administration's Mexican policy.[26]

This pacification was at best only temporary. The *Chicago Tribune* spoke for administration critics in late December 1866 by declaring "the recent management of the Mexican question" would not "add to Mr. Seward's reputation as a statesman." Even as the *Tribune* taunted the secretary, his restrained but persistent pressure was about to obtain the ultimate objective—French departure from Mexico. Faced with financial difficulties, domestic French political opposition, European strategic concerns, staunch resistance from Juárez and liberal Mexican forces, and Emperor Maximilian's missteps and general ineptness, the French emperor's Mexican policy met its final demise. Seward had been fully aware of these collateral realities as he implemented US policy, and his efforts proved successful when the last French forces departed from Mexico in March 1867. From 1862 forward, the secretary had made US dissatisfaction clear and had steadily upped the geopolitical ante as US military situations allowed, but he had also left Napoleon an escape route—even "graciously" holding the "door" for the French "departure." Three months after that departure, Maximilian was executed by a Mexican firing squad. Seward had repulsed this major "ideological and geopolitical challenge" to the Monroe Doctrine and its ban on the establishment of European monarchies in the Western Hemisphere without mentioning the Doctrine by name and without military intervention in Mexico or the loss of a single US soldier. Late nineteenth-century historian Frederick Bancroft, with some hyperbole, pronounced this outcome Seward's "most perfect achievement in diplomacy."[27]

III.

While helping orchestrate the French expulsion from Mexico may not have been Seward's foremost diplomatic achievement, it did allow him to devote full attention to "laying the foundations of a great empire." Seward's cabinet adversary, Secretary of the Navy Gideon Welles, ranted that he had "become almost a monomaniac on the subject of territorial acquisition," that he sought new territory indiscriminately; and the secretary of states' old political ally and friend Charles Francis Adams lamented in 1867, "Mr. Seward's thirst for more land seems insatiable." Subsequent historians have asserted that his "imperialism had a buckshot quality to it" and that he sought "public acclaim," personal "power," and "historical reputation" rather than "well-defined policy goals." Without denying that Seward valued all of these possible personal outcomes, he adhered rather consistently to the imperial vision he had formulated and articulated in the 1850s. Each facet of his postwar imperial pursuit was, as he informed John Bigelow in March 1867, "part of a system of negotiations" or, as he wrote into President Johnson's December 1868 annual message, part of "a comprehensive national policy."[28]

Seward remained convinced that only a strong, consolidated United States could compete successfully in the international pursuit of power. Development of this coherent, powerful nation had prompted his pre–Civil War championing of the Homestead Act, liberal immigration policies, and the transcontinental railroad. This goal also fueled his determination to defeat the South and preserve one powerful nation and to reintegrate Dixie rapidly back into the Union. Seward similarly retained his conviction that becoming a great nation required not just military and economic power but also an elevated moral standing. Americans were "charged with responsibilities of establishing on the American continent a higher condition of civilization and freedom than has ever before been attained in any part of the world." From this perspective, expunging the moral burden of slavery had been a principal reason for war, and the North's victory had enhanced the nation's respectability and removed a major obstacle to expansion into the Caribbean. Union victory had also sustained the US experiment in democracy and its mission to promote republicanism at home and abroad—the message President Lincoln had so eloquently propounded and Seward had echoed during the conflict.[29]

Although Seward became more amenable to territorial expansion after 1865, commercial expansion remained his primary objective. US "commercial ascendancy," or the domination of international trade and markets, would, he asserted, make the United States "the great power of the earth" and enable the nation to beget benign changes worldwide by disseminating American "civilization." He was confident that American republican values, institutions, and commerce would attract other territories into the US orbit peacefully, without the forceful overseas conquest the secretary disdained. Capturing East Asian trade was his ultimate objective and the key to US commercial supremacy. From this perspective, California afforded the crucial ports and frontage on the Pacific Ocean; Caribbean islands constituted "a halfway station [for] our national commerce with South America and the Pacific Coast" and naval stations "for our squadrons of war"; a canal through Panama, the "Great American Route," would afford the United States a "decided advantage" over the French and British and their use of the Suez Canal in trading with China and Japan; Alaska would become a "foothold for commercial and naval operations accessible from the Pacific States" and augment trade with Asia; and Hawaii would furnish the same strategic and economic outpost in the Pacific that Seward projected for Caribbean islands in the Atlantic.[30]

The United States' purchase of Alaska was the most significant achievement in Seward's pursuit of empire. While his contemporaries often ridiculed "Seward's Folly" or "Seward's Icebox," the annexation of this vast territory, replete with rich natural resources and great strategic utility, must be included among Seward's greatest achievements as secretary of state. Acquisition of the Russian colony accorded nicely with Seward's conviction that the seat of world empire was moving inevitably westward and that it was coming to reside in the United States. Mastery of East Asian commerce was the key to that outcome. These assumptions help explain Seward's determination to make California a state and to employ its excellent ports to dominate Pacific trade. These guiding principles also account for his energetic work on behalf of the telegraph line that Perry McDonough Collins attempted to build from California to Europe via British Columbia, Alaska, the Bering Strait, and Siberia. The secretary of state eyed Russian North America from this same imperial perspective. As early as 1852, he had introduced legislation calling on the US government to conduct an oceanic survey designed to promote whaling in the Bering Sea region and US-Asian commerce generally. Two years later, Seward suggested the possible US purchase of the territory in a Senate speech, and in 1860 he encouraged Russia to "build up" its "outposts all along the coast, up even to the Arctic Ocean" since they would eventually "become the outposts of my country."[31]

Although Seward had deferred his imperial aspirations, including a possible purchase of Alaska during the war years, cordial US-Russian relations between 1861 and 1865 ultimately facilitated postwar negotiations. These interactions derived from complementary national interests. Russia viewed the United States as a counterweight to Britain in the European balance of power, and Washington was grateful for Russia's refusal to cooperate in 1862 and 1863 with Anglo-French overtures to recognize the Confederacy and for the Russian fleet's visits to New York and San Francisco in 1863. Seward reciprocated that same year when he rebuffed joint British-French overtures to intervene on the side of nationalistic Poles who were rebelling against Russian control.[32]

When northern victory appeared likely in December 1864, Seward invited Grand Duke Constantine, the brother of the czar and the most important Russian proponent of the colony's sale, to visit the United States. In his instructions to the US minister in St. Petersburg, the secretary did not specify his reasons for the invitation, but added, "They will readily occur to you as they would to His Imperial Highness." Constantine did not make the trip, but Seward's interest in the territory persisted. In early 1866 he employed a Washington territorial legislature's petition on fishing rights as the occasion for suggesting to Eduard de Stoeckl, Russia's minister to the United States, that the two nations should make "early and comprehensive arrangements . . . to prevent the growth of difficulties in the Russian possessions." When Stoeckl offered to conclude such an agreement the following year, he fully understood that Seward would be an enthusiastic negotiating partner.[33]

Following nearly a decade of intragovernmental debate after Russia's defeat in the Crimean War (1854–1855), Czar Alexander II opted to sell his North American colony for the best possible price rather than risk losing the territory to ever-increasing US expansionist pressure. Prince Constantine had noted his country's sizable postwar debt as early as 1857 when he recommended the sale. These fiscal pressures and important strategic considerations in Europe and Asia precluded the financial and military investments needed to safeguard the region. When Alexander's government secured valuable territory in the lower Amur Valley in 1866 and, with it, commercial access to Beijing, the American colony, which ran a debilitating deficit throughout the 1860s, was no longer essential to Russian commercial expansion in the region. Minister Stoeckl also warned that US commercial and population pressures were unrelenting and, likely, irresistible. Russia, he argued, needed to sell its colony or risk it being overrun by Americans. By late 1866, a reluctant Prince Alexander Gorchakov, the Russian foreign minister, agreed and, along with Constantine and Stoeckl, recommended the sale to Czar Alexander. On December 16, 1866, the czar instructed Stoeckl, who was at home on leave, to return to the United States, begin negotiations, and accept no less than $5 million.[34]

Minister Stoeckl arrived in New York City on February 15, 1867, but a foot injury suffered during the rough transatlantic crossing delayed his arrival in Washington for another three weeks. In the interim, he dispatched one of Seward's close "political friends," probably Thurlow Weed, to prepare the way for the negotiations. On March 11 Stoeckl called upon Seward at the

State Department. After some initial sparring over American encroachments into Russian territory and conflicts over fishing rights, Seward broached the possibility of the US purchase. Stoeckl responded that he was authorized to consider a US offer, but the secretary replied that he needed to secure the approval of President Johnson and the cabinet before commencing substantive negotiations.[35]

The secretary conferred with Johnson, whom he described misleadingly to Stoeckl as "not inclined to the transaction" but willing to allow discussions to proceed. Seward and Stoeckl met again on March 14. Although Seward claimed he could make no official offers without cabinet sanction, he cited $5 million as a possible price and then declared the United States could pay no more than $5.5 million. Stoeckl, who had represented Russia in Washington since 1850, suggested that he might lobby some of his friends in Congress while Seward consulted the cabinet, an offer the secretary decisively rejected. Given his unpopularity among both Democrats and Republicans, Seward wisely advised, "This negotiation must be conducted in the greatest secrecy. Let us first see if we can agree. It will be time then to consult Congress." He fully understood that an earlier disclosure of the negotiations would subject them to attacks from all sides; better to provide potential critics with the finished product.[36]

After Seward secured cabinet approval of a draft treaty with a purchase price of $7 million, he resumed talks with Stoeckl. By March 23, the secretary and Russian diplomat agreed to a figure of $7.2 million. As Stoeckl noted, Seward had certainly not driven a hard bargain, but the secretary ultimately prevailed on three important points. The purchase would come without any claims by the Russian American Company; the US payment would be made in Washington rather than London; and the transfer of the property would occur when the two sides signed the treaty rather than upon the actual US payment. Seward argued successfully that the House of Representatives could not appropriate the funds until December. The timing of the transfer proved particularly influential since it became virtually impossible for Seward's opponents in the House to block the appropriation once the United States had physically taken control of the territory. It was also significant that the final draft of the treaty extended the constitutional rights enjoyed by US citizens to Russian residents of Alaska. By contrast, the region's "uncivilized native tribes" were specifically denied these rights. This same assumption of indigenous Alaskans' racial and cultural inferiority, an assumption that characterized the Lincoln administration's interactions with American Indians, was apparent in Seward's visit to Alaska in 1869 when he was said to have encountered some natives who had "discarded savage" ways and adopted aspects of "civilized life" despite their "semi-civilized, semi-savage surroundings."[37]

At Seward's urging, Stoeckl sent a long telegram to St. Petersburg that detailed the treaty terms and requested Czar Alexander's prompt approval. When the Russian minister received a positive response on the evening of Friday, March 29, he went to Seward's home to deliver the good news. Stoeckl found the secretary and several family members playing cards, informed him of the czar's endorsement, and suggested he would come to the State Department on Saturday to consummate the treaty. Since it was nearly 10 p.m., Seward's response startled him.

"Why wait until tomorrow, Mr. Stoeckl? Let us make the treaty tonight."

"But your department is closed," Stoeckl replied. "You have no clerks, and my secretaries are scattered about the town."

"Never mind that," Seward asserted. "If you can muster your legation together before midnight, you will find me awaiting you at the department, which will be open and ready for business."[38]

Having reached an agreement with Russia, Seward not only moved promptly to finalize the treaty, he also contacted Senator Charles Sumner, the chairman of the Senate Foreign Relations Committee (SFRC). Although Seward and Sumner had a complicated, often troubled relationship, the secretary fully understood that the Massachusetts senator's support was indispensable to Senate ratification of the treaty. The elder Seward sent his son and assistant secretary of state, Frederick, to Sumner's house with a note requesting the senator to come to the Seward residence "at once" to consider a "matter of public business." Sumner was out, but when he returned home and found the note, he complied with Seward's request.[39]

When Sumner arrived, Secretary Seward had already gone to the State Department, but Stoeckl and Frederick briefed the senator on the agreement. Sumner listened attentively, but made no commitment to back the treaty, about which he had mixed feelings. A proponent of northward US expansion that was uncomplicated by the potential expansion of slavery and particularly interested in acquiring Canada, he recognized that annexing Alaska might help the United States to "squeeze England out of the continent." But Sumner was annoyed because he had not been kept informed of the negotiations and worried that his endorsement of the treaty could be interpreted as more general support for Seward and the Johnson administration. Finally, he feared the purchase of Alaska would reinforce Seward's pursuit of what Sumner considered "indiscriminate and costly annexation" efforts.[40]

Seward and Stoeckl signed the final draft of the treaty at 4 a.m. on March 30. Six hours later, Seward was on the floor of the Senate to aggressively lobby senators who, save Sumner, knew nothing about the negotiations or the resulting treaty. Were this effort to ram the treaty through on the Senate's final day of the congressional session not a sufficient impediment, any Johnson administration proposal faced dire prospects in the spring of 1867. The Republican Congress had already legislated military reconstruction of the South over Johnson's veto, circumscribed the president's appointment power with the Tenure of Office Act, and soundly rejected Secretary Seward's requests for increased State Department funding. This hostile political climate led Senator Sumner to warn Stoeckl that the treaty "had no chance of being confirmed."[41]

The SFRC chairman had the treaty referred to his committee, and perhaps to oblivion, but President Johnson promptly called the Senate back into a special session on April 1 to consider the agreement. Fully aware of his and Johnson's unpopularity, Seward said little publicly; but over the ensuing ten days, the secretary, who was described as a "careless looking old man" who "speaks and thinks slowly," orchestrated a highly effective lobbying campaign on behalf of his treaty. This campaign, which closely resembled his artful public diplomacy during the war and after, defied such pessimistic assessments of his competence and demonstrated that he remained surprisingly energetic, mentally acute, and politically astute.[42]

Seward's lobbying efforts were multifaceted. Beginning on the evening of March 30, the day the treaty was made public, he hosted a series of lavish dinner parties for senators and cabinet members. Over excellent food accompanied by his seemingly limitless supply of imported wine, Seward elucidated the strategic, diplomatic, and commercial merits of the purchase. Although one newspaper correspondent observed sarcastically that "Terrapin and Chateau Marguax" would undoubtedly clarify "this already knotty subject," another reported more accurately that Seward was providing a "diplomatic symposium" for legislators who would decide the treaty's fate. These "seductive dinners" did not, as some critics asserted, "corrupt Senators and Representatives into voting" for the annexation of Alaska, but they did provide Seward's guests with a lucid presentation of the region's enormous geographical expanse and the tangible benefits of the Alaska territory.[43]

The secretary supplemented these personal overtures with a robust press campaign. His principal allies in this realm were two long-time political associates, Thurlow Weed, the editor of the *New York Commercial Advertiser,* and Henry J. Raymond, the editor of the *New York Times.* Weed published the first account of the treaty on March 30, and the *Commercial Advertiser* and the *Times* remained the principal newspaper advocates of the purchase over the next year. Together, these papers emphasized that the new territory enhanced commercial access to Asia, augmented the US fishing and whaling industries, possessed abundant natural resources, and would pressure Great Britain to withdraw from British Columbia. These arguments were representative of majority press opinion in April 1867, with the *New York Herald,* the *Daily Alta California,* and the normally anti-Seward *Chicago Tribune* also endorsing the treaty.[44]

The most conspicuous and important exception to these pro-treaty responses came from the *New York Tribune,* which was edited by Horace Greeley, who had been at odds with Seward since at least 1863. The *Tribune,* like other hostile papers such as the *Cincinnati Daily Gazette,* contended that Seward and the Johnson administration sought to divert attention from "failures at home." Greeley warned that the purchase promised to cause difficulties with Great Britain, while yielding no compensatory advantages from Russia. Anticipating language that became prominent later in the year, the *Tribune* declared there was "not, in the history of diplomacy, such insensate folly as this treaty," and the *New York Herald,* despite its overall endorsement of the acquisition, added terms such as "an ice house, a worthless desert."[45]

To bolster his work with individual senators and the press, Seward solicited and circulated the pro-treaty endorsements by important military figures and scientific authorities. Commodore John Rodgers, Quartermaster General Montgomery Meigs, General Henry Halleck, and Smithsonian Institution official Spencer Baird responded positively to the secretary's overtures. Under Seward's oversight, their letters were first printed in newspapers and then included in a State Department publication with the unwieldy title *Purchase of the Russian Possessions in North America by the United States; Papers Relating to the Value and Resources of the Country.* Collectively, these treaty proponents lauded the region's fishing and whaling prospects; timber, coal, and other resources; and reported gold discoveries.[46]

Although Seward's lobbying efforts helped form the public's perception of the treaty and furnished the House and Senate with a powerful pro-treaty brief, the support of Congressman Thaddeus Stevens and Senator Sumner, both Radical Republicans and harsh critics of the secretary's domestic political positions, was crucial to the US acquisition of Russian America. The chairman of the House Committee on Appropriations, Stevens played an essential role through his endorsement of the treaty and subsequent aid in funding the $7.2 million cost. Stevens had reportedly lamented that Lewis Powell had been such a "bungler" in his attempt to assassinate Seward in 1865 and to have mocked the secretary as Johnson's "chief clown," but his commitment to US territorial expansion made him receptive to Seward's overtures. From April through December 1867, these usual adversaries worked harmoniously on behalf of the treaty's ratification and funding.[47]

Sumner's role was even more significant. Despite his personal dislike for Seward, disdain for the secretary's politics, and persistent attempts to undermine his rival's diplomatic policies, the chair of the SFRC threw his decisive influence behind the treaty. Pressure from New England merchant, fishing, and shipping interests; a growing comprehension of the territory's abundant resources; a reluctance to alienate Russia by rejecting the agreement; and his proclivity to support any openings for expansion on the North American continent explain his pro-treaty position. Sumner's influence was crucial in securing a 4–2 vote in favor of the treaty from the Foreign Relations Committee. This vote overcame the opposition of an infuriated Fessenden, who despised Seward and his treaty. The Maine senator's disgust was evident in a comment, offered only partly in jest, that he would vote for the treaty if "the Secretary of State" were "compelled to live there, and the Russian government be required to keep him there."[48]

Armed with the SFRC's positive vote, Sumner reported the treaty to the full Senate on April 8 and then delivered a three-hour, pro-treaty speech, which drew on only one page of notes. The following day, the Senate approved the pact by a 37–2 margin, despite Fessenden's continued opposition. Sumner declared correctly and with characteristic self-importance, "My course had a decisive influence." Ironically, the senator's decisive influence had been indispensable to the realization of his old rival's most important expansionist accomplishment.[49]

Even if Seward may not have immediately grasped the irony of Sumner's role in the Senate approval of this momentous accomplishment, he certainly relished the praise that accompanied the treaty's ratification. From Thaddeus Stevens, "I congratulate you and rejoice at your safe deliverance" and "hope the afterbirth [funding by the House] is easy." US minister in St. Petersburg, Cassius Clay, was equally laudatory, declaring, "Hereafter the wonder will be we got it at all." Still, the secretary recognized that convincing the House of Representatives to appropriate the $7.2 million would be far from easy.[50]

With that arduous task in view, he took steps to make it virtually impossible for the House to reject the purchase. On June 20, he and the Russian minister exchanged signed copies of the treaty. Seward then dispatched a US revenue cutter carrying Smithsonian personnel to conduct a study of Alaska's resources; and he subsequently combined the Smithsonian findings with Sumner's speech and other supporting documents into a 380-page report to Congress in February 1868. Even more significant, on October 18, 1867, US Brigadier General Lovell H. Rousseau and 250 American troops formally took possession of the territory and raised the American flag. Fully grasping the impact of this final, strategic action, the *New York Times* declared that the United States was "honor bound" to fund the purchase. The *Washington Daily Morning Chronicle* asserted that the failure to allocate the $7.2 million would constitute "an open violation of a distinct clause of the treaty" and asked what the "Great Powers of the world" would "think of us should we violate" this "most sacred obligation." Congressman Godlove Orth warned, "Palsied be the hand that would dare to remove" the American flag.[51]

Seward's strategic maneuvers during the summer and fall of 1867 made it exceedingly difficult for the House to deny the requisite funds, but consummation of the Alaska purchase was hardly assured and was not concluded until July 27, 1868. Congress came back into session in December, but most of the legislators' attention over the ensuing seven months was focused on the Republican attempt to impeach Andrew Johnson—an attempt that failed when the Senate voted on May 26, 1868, not to remove him from office. Opposition to Seward and his simultaneous attempts to annex islands in the West Indies and even his expressed interest in Greenland and Iceland also impeded a positive House vote on Alaska. Although numerous Republican congressmen loathed Seward, his association with President Johnson, and his expansionist agenda, Representative Cadwallader C. Washburn of Wisconsin was the most strident and vocal antagonist. Washburn voiced the frustration and resentment of House members more generally by asking whether Congress would "allow itself to be coerced" by Seward's pre-December 1867 maneuvers. The Wisconsin representative also warned that Alaska could be only the first of the secretary's potential acquisitions. "Pass this appropriation," he raged, and "it will be but a few days before you will hear of" the Senate ratification of treaties calling for "the purchase of St. Thomas . . . Greenland and Iceland." In an attempt to forestall such additional annexations, Washburn sponsored a resolution in November 1867 stating the House would not pay for the purchase of the Danish West Indies or any other acquisition that Seward negotiated "on his own motion" without consulting the House and Senate. Washburn explicitly omitted Alaska from this prohibition, but he left no doubt about his assessment of the purchase by referring disparagingly to "Walrussia."[52]

Seward left nothing to chance as he continued his campaign for the treaty's ratification. In January 1868 he solicited the aid of veteran lobbyist Robert J. Walker, who was described as "one of the best talkers" in Washington and had been a player in national politics since the 1830s. Over the preceding three decades, he had served as a US senator, cabinet member in the Polk administration, governor of the Kansas Territory in the 1850s, newspaperman, and US Treasury agent and had established close associations across the political spectrum. A self-described "life-long expansionist," Walker was an enthusiastic supporter of acquiring Alaska. At Seward's behest, he wrote a long pro-annexation letter for the *Washington Daily Morning Chronicle* and subsequently printed ten thousand copies of the article, which he and the secretary circulated widely. The secretary also arranged for the broad dissemination of a letter from San Francisco reporting that gold had been discovered in Alaska.[53]

When Stoeckl grew increasingly alarmed at the House's delay in acting on the Alaska appropriation, Seward suggested in May that the Russian diplomat also work with Walker. Stoeckl had previously noted that Seward had been cooperating "persistently" and with "the greatest circumspections" with Walker, and he acted promptly on Seward's advice. The Russian minister ultimately paid Walker and an associate $26,000 for their services, which included the lobbying of key congressmen, such as Nathaniel Banks and Thaddeus Stevens, and the insertion of pro-Alaska articles into the *Daily Morning Chronicle* and *National Intelligencer.* Stoeckl also paid $30,000 to D. C. and John Forney, the proprietor and editor, respectively, of the *Daily Morning Chronicle* and distributed another $73,000 in "expenses" to selected US congressmen. On July 14, these cumulative efforts bore fruit when the

House voted 113 to 43, with 44 abstentions, to appropriate the $7.2 million. That 41 of the 43 "no" votes were cast by congressmen who had voted to impeach Johnson afforded a telling commentary on the political opposition Seward had encountered.[54]

Along with the approval of the appropriation came rumors of bribes and payoffs, extensive newspaper charges and speculation about alleged corruption, and a two-month congressional investigation in February and March 1869. From his close cooperation with Walker and Stoeckl, Seward had acquired considerable knowledge of the Russian minister's monetary payments. During September 1868, the secretary discussed the matter with President Johnson and John Bigelow. Seward provided them slightly different accounts, but both versions cited the conveyance of funds to Walker, the Forneys, Congressman Stevens, and other unnamed legislators. When called before the congressional committee, Seward claimed to "know nothing whatever" about the Russian minister's payments. The secretary had essentially committed perjury, rather than publicly impugn Stoeckl and Walker or sully further his foremost expansionist accomplishment. Historian Paul Holbo has argued that the dubious actions facilitating the Alaska purchase rendered it a "tainted act," which negatively impacted the secretary's other imperial projects and subsequent US expansionist efforts during the late nineteenth century.[55]

IV.

Representative Washburn and other Seward critics were correct in their fear that the secretary's expansionist agenda stretched well beyond Alaska. In a clear exaggeration, the editor of the *Hartford Courant* warned that Seward would "buy up the whole hemisphere from the glaciers of Greenland to the volcanoes of Tierra del Fuego if he only lives long enough and the credit of the nation holds out," but the secretary's imperialist vista was certainly vast.[56]

Like Senator Sumner, Seward had seen that the purchase of Alaska might provide the leverage for pressuring Great Britain to yield British Columbia to US westward expansion, or, as the secretary observed, to "round off our North Western territory" and US frontage on the Pacific. Seward also agreed with Sumner that the United States might obtain this territory as compensation for US claims for damages against Britain for its role in the construction of the *Alabama* and other Confederate cruisers and those ships' attacks on American commerce. The secretary had begun to think in these terms as early as mid-1866, and, by early 1867, he instructed Minister Adams that US claims should include not only the direct maritime costs but also indirect damages that resulted from other British actions such as the recognition of Confederate belligerency in 1861. Seward had long asserted that this British recognition, sale of war materials, and naval construction had prolonged the war and greatly increased its costs. By citing these inclusive damages, Seward projected total claims that might be exchanged for British Columbia. He admitted as much in early 1868: All "grievances on both sides" could "be thrown into a heap and would be taken out to balance [one] another. . . . In this way we would pay for Columbia with the *Alabama* claims." When neither the British nor the residents of British Columbia showed any enthusiasm for such an exchange, Seward's pursuit of additional continental territory facing Asia came to naught.[57]

His attempts to acquire islands in the Caribbean were no more successful. Having observed the need for commercial and naval outposts during the war and no longer encumbered by the potential expansion of slavery, Seward aggressively sought to expand into the Caribbean. Even before he and Lincoln met the Confederate representatives at the Hampton Roads Conference in early February 1865, Seward had inquired whether Denmark might be willing to sell St. Thomas in the West Indies. The following January, the secretary, accompanied by Frederick and Anna, embarked on a reported family vacation, which lasted four weeks and included visits to St. Thomas, Samana Bay in the Dominican Republic, Port-au-Prince in Haiti, and Havana, Cuba. At each stop, he met with local officials and assessed the location's potential utility as a port for furthering US trade and naval power in the Caribbean. Upon his return home, he opened negotiations with Waldemar Raasloff, the Danish minister in Washington, to purchase St. Thomas. These negotiations culminated in the summer of 1867 with a treaty in which the United States agreed to pay Denmark $7.5 million for the islands of St. Thomas and St. John.[58]

The treaty faced stiff opposition from Washburn, other congressional critics, and hostile newspapers. Opponents in the press disparaged Seward's inclination to purchase "outlandish possessions" and emphasized the nation's unprecedented national debt. The secretary countered with a coordinated public response. He worked with Samuel S. Cox, a New York attorney and politician, to secure endorsements of the treaty from the New York City

Commercial Council and Board of Aldermen, cultivated similar backing in Philadelphia and from the *Army and Navy Journal,* induced Vice-Admiral David D. Porter to lobby key senators, and personally interceded with Senator Sumner. All these efforts failed. While the treaty was before the Senate in early 1868, a hurricane devastated St. Thomas and an earthquake rocked nearby St. Croix. These natural disasters, combined with the political fallout from the ongoing Republican efforts to impeach President Johnson, the bitterness accompanying Seward's Alaska manipulations, and scathing ridicule of the treaty from Mark Twain, convinced Sumner to back away from the project.[59]

Seward's other efforts to acquire a Caribbean port met a similar fate. He had expressed interest in Samana Bay in 1864, and his January 1866 visit further whetted his annexationist appetite. In December 1866 he sent his son Frederick and Vice-Admiral Porter to negotiate an agreement for US use of the port. This effort fell short, as did Seward's ongoing attempts during the remainder of the Johnson administration to gain control over this port or to obtain a protectorate over Hispaniola, the island that was home to both the Dominican Republic and Haiti. Seward's conviction that a US insular base in the Caribbean was essential to the nation's self-defense and commercial advancement also led him to monitor the possibility of annexing Puerto Rico or Cuba and even to investigate the merits of adding Greenland and Iceland to the national domain—despite their location in the North Atlantic.[60]

This pattern of frustration persisted when Seward pushed for the construction of a US-controlled ship canal through Central America. As with other components of his imperial design, Seward had first extolled "our Panama route to China" in the 1850s. Following the end of the Civil War, he began discussions with the Colombian minister to Washington regarding a US canal through the isthmus. By January 1869, these talks had produced no tangible results. With the Johnson administration and Seward's term as secretary of state about to end, he dispatched veteran statesman and diplomat Caleb Cushing to Bogota in one last effort to negotiate a treaty. Seward also worked to secure funding for a canal. Recognizing that he had no chance of convincing Congress to fund the construction, he recruited a group of New York capitalists, who formed the Isthmian Canal Company in September 1868. The following month these businessmen assured the secretary that "men of wealth and enterprise were ready to invest millions." Only the absence of a treaty with Colombia seemed to preclude moving ahead with the canal's construction when Cushing returned to Washington in mid-February 1869 with a signed agreement. Seward thought he had cleared both the diplomatic and financial hurdles to construction of a US canal that countered the French project in Suez and guaranteed American domination of Pacific and East Asian trade. His hopes were dashed when Colombia reneged on the agreement and demanded a higher US payment and the Senate refused to consider the treaty. Still, Seward's contention that this waterway linking the Atlantic and Pacific would become "transcendently profitable and transcendently useful" proved farsighted and accurate.[61]

As Seward envisioned commercial empire in the Pacific, he also coveted the Sandwich Islands, as Hawaii was then called. These islands, Seward believed, could provide the same naval station and commercial entrepôt in the Pacific that he had sought to obtain by acquiring bases in the Caribbean. Following the Civil War, he had rejected a British offer to jointly protect Hawaiian independence. Seward was unwilling to accept a self-denying obstacle to ultimate annexation, a goal he made perfectly clear as he advocated a reciprocity treaty with Hawaii in 1867: "If the policy of annexation" conflicted "with the policy of reciprocity," he instructed an American diplomat, "annexation" was "in every case to be preferred." He secured neither reciprocity nor annexation. His 1867 treaty died in the Senate, the victim of opposition from domestic sugar and rice growers, budget hawks who feared the loss of tariff revenue, anti-expansionists who recognized Seward's ultimate objective, Radical Republicans who objected to the colonization of nonwhites, and Johnson and Seward's political opponents.[62]

Consistent with his ambitious, if largely unfulfilled, expansionist efforts in the Caribbean, Central America, Hawaii, and Alaska, Seward sought a preeminent American presence in East Asia, the ultimate commercial prize in his imperial project. Without the requisite military and naval power to impose US will on either China or Japan, the secretary implemented a proto–Open Door policy designed to guarantee equal US access to these potentially vast Asian markets. His efforts built on the US-Chinese Treaty of 1844, which had granted the United States commercial entry through five treaty ports, and the subsequent Treaties of Tianjin, which had been imposed on the Chinese Manchu dynasty during the Second Opium War (1856–1860). The latter agreements had opened additional ports and proclaimed religious freedom in China. Through cooperation with the British and French and the selective use of force, Seward attempted to preserve this equality of commercial opportunity, an arrangement that he believed would ultimately enable the United States to outpace its European rivals and dominate trade with China and Japan. He based this predicted outcome on the superiority of American enterprise and productivity. Seward also anticipated the US ability to rouse the Asian nations "from the lethargy of superstition and caste" and to provide a "protective tutorship" for "decaying Asiatic states." This tutorship, he opined, would yield "mutual sympathy and respect between the protectors and the protected" and redound to the benefit of the "American benefactors." Both his cultural and commercial assumptions remained injurious staples of the American foreign relations with East Asia well into the twentieth century.[63]

Seward's diplomacy worked best with China, whose leaders were outwardly more receptive than the Japanese to western commercial and ideological overtures. The Manchus, intent upon survival, made overtures to the United States as part of their strategy to play western nations off against one another. Seward and the United States, in turn, had no desire to acquire Chinese territory and viewed Chinese stability as favorable to the prospects of American merchants and missionaries. Seward instructed US diplomats to push for all possible commercial "concessions," but not to imperil "the stability of the present Government or the internal peace and tranquility of China." These policies, together with the skilled intercession of Anson Burlingame, the US minister to China, yielded a mutually beneficial treaty in 1868 that reinforced Seward's objective of capturing the China market.[64]

Burlingame had served admirably as the US minister to Beijing beginning in June 1861, and when he resigned from this position in November 1867, the Chinese government asked him to represent it with the United States and the other major western nations. He accepted this assignment and arrived in Washington in June 1868 with some thirty Chinese officials in tow. His talks with Seward produced the "Burlingame Treaty," although the secretary had drafted the document in advance. Unsurprisingly, given the treaty's provenance, the pact embodied Seward's "mature thinking" on China's "future prospects": an endorsement of China's territorial and administrative integrity, provision for the ongoing pursuit of equal US commercial opportunity in the celestial empire, and the "free migration and immigration" of the Chinese and Americans between the two countries. The latter reflected Seward's long-held belief that immigrant labor was an essential component of US national development. In typical Seward fashion, he rescued the Chinese delegation from Washington's summer heat and led them on a tour that included a visit to Niagara Falls and his home in Auburn, where sixteen of the visitors stayed in his house.[65]

The secretary oversaw far less cordial US relations with Japan and Korea. In decided contrast to China, Japanese leaders exhibited no interest in being tutored by the West. According to one biographer, Seward deemed the Japanese "semi-barbarous." He was particularly disturbed by Japan's hostile treatment of Christian missionaries and refusal to open the port of Yedo to western commerce. The former challenged his conviction that "the continually extending sway for the Christian religion" carried great benefits for humanity, and the latter impeded the expansion of US commerce and the role of trade as the "chief fertilizer" of Japanese economic and cultural development.[66]

While adopting a more adversarial posture toward Japan, Seward sustained his cooperation with the British and French. Following the burning of the American legation in Yedo in May 1863; an attack on the *Pembroke,* an American merchant ship, the following month; and an exchange of gunfire between the USS *Wyoming* and Japanese shore batteries soon thereafter, the United States joined the British and French in a four-day bombardment of Japanese positions in the Straits of Shimonoseki in September 1863. Seward was equally willing to employ force against Korea after its residents attacked and killed the crew of the *General Sherman,* another American merchant vessel, in August 1866. This campaign did not materialize, but the secretary's overtures to the French for a joint expedition further illustrated his willingness to use force to protect American citizens and commerce. Despite these Seward-condoned uses of force, his preference for a softer diplomatic touch was evident when two Japanese commissioners visited the United States in May 1867. The secretary squired them around Washington, facilitated their purchase of a warship, and arranged for them to visit the Annapolis naval yard.[67]

The decidedly mixed results of Seward's East Asia diplomacy were representative of the overall record of his imperial agenda. On October 10, 1872, three and a half years after the end of his tenure as secretary of state and one year after he completed his around the world trip, Seward died peacefully in the library of his Auburn home at the age of seventy-one. Fittingly, he had worked earlier in the day on the account of this last trip. Both the trip and the resulting travelogue demonstrated his ever-evolving interest in the international environment and the United States' place therein. The purchase of Alaska, which Seward valued primarily as the northern outpost for US access to Asian commerce, but which ultimately yielded vast stores of enormously valuable natural resources, had been his one great expansionist achievement. The only other territorial acquisition had been Midway Island in the South Pacific, which the US Navy formally occupied in 1867.

Seward, who relished the opportunity of "laying the foundations of a great [US] empire," was deeply disappointed not to have acquired naval and commercial bases in the Caribbean, built an isthmian canal, or annexed Hawaii. As his term as secretary wound down, he lamented, "How sadly domestic disturbances of ours demoralize the national ambition." His reference to Reconstruction's bitter and highly partisan political environment was appropriate. Truly a man without a party, long detested by Democrats and disowned during and after the war by most Republicans, Seward's expansionist projects met with fierce domestic opposition simply because he had proposed them. Opponents also argued that the United States could not afford to purchase new territories, given the national debt incurred during the war and the looming costs of rebuilding the South. As Seward acknowledged in 1867, "We have already come to value dollars more, and dominion less."[68]

Anti-expansionists deemed such expenditures for new land unnecessary, since the United States was not "at the moment, pressed for want of room" and had "territory enough to last the present century out." These critics raised constitutional objections and argued that Seward overstepped executive authority and ignored Congress. They also warned that the United States could not retain its position as the world's foremost democratic republic if it imposed colonial control on new island territories. As was true for the debate over Reconstruction, race was a constant consideration in foreign policy discussions. Secretary of the Navy Gideon Welles decried the proposed purchase of St. Thomas and St. John because their "population" was "not American;" and, from an opposing racial perspective, Radicals such as Charles Sumner were uneasy at the prospect of imposing US dominion on nonwhites in Hawaii. Alaska, with a negligible nonwhite population by 1867, escaped any race-based objection to its annexation. Finally, Seward and the United States lacked the requisite naval power in the late 1860s to obtain, oversee, and take full advantage of a canal and a sprawling insular empire.[69]

Given these myriad obstacles to Seward's "fixed idea" of expansion, Henry Adams observed correctly that the secretary's imperial aspirations "went somewhat too far and too fast for the public"—and, one might add, for the contemporary political establishment. A more recent student of the secretary's work has offered the complementary criticism that "the most consummate diplomats are those who practice the art of the possible." However, "the possible" can only be determined in retrospect after the foreign policy effort has been made. Alaska, Seward's greatest imperial success, provides a telling example. Charles Sumner, the highly informed and centrally placed chairman of the Senate Foreign Relations Committee, predicted that the Senate would not ratify the treaty enabling the US purchase. Had Seward accepted this appraisal of the possible, his most significant post-1865 foreign policy achievement and its great benefits for the nation would not have been realized.[70]

Although Alaska and Midway were the only tangible portions of Seward's imperial vision that came to fruition during his second term as secretary of state, the vision itself was of great importance. Seward, who thought in global terms long before the concept of globalization gained international currency, devised "not only a road map but an ideology" for the empire that the United States acquired at the turn of the twentieth century. Whether one condemns or applauds the subsequent US imperial policies and acquisitions, their fulfillment of Seward's vision is evident. He has been termed the "central figure of nineteenth-century American imperialism" and the "prince of players" in the United States' transition from the pursuit of territorial to commercial empire, a transition that began with his diplomacy and ended in the late nineteenth and early twentieth centuries when the United States acquired Hawaii, the Danish West Indies, the Philippines, and Puerto Rico; constructed the Panama Canal; imposed a protectorate over Cuba; and practiced Open Door diplomacy in China. The Open Door was designed to preserve Chinese territorial and political integrity and to guarantee the United States equal commercial opportunities. US proponents of these later imperial actions not only fulfilled the specific objectives of Seward's agenda, they also adopted much of his strategic and commercial ideology and his belief that the United States' presence, even dominance, in these far-flung places would enhance the well-being of their residents.[71]

Seward's confidence that the United States embodied the nineteenth century's leading democracy and republican government recalled his unlikely friendship and foreign policy partnership with Abraham Lincoln. Together, they had crafted foreign policies that were central to the North's victory in the Civil War and the preservation of the Union. In the process, Lincoln had brilliantly joined the causes of freedom, liberal democracy, and US nationalism. The North's victory had not only preserved the Union and the republican experiment, it had yielded one very powerful nation, rather than two weaker ones. That one increasingly powerful nation would, by the end of the century, emerge as both a great and an imperial power. Seward's service during the Johnson administration provided the blueprint for US ascension to world power status over the ensuing fifty years. Combined with his Civil War diplomacy and his deft handling of the French occupation of Mexico, this imperial vision has led most historians of US foreign relations to rank him behind only his idol, John Quincy Adams, among American secretaries of state. It was only appropriate that his foreign policy partnership with Lincoln, America's greatest president, played a decisive role in preserving and expanding the nation.

CONCLUSION

President Abraham Lincoln and Secretary of State William Henry Seward confronted the greatest foreign policy challenge of their young, and still impermanent, nation's existence. With the South's secession and potential European intervention in the Civil War, national survival was literally at stake. Neither President Lincoln nor Secretary of State Seward could boast of the relevant foreign policy background and experience of several of their better-prepared predecessors, such as John Adams, Thomas Jefferson, James Madison, or John Quincy Adams. Still, both were highly intelligent, well-read, shrewd political operatives, who had developed great skill in managing difficult contemporaries and complex public issues and problems. They were also quick studies who learned from both successes and failures.

Even more important, they formed a superb foreign policy partnership. Ultimately grounded in genuine, mutual respect and affection and strong agreement on essential diplomatic principles and objectives, the alliance originated in Lincoln's pursuit of Republican Party and northern political solidarity and his obligation to reward and retain the loyalty of the party's second most important figure. Seward, in turn, sought to sustain his public career and personal importance and to contribute to national salvation. Once Lincoln established his position as the unquestioned senior partner, these two talented, forceful personalities conducted a well-coordinated and highly successful foreign policy.

As Lincoln and Seward initiated this partnership, they agreed that the United States was conducting a grand experiment in republican government and that their country had the potential to become a major international power with vast ideological, economic, and geopolitical influence. They also agreed that realizing this multifaceted influence depended on defeating the South and restoring the Union. Were southern secession to succeed, slavery would be preserved, the republican experiment discredited, and a balkanized North America left vulnerable to repeated interventions by European nations.

Forestalling the South's bid for independence and preserving the Union required the prevention of decisive European intervention on the side of the Confederacy, and this became the cornerstone of the Lincoln-Seward foreign policy. Lincoln instituted and Seward skillfully implemented this fundamental objective. Significantly, they did so while achieving the president's maxim: no second war with one of the major European powers. Lincoln eloquently articulated the international importance of preserving the US republican experiment and, with the Emancipation Proclamation, tied the freeing of the slaves to a Union victory. Both of these ideological and institutional positions rendered intervention far more difficult for Britain and France. As he delivered his masterful speeches, issued the Emancipation Proclamation, and wrote letters meant for publication, Lincoln practiced public diplomacy aimed at influencing both the American and European populace and leaders. Lincoln further recognized the crucial connection between US military power and the deterrence of European meddling. Therefore, his progressive mastery of military strategy and growing confidence as commander in chief not only contributed to the Union battlefield victories, but also reinforced the North's warnings that European intervention would mean destructive war with the North.

Seward's purposeful blustering and brinkmanship during the war's first seven months, and his periodic blunt warnings thereafter that European intervention meant war with the Union, employed this US threat to great, perhaps decisive, diplomatic advantage. Over the first two years of the war, European diplomats and statesmen were never completely sure how seriously to take the secretary's fulminations, and this uncertainty was central to their continued restraint. By mid-1863, when the British and French shut down Confederate shipbuilding in their countries, the US victories at Gettysburg and Vicksburg left no doubt that the secretary's threats were backed by ever-increasing and menacing US military power. Seward tempered these aggressive admonitions with successful efforts to cultivate workable personal relationships with Lord Lyons and Henri Mercier, the British and French ambassadors in Washington, respectively. The secretary's far less assertive posture on other issues, such as the *Trent* affair, the British role in Confederate blockade running, and the French intervention in Mexico, demonstrated his willingness to compromise when necessary and his primary goal to prevent European intervention, while avoiding a second war.

Seward's effective combination of threat and conciliation raises the question of whether he and Lincoln would have responded militarily to significant, direct European intervention in the American war. This classic "what if" question is, of course, ultimately unanswerable. That Palmerston, Russell, Napoleon III, and Thouvenel were never quite sure how to interpret Seward's fulminations argues for similar caution among historians. Still, given Lincoln and Seward's guiding geopolitical assumptions and practices, a US military response would have been highly unlikely. Most importantly, Lincoln and Seward were committed to fight only one war at a time, and both partners recognized that a second military involvement would have jeopardized, if not destroyed, Union chances of defeating the Confederacy. This was especially the case over the first two and one-half years of the war before the United States demonstrated the military power and secured the geopolitical position that presaged victory. Even in early 1864, with the North's greatly enhanced military capacity and a US triumph more clearly in sight, Lincoln and Seward sustained the one-war policy and declined to intervene in Mexico in response to Napoleon's blatant provocations. Seward's decided preference not to use force in international relations and his expressed understanding that military interventions came with unpredictable outcomes—that withdrawal could be far more difficult than intervention—reinforced the presumption that he and Lincoln would not have responded with force to a significant defiance of the secretary's warnings.

The secretary's handling of Napoleon's attempt to install a European monarchy in Mexico provided a revealing example of his priorities and statecraft. The secretary consistently increased the diplomatic pressure on Napoleon III after 1862, as the US foreign policy and military situations allowed. This pressure, together with Mexican resistance and France's domestic and European foreign policy involvements, led to French withdrawal in 1867 without US military involvement or loss of life. Over this five-year period, Seward was acutely aware of the French leader's competing foreign policy concerns in Europe and other parts of the world. Seward built this same consideration into his policies toward the British and French during the Civil War, when both of these potential interlopers placed a higher priority on

European developments than the American war. In addition, Seward's periodic publication of his diplomatic correspondence with France embodied his practice of public diplomacy, as did his purposeful provision of information to friendly US journalists and more general publication of important dispatches during the Civil War. Together, Lincoln and Seward conceived of and implemented a most successful foreign policy that was critical to the victory over the South and preservation of the Union.

This United States victory advanced the cause of nationalism and republicanism in the western world. It also enabled the United States to resume its imperial expansion and path toward great power status. Although Lincoln and Seward had opposed slavery's extension into the New West and denounced the aggressive aspects of the Mexican American War, they accepted the more general course of US imperial expansion at the expense of the British, French, Spanish, Native Americans, and Mexicans as a natural feature of the United States' national growth toward its destiny as an important country in the international arena. Lincoln's sanction of the Union's military suppression of Indians during the Civil War reflected not just strategic responses to Confederate military and diplomatic initiatives, but also his endorsement of American westward expansion and the cultural assumptions that provided the rationale for confining Native Americans to reservations and forcing them to adopt settled agriculture and Christianity.

Seward shared Lincoln's belief that the United States should instruct other, ostensibly inferior, peoples in the attributes of American culture, and he aspired unsuccessfully to extend the practice beyond the North American continent to Asia. His overall imperial vision and aspirations were similarly expansive. Following the Civil War and Lincoln's assassination, the secretary of state retained his position in the administration of President Andrew Johnson. During those four years, Seward sought to implement the imperial blueprint he had first articulated in the 1850s. The purchase of Alaska from Russia was his only significant territorial acquisition, but he viewed even this vast, resource-rich region as part of an overall scheme designed to dominate commerce with China and Japan. When combined with California, Alaska would, from the secretary's perspective, have afforded the United States vital frontage on the Pacific and enhanced trade with East Asia. His abortive efforts to acquire Hawaii, islands in the Caribbean, and British Columbia, and to build an isthmian canal were also meant to facilitate US commercial dominance. While none of these latter projects came to fruition, Seward's imperial vision and work under Johnson embodied the US transition from the construction of a landed to a commercial empire, demonstrated his prescient grasp of the economic process that would come to be termed globalization, and provided an uncanny forecast of the nation's actions at the turn of the twentieth century. Indeed, Seward and his senior foreign policy partner, Abraham Lincoln, devised and conducted foreign policies that were indispensable to the preservation and expansion of the Union during the critical period of the 1860s.

ACKNOWLEDGMENTS

Since this book is a synthesis based on an extensive and rich historical literature, I must first acknowledge and thank the talented scholars whose work I have consulted to recount and analyze Lincoln, Seward, and their foreign policy partnership.

While absolving them of any errors, dubious assertions, or scholarly shortcomings that remain in this book, I would like to thank Ed Crapol, Tom Wright, Jeff Matthews, and Mike Green for their indispensable help. All four read the entire manuscript and offered incisive and exceedingly useful suggestions. Tom recently characterized me as "long suffering" in my reading of his scholarship on Latin America. Ed, Tom, and Jeff have more than earned this same moniker based on the aid they have afforded me over the past three-plus decades. Mike is the conspicuous and welcome addition to these usual suspects. A former UNLV undergraduate and MA student, an expert on Lincoln and the Civil War era, and now an esteemed member of the UNLV History Department, he tutored me on Lincoln scholarship, suggested important thematic approaches, and saved me from numerous embarrassing errors.

Mike's support is characteristic of that provided by the UNLV History Department, whose last two chairpersons, Paul Werth and Andy Kirk, have graciously furnished office space to a former department member. Similarly, the department's expert staff, Annette Amdal, Heather Nepa, and Shontai Wilson-Beltran, have cheerfully and most helpfully responded to my key requests, computer problems, and copy machine difficulties. More generally, they make the History Department a welcoming and enjoyable place to work.

University Press of Kentucky personnel have been equally tolerant and supportive. Senior Acquisitions Editor Melissa Hammer oversaw a seamless transition from the previous UPKY press administration and secured two exceedingly knowledgeable and helpful reviewers for the manuscript. They, too, saved me from errors, challenged my thematic assertions, and suggested provocative, alternative analytical approaches. I carefully contemplated all of their observations, accepted most of them, and probably should have incorporated the remainder. Natalie O'Neal, Melissa's primary assistant, skillfully guided me through the provision of key words, chapter abstracts, and illustrations; Jackie Wilson, the press's marketing assistant, provided similar assistance as I worked on the marketing questionnaires; and Sarah Olson, the book's project editor, expertly directed the production process. I must also acknowledge my copyeditor, Janet Yoe, who has carefully scrutinized the manuscript, inserted important corrections and clarifications, and prompted me to assess key aspects of my prose.

I would like to thank my family: my wife of fifty years, Sandy; our son, Bryan; and his wife, Lael. They have shown far more interest in this project than it probably deserved. That said, their love and support have been unwavering, indispensable, and greatly appreciated.

In closing, I am dedicating this book to my great friend, Ron "Bear" Kyle. We met while playing on opposing high school baseball teams in 1964, subsequently were college basketball teammates for four years, roomed together for three of those years, and have remained dear friends over the intervening five decades. Ron is the brother I never had, but I love and value him as if he had been born a Fry or I a Kyle.

NOTES

Introduction

1. Thomas Bender, *A Nation among Nations: America's Place in World History* (New York: Hill and Wang, 2006), 131 (quotes); Don H. Doyle, *The Cause of All Nations: An International History of the American Civil War* (New York: Basic Books, 2015), 1–10; David M. Potter, *The South and the Sectional Conflict* (Baton Rouge: Louisiana State University Press, 1968), 291, 294–95, 298; David Armitage, Thomas Bender, Leslie Butler, Don H. Doyle, Susan-Mary Grant, Charles S. Maier, Jörg Nagler, Paul Quigley, and Jay Sexton, "Interchange: Nationalism and Internationalism in the Era of the Civil War," *Journal of American History* 98 (September 2011): 458, 464, 469, 470. See also Douglas R. Egerton, "Rethinking Atlantic Historiography in a Postcolonial Era: The Civil War in a Global Perspective," *Journal of the Civil War Era* 1 (March 2011): 79–95 and Jay Sexton, "Toward a Synthesis of Foreign Relations in the Civil War Era, 1848–77," *American Nineteenth Century History* 5 (Autumn 2004): 50–73.

2. Robert Kagan, *Dangerous Nation* (New York: Alfred A. Knopf, 2006), 233 (competition); D. P. Crook, *Diplomacy during the American Civil War* (New York: John Wiley and Sons, 1975), 9; for an overview of US imperial ascent and sectional competition, see Joseph A. Fry, "Diplomatic Milestones, 1770s–1898: History and Analysis of the Foreign Policy Developments in the New Nation," in *U.S. Foreign Policy: A Diplomatic History,* ed. Robert J. McMahon and Thomas W. Zeiler (2 vols.; Los Angeles: CQ Press and SAGE Publications, 2012), 1: 67–85; Joseph A. Fry, *Dixie Looks Abroad: The South and U.S. Foreign Relations, 1789–1973* (Baton Rouge: Louisiana State University Press, 2002), 40–74; Walter Nugent, *Habits of Empire: A History of American Expansion* (New York: Alfred A. Knopf, 2008); Robert E. May, *Slavery, Race, and Conquest in the Tropics: Lincoln, Douglas, and the Future of Latin America* (New York: Cambridge University Press, 2013); Matthew Karp, *This Vast Southern Empire: Slaveholders at the Helm of American Foreign Policy* (Cambridge: Harvard University Press, 2016).

3. Richard N. Current, "God and the Strongest Battalions," in *Why the North Won the Civil War,* ed. David Donald (Baton Rouge: Louisiana State University Press, 1960), 22.

4. Joshua Wolf Shenk, *Powers of Two*: *Finding the Essence of Innovation in Creative Pairs* (Boston: Houghton Mifflin, 2014), xxii–iii, 21, 33, 99, 153, 163, 171, 173, and 175 (quotes), 192. Shenk does not include Lincoln and Seward among his illustrative examples, but his analysis is applicable.

5. Kinley J. Brauer, "Seward's 'Foreign War Panacea': An Interpretation," *New York History* 55 (April 1974): 137 (crisis); Dean B. Mahin, *One War at a Time*: *The International Dimensions of the American Civil War* (Washington, D.C.: Brassey's, 1999), 7.

6. For the concept and practice of public diplomacy during the Civil War, see Doyle, *Cause of All Nations,* 3–5 and *passim;* Peter S. Onuf, "Imperialism and Nationalism in the Early American Republic," in *Empire's Twin*: *U.S. Anti-Imperialism from the Founding Era to the Age of Terrorism,*" ed. Ian Tyrrell and Jay Sexton (Ithaca: Cornell University Press, 2015), 23, 40 (American Creed).

7. Eric Foner, *Free Soil, Free Labor, Free Men*: *The Ideology of the Republican Party before the Civil War* (New York: Oxford University Press, 1970), 316 (modest); Steven Hahn, *A Nation without Borders*: *The United States and Its World in an Age of Civil Wars* (New York: Viking, 2016), 193 (slowly unfolding).

8. Edward P. Crapol, "Coming to Terms with Empire: The Historiography of Late-Nineteenth-Century American Foreign Relations," *Diplomatic History* 16 (October 1992): 573–97; Walter La Feber, *The New Cambridge History of American Foreign Relations, Volume 2*: *The American Search for Opportunity, 1865–1913,* 2nd ed. (New York: Cambridge University Press, 2015); Walter La Feber, *The New Empire*: *An Interpretation of American Expansion, 1860–1898* (Ithaca: Cornell University Press, 1998).

9. Seward quoted in Norman B. Ferris, *Desperate Diplomacy*: *William Henry Seward's Foreign Policy, 1861* (Knoxville: University of Tennessee Press, 1976), vii.

10. Joseph A. Fry, *Henry Shelton Sanford*: *Diplomacy and Business in Nineteenth-Century America* (Reno: University of Nevada Press, 1982); *John Tyler Morgan and the Search for Southern Autonomy* (Knoxville: University of Tennessee Press, 1992); *Dixie Looks Abroad; The American South and the Vietnam War*: *Belligerence, Protest, and Agony in Dixie* (Lexington: University Press of Kentucky, 2015).

1. Origins of the Foreign Policy Partnership, 1801–1861

1. Walter Stahr, *Seward*: *Lincoln's Indispensable Man* (New York: Simon and Schuster, 2012), 8 (Seward Mansion); Glyndon G. Van Deusen, *William Henry Seward* (New York: Oxford University Press, 1967), 3. For Seward's youth, education, early career, and marriage, see Stahr, *Seward,* 9–20 and Van Deusen, *William Henry Seward,* 3–10.

2. For Lincoln's early life, self-education, business dealings, and legal career

through 1841, see Ronald C. White Jr., *A. Lincoln: A Biography* (New York: Random House, 2009), 3–112 and William E. Gienapp, *Abraham Lincoln and Civil War America* (New York: Oxford University Press, 2002), 1–37.

3. White, *A. Lincoln,* 30–31 (quotes); William Lee Miller, *Lincoln's Virtues: An Ethical Biography* (New York: Alfred A. Knopf, 2002), 27–35, 44–57.

4. Joshua Wolf Shenk, *Lincoln's Melancholy: How Depression Challenged a President and Fueled His Greatness* (Boston: Houghton Mifflin Company, 2005), 4, 89, 111.

5. Gienapp, *Abraham Lincoln and Civil War America,* 21; Kevin Peraino, *Lincoln in the World: The Making of a Statesman and the Dawn of American Power* (New York: Crown Publishers, 2013), 29 (Mary Lincoln).

6. White, *A. Lincoln,* 125–26; Gienapp, *Abraham Lincoln and Civil War America,* 47; Stahr, *Seward,* 19, 86–87; Van Deusen, *William Henry Seward,* 87–88; Doris Kearns Goodwin, *Team of Rivals: The Political Genius of Abraham Lincoln* (New York: Simon and Schuster, 2005), 11–12.

7. For US population and economic growth, see James M. McPherson, *Battle Cry of Freedom: The Civil War Era* (New York: Oxford University Press, 1988), 10–20; Eric Foner, *Give Me Liberty! An American History* (2 vols.; New York: W. W. Norton and Company, 2014), 1:232, 324, 329, 489.

8. Brian Schoen, *The Fragile Fabric of Union: Cotton, Federal Politics and the Global Origins of the Civil War* (Baltimore: Johns Hopkins University Press, 2009), 122–23; Walter Johnson, *River of Dark Dreams: Slavery and Empire in the Cotton Kingdom* (Cambridge: Harvard University Press, 2013), 10; Sven Beckert, *Empire of Cotton: A Global History* (New York: Alfred A. Knopf, 2015), 205–6, 225; Hahn, *Nation without Borders,* 111–13.

9. For the political environment, see McPherson, *Battle Cry of Freedom,* 26–39; Hahn, *Nation without Borders,* 108–10, 113, 123–24; Thomas R. Hietala, *Manifest Design: American "Exceptionalism" & Empire,* rev. ed. (Ithaca: Cornell University Press, 2003), 1–131; Michael F. Holt, *The Rise and Fall of the American Whig Party: Jacksonian Politics and the Onset of the Civil War* (New York: Oxford University Press, 1999), 13, 31, 117; Michael A. Morrison, "Westward the Curse of Empire: Texas Annexation and the America Whig Party," *Journal of the Early Republic* 10 (Summer 1990): 221–49.

10. McPherson, *Battle Cry of Freedom,* 30; Van Deusen, *William Henry Seward,* 12–14. Most northern Whigs moved to the Republican Party in the mid-1850s.

11. Van Deusen, *William Henry Seward,* 9, 13, 17, 33 (wizard); Stahr, *Seward,* 20–40.

12. Van Deusen, *William Henry Seward,* 55–86; Stahr, *Seward,* 52–85.

13. Van Deusen, *William Henry Seward,* 65–67 (quote).

14. Stahr, *Seward,* 76–80.

15. Van Deusen, *William Henry Seward,* 99 (public life); Stahr, *Seward,* 231–32 (history).

16. White, *A. Lincoln,* 59–97; Gienapp, *Abraham Lincoln and Civil War America,* 16–37; Miller, *Lincoln's Virtues,* 4.

17. Gienapp, *Abraham Lincoln and Civil War America,* 29 (10 or 12 feet), 32 (deepest regret); White, *A. Lincoln,* 94 (skinning).

18. White, *A. Lincoln,* 75–76.

19. Anders Stephanson, *Manifest Destiny: American Expansion and the Empire of Right* (New York: Hill and Wang, 1995), 40, 42 (quotes); Michael H. Hunt, *Ideology and U.S. Foreign Policy* (New Haven: Yale University Press, 1987), 29–36. For an excellent analysis of southern expansionist thought and actions and the sectional backdrop, see Edward P. Crapol, *John Tyler: The Accidental President* (Chapel Hill: University of North Carolina Press, 2006).

20. Hietala, *Manifest Design,* 1–9; Michael A. Morrison, *Slavery and the American West: The Eclipse of Manifest Destiny and the Coming of the Civil War* (Chapel Hill: University of North Carolina Press, 1997), 66–95; Major L. Wilson, "Ideological Fruits of Manifest Destiny: The Geopolitics of Slavery Expansion in the Crisis of 1850," *Journal of the Illinois State Historical Society* 77 (Summer 1970): 132–57.

21. Gordon H. Warren, "Imperial Dreamer: William Henry Seward and American Destiny," in *Makers of American Diplomacy: From Benjamin Franklin to Alfred Thayer Mahan,* ed. Frank J. Merli and Theodore A. Wilson (New York: Charles Scribner's Sons, 1974), 200–201.

22. Van Deusen, *William Henry Seward,* 102 (secession); Richard H. Immerman, *Empire for Liberty: A History of American Imperialism from Benjamin Franklin to Paul Wolfowitz* (Princeton: Princeton University Press, 2010), 104 (bastard); Ernest N. Paolino, *The Foundations of the American Empire: William Henry Seward and U.S. Foreign Policy* (Ithaca: Cornell University Press, 1973), 11 (want no war).

23. Amy S. Greenberg, *A Wicked War: Polk, Clay, Lincoln, and the 1846 U.S. Invasion of Mexico* (New York: Alfred A. Knopf, 2012), 268; Stahr, *Seward,* 111–12 (Seward); Goodwin, *Team of Rivals,* 133–34 (Seward, neck).

24. Gienapp, *Abraham Lincoln and Civil War America,* 38–39 (Lincoln quotes); Peraino, *Lincoln in the World,* 50 (Lincoln, "necessity"); Greenberg, *A Wicked War,* 237, 248 (pro-war fervor).

25. Peraino, *Lincoln in the World,* 47, 54; White, *A. Lincoln,* 150–52; Goodwin, *Team of Rivals,* 121–23: Greenberg, *A Wicked War,* 254 (Herndon).

26. Greenberg, *A Wicked War,* 254, 270 (for Democrats); Peraino, *Lincoln in the World,* 54; White, *A. Lincoln,* 152.

27. White, *A. Lincoln,* 157–58; David A. Nichols, *Lincoln and the Indians: Civil War Policy and Politics* (Columbia: University of Missouri Press, 1978), 3.

28. Fry, *Dixie Looks Abroad,* 42, 51; Robert E. May, *The Southern Dream of a Caribbean Empire, 1854–1861* (Athens: University of Georgia Press, 1989), 265, 269–70.

29. Fry, *Dixie Looks Abroad,* 63 (quotes); Morrison, *Slavery and the American West,* 6.

30. Kagan, *Dangerous Nation,* 233 (imperial competition); Paul Quigley, *Shifting Grounds: Nationalism and the American South, 1848–1865* (New York: Oxford University Press, 2012), 55, 58; Fry, *Dixie Looks Abroad,* 65–66; William J. Cooper

Jr., *The South and the Politics of Slavery, 1828–1856* (Baton Rouge: Louisiana State University Press, 1978), 6.

31. Schoen, *Fragile Fabric of Union,* 183, 226; Johnson, *River of Dark Dreams,* 288–92.

32. Johnson, *River of Dark Dreams,* 14 (military action), 399–400, 405; Don E. Fehrenbacher (completed and edited by Ward M. McAfee), *The Slaveholding Republic: An Account of the United States Government's Relations to Slavery* (New York: Oxford University Press, 2001), 127 (Brown); McPherson, *Battle Cry of Freedom,* 106 (*DeBow's Review*); Karp, *Vast Southern Empire,* 197 (march of conquest); May, *Slavery, Race, and Conquest in the Tropics,* 57–103; Robert E. May, "The Irony of Confederate Diplomacy: Visions of Empire, the Monroe Doctrine, and the Quest for Nationhood," *Journal of Southern History* 83 (February 2017), 69–71.

33. Kagan, *Dangerous Nation,* 196 (Adams); Fehrenbacher, *Slaveholding Republic,* 132; Karp, *Vast Southern Empire,* 7, 31 (foreign policy of slavery); Crapol, *John Tyler,* 58 (proslavery president), 58; Leonard L. Richards, *The Slave Power: The Free North and Southern Domination, 1780–1860* (Baton Rouge: Louisiana State University Press, 2000), 4–16, 62; James McPherson, *The War That Forged A Nation: Why the Civil War Still Matters* (New York: Oxford University Press, 2015), 7.

34. Van Deusen, *William Henry Seward,* 123, 128 (political leader); Stahr, *Seward,* 124.

35. Hahn, *Nation without Borders,* 167; Van Deusen, *William Henry Seward,* 189, 193; Stahr, *Seward,* 142, 174–75.

36. Stahr, *Seward,* 154; Van Deusen, *William Henry Seward,* 205, 428; Immerman, *Empire for Liberty,* 112 (quotes).

37. Norman B. Ferris, "William H. Seward and the Faith of a Nation," in *Traditions and Values: American Diplomacy, 1790–1865,* ed. Norman A. Graebner (Lanham, MD: University Press of America, 1985), 154–55, 157; Paolino, *Foundations of the American Empire,* 3–5, 30; Immerman, *Empire for Liberty,* 114–15.

38. Paolino, *Foundations of the American Empire,* 26–27; Immerman, *Empire for Liberty,* 108, 113; Jay Sexton, "William H. Seward in the World," *Journal of the Civil War Era* 4 (September 2014): 398–99.

39. Immerman, *Empire for Liberty,* 113–14; Paolino, *Foundations of the American Empire,* 27, 35–41.

40. Immerman, *Empire for Liberty,* 114; Paolino, *Foundations of the American Empire,* 37; Stahr, *Seward,* 136.

41. Gienapp, *Lincoln and Civil War America,* 40–48, 48 (quote); White, *A. Lincoln,* 167–96.

42. White, *A. Lincoln,* 188.

43. White, *A. Lincoln,* 199; Goodwin, *Team of Rivals,* 167.

44. White, *A. Lincoln,* 203–12, 224 (quote); Gienapp, *Abraham Lincoln and Civil War America,* 52–56.

45. White, *A. Lincoln,* 251–52; McPherson, *Battle Cry of Freedom,* 179–81; Gienapp, *Abraham Lincoln and Civil War America,* 61

46. May, *Slavery, Race, and Conquest in the Tropics,* 146–47 (quote); McPherson, *Battle Cry of Freedom,* 184–85.

47. May, *Slavery, Race and Conquest in the Tropics,* 147, 149 (quote).

48. Roy P. Basler, ed., *The Collected Works of Abraham Lincoln* (9 vols.; Springfield, IL: The Abraham Lincoln Association, 1953), 2:364 (empire); Richard Carwardine, "Lincoln's Horizons: The Nationalist as Universalist," in *The Global Lincoln,* ed. Richard Carwardine and Jay Sexton (New York: Oxford University Press, 2011), 36 (new country), 37 (white people); Richard W. Etulain, "Abraham Lincoln and the Trans-Mississippi West: An Introductory Overview," in *Lincoln Looks West: From the Mississippi to the Pacific,* ed. Richard W. Etulain (Carbondale: Southern Illinois University Press, 2010), 50 (*western*), 58 (expansionist of another kind); Foner, *Free Soil, Free Labor, Free Men,* 316.

49. McPherson, *Battle Cry of Freedom,* 184–87; White, *A. Lincoln,* 266, 271; Goodwin, *Team of Rivals,* 204–5; Gienapp, *Abraham Lincoln and Civil War America,* 58; May, *Slavery, Race, and Conquest in the Tropics,* 84–85.

50. Gienapp, *Abraham Lincoln and Civil War America,* 52; Goodwin, *Team of Rivals,* 204; May, *Slavery, Race, and Conquest in the Tropics,* 80–81.

51. White, *A. Lincoln,* 287–88.

52. White, *A. Lincoln,* 252; Michael S. Green, *Lincoln and the Election of 1860* (Carbondale and Edwardsville: Southern Illinois University Press, 2011), 28–38.

53. Stahr, *Seward,* 177 (quote); Goodwin, *Team of Rivals,* 212–14.

54. Green, *Lincoln and the Election of 1860,* 21, 43 (offense)-44; 57 (contracts), 58 (lied); McPherson, *Battle Cry of Freedom,* 216–21.

55. Gienapp, *Abraham Lincoln and Civil War America,* 69; McPherson, *Battle Cry of Freedom,* 216–21; Miller, *Lincoln's Virtues,* 391–95; Walter Stahr, "Seward and Lincoln: A Second Look," in *Exploring Lincoln: Great Historians Appraise our Greatest President,* ed. Harold Holzer (New York: Fordham University Press, 2015), 51.

56. David Herbert Donald, *"We Are Lincoln Men": Abraham Lincoln and His Friends* (New York: Simon and Schuster, 2003), 147 (disappointment); Stahr, *Seward,* 209 (final quotes).

57. Foner, *Give Me Liberty,* 1:501–3.

58. White, *A. Lincoln,* 361 (*Richmond Enquirer*); McPherson, *Battle Cry of Freedom,* 231 (New Orleans paper); Quigley, *Shifting Grounds,* 107 (Curry); Karp, *Vast Southern Empire,* 228 (men like Lincoln and Seward).

59. Morrison, *Slavery and the American West,* 260 (foreign tyrant and hostile people); Harold Holzer, *Lincoln President-Elect: Abraham Lincoln and the Great Secession Winter, 1860–1861* (New York: Simon and Schuster, 2008), 17, 223–24, 240 (Lincoln); Gienapp, *Abraham Lincoln and Civil War America,* 78 (Lincoln); Miller, *Lincoln's Virtues,* 434–40; Daniel W. Crofts, *Reluctant Confederates: Upper South Unionists in the Secession Crisis* (Chapel Hill: University of North Carolina Press, 1989), 283. Northerners had also come to view the South as "another country." See William Earl Weeks, *The New Cambridge History of American Foreign Rela-*

tions, Volume I: Dimensions of the Early American Empire, 1754–1865, 2nd ed. (New York: Cambridge University Press, 2015), 231.

60. Goodwin, *Team of Rivals,* 274 (people of the South); Holzer, *Lincoln President-Elect,* 112 (Disunionists); Croft, *Reluctant Confederates,* 283, 285; White, *A. Lincoln,* 351–52; David W. Blight, "Hating and Loving the 'Real' Abe Lincolns: Lincoln and the American South," Carwardine and Sexton, eds., *Global Lincoln,* 273.

61. Holzer, *Lincoln President-Elect,* 163 (now held); May, *Slavery, Race, and Conquest in the Tropics,* 212 (Breckenridge), 215 (Lincoln).

62. Ferris, "William H. Seward and the Faith of a Nation," 154 and 160 (quotes); Kinley J. Brauer, "Seward's 'Foreign War Panacea,'" 137 (quotes); Kagan, *Dangerous Nation,* 266.

63. Lawrence M. Denton, *William Henry Seward and the Secession Crisis: The Effort to Prevent Civil War* (Jefferson, NC: McFarland, 2009), 66–108; Stahr, *Seward,* 223–47; Van Deusen, *William Henry Seward,* 242–53, 276–86.

64. Stahr, *Seward,* 211 and 217 (quotes), 224; Peraino, *Lincoln in the World,* 95–96.

65. Peraino, *Lincoln in the World,* 96–97 (overpleased, inflexible); Croft, *Reluctant Confederates,* 241 (Seward); Stahr, *Seward,* 235 (Seward and Lincoln).

66. Stahr, *Seward,* 236 (leader), 243–46; Donald, *"We are Lincoln Men,"* 149 (Lincoln); Crofts, *Reluctant Confederates,* 254.

67. Goodwin, *Team of Rivals,* 328 (hold); Crofts, *Reluctant Confederates,* 127; Peraino, *Lincoln in the World,* 110–11; Denton, *William Henry Seward and the Secession Crisis,* 81–82, 84.

68. Peraino, *Lincoln in the World,* 111 (Lincoln); Crofts, *Reluctant Confederates,* 248, 285; Goodwin, *Team of Rivals,* 335–38.

69. Norman B. Ferris, "Lincoln and Seward in Civil War Diplomacy: Their Relationship at the Outset Reexamined," *Journal of the Abraham Lincoln Association* 12 (1991): 4–5 (accessed via http://hdl.handle.net/2027/sp0.2629860.0012.1050); Brauer, "Seward's 'Foreign War Panacea,'" 133–57; Stahr, *Seward,* 269–73; Van Deusen, *William Henry Seward,* 281–84.

70. Stahr, *Seward,* 269–70, (quotes); Ferris, "Lincoln and Seward in Civil War Diplomacy," 4–5; Brauer, "Seward's 'Foreign War Panacea,'" 133–34.

71. Stahr, *Seward,* 271–72 and Brauer, "Seward's 'Foreign War Panacea,'" 150–57 for the "foreign crisis" analysis.

72. Goodwin, *Team of Rivals,* 315 (Rives); Gienapp, *Abraham Lincoln and Civil War America,* 81 (I must do it).

2. The First Perilous Year, 1861

1. Peraino, *Lincoln in the World,* 102; Stahr, *Seward,* 253; Doyle, *Cause of All Nations,* 61.

2. Howard Jones, *Blue and Gray Diplomacy: A History of Union and Confederate*

Foreign Relations (Chapel Hill: University of North Carolina Press, 2010), 21 (diplomatist); Peraino, *Lincoln in the World,* 116 (master). For insight into the Lincoln-Seward relationship, see Shenk, *Powers of Two.* Although Shenk does not include Lincoln and Seward among his examples of this dynamic process, his analysis provides useful insight into their highly productive foreign policy partnership.

3. Donald, *"We Are Lincoln Men,"* 154 (useful friends); Jones, *Blue and Gray Diplomacy,* 38 (close harmony); Stahr, *Seward,* 266, 303, 356 (Mary Lincoln).

4. Peraino, *Lincoln in the World,* 1 (Hellcat); Stahr, *Seward,* 266–68.

5. White, *A. Lincoln,* 479.

6. Van Deusen, *William Henry Seward,* 256.

7. Goodwin, *Team of Rivals,* 364 (Seward), 387–88; Ferris, "Lincoln and Seward in Civil War Diplomacy," 2, 11; Donald, *"We Are Lincoln Men,"* 140–76.

8. Fry, *Dixie Looks Abroad,* 76.

9. McPherson, *War That Forged a Nation,* 65; Doyle, *Cause of All Nations,* 5–6.

10. Howard Jones, *Abraham Lincoln and a New Birth of Freedom* (Lincoln: University of Nebraska Press, 1999), 4; D. P. Crook, *The North, the South, and the Powers, 1861–1865* (New York: John Wiley & Sons, 1974), 9–13; Jay Sexton, *Dollar Diplomacy: Finance and American Foreign Relations in the Civil War Era, 1837–1873* (Oxford, UK: Oxford University Press, 2005), 58–60, 78.

11. Ferris, *Desperate Diplomacy,* 39 (Russell); Peraino, *Lincoln in the World,* 128–29 (Palmerston).

12. Henry Blumenthal, *A Reappraisal of Franco-American Relations, 1830–1871* (Chapel Hill: University of North Carolina Press, 1959), 143 (Napoleon); James M. McPherson, "'The Whole Family of Man': Lincoln and the Last Best Hope Abroad," in *The Union, the Confederacy, and the Atlantic Rim,* ed. Robert E. May, rev. ed. (Gainesville: University of Florida Press, 2013), 152 (exile); Doyle, *Cause of all Nations,* 8, 107–8; Jones, *Blue and Gray Diplomacy,* 72–77.

13. Lynn M. Case and Warren F. Spencer, *The United States and France: Civil War Diplomacy* (Philadelphia: University of Pennsylvania Press, 1970), 31, 38–44, 50–51; Blumenthal, *Reappraisal of Franco-American Relations,* 100–107, 123–27, 133–37.

14. Lawrence Goldman, "'A Total Misconception': Lincoln, the Civil War, and the British, 1860–1865," Carwardine and Sexton, eds., *Global Lincoln,* 119 (Herndon); Van Deusen, *William Henry Seward,* 30.

15. Goldman, "'A Total Misconception,'" 112 (Lyons); Daniel B. Carroll, *Henri Mercier and the American Civil War* (Princeton: Princeton University Press, 1971), 42–43; Peraino, *Lincoln in the World,* 103 (Stoeckl).

16. Ferris, *Desperate Diplomacy,* 13, 20, 48 (Lyons and Stoeckl); Carroll, *Mercier,* 74.

17. Van Deusen, *William Henry Seward,* 294 (Russell); Amanda Foreman, *A World on Fire: Britain's Role in the American Civil War* (New York: Random House,

2010), 46 (Palmerston); Gordon H. Warren, *Fountain of Discontent: The Trent Affair and Freedom of the Seas* (Boston: Northeastern University Press, 1981), 86 (Palmerston); Norman B. Ferris, *The Trent Affair: A Diplomatic Crisis* (Knoxville: University of Tennessee Press, 1977), 86.

18. Stahr, *Seward,* 317 (Seward); Foreman, *World on Fire,* 59; Van Deusen, *William Henry Seward,* 293 (Lyons).

19. Stahr, *Seward,* 266; Crook, *The North, the South, and the Powers,* 50.

20. David Herbert Donald, *Sumner* (New York: Da Capo Press, 1996), part 1: 368–84; part 2:14, 16–17, 20 (cunning); Ferris, *Desperate Diplomacy,* 62 (force); Stahr, *Seward,* 295 (evil).

21. Crook, *The North, the South, and the Powers,* 49–50 (quotes), 51; Brauer, "Seward's 'Foreign War Panacea,'" 142–43.

22. Crook, *The North, the South, and the Powers,* 54–55 (*Daily Journal*); Doyle, *Cause of All Nations,* 106, 109–12; Wayne H. Bowen, *Spain and the American Civil War* (Columbia: University of Missouri Press, 2011), 84–92.

23. Warren, *Fountain of Discontent,* 62 (foxy); Crook, *The North, the South, and the Powers,* 60 (brinkmanship).

24. Warren, *Fountain of Discontent,* 62–63 (harm); Foreman, *World on Fire,* 123; Donald, *Sumner,* 2:23; Case and Spencer, *United States and France,* 152.

25. Doyle, *Cause of All Nations,* 55 (Lincoln); Ferris, *Desperate Diplomacy,* 182–83 (Seward); Jones, *Blue and Gray Diplomacy,* 28–29; Stahr, *Seward,* 303.

26. Gienapp, *Abraham Lincoln and Civil War America,* 89 (Kentucky); Jones, *Blue and Gray Diplomacy,* 15.

27. McPherson, *Battle Cry of Freedom,* 356 (*damn*); Peraino, *Lincoln in the World,* 191 (god); Goodwin, *Team of Rivals,* 368 (listens).

28. Doyle, *Cause of All Nations,* 69, 212 (Schurz); Kinley J. Brauer, "The Slavery Problem in the Diplomacy of the American Civil War," *Pacific Historical* Review 46 (August 1977): 447–48 (Schurz); Ferris, *Desperate Diplomacy,* 184 (Sanford and Clay).

29. Doyle, *Cause of All Nations,* 29 (quote); Jones, *Blue and Gray Diplomacy,* 9, 38–39, 52.

30. Jones, *Blue and Gray Diplomacy,* 54 (measure); Peraino, *Lincoln in the World,* 118 (life and limb). Lincoln was discussing the suspension of habeas corpus, but these assumptions applied equally well to the blockade.

31. Jones, *Blue and Gray Diplomacy,* 52–53; Case and Spencer, *United States and France,* 29.

32. Doyle, *Cause of All Nations,* 28.

33. Jones, *Blue and Gray Diplomacy,* 53; Warren, *Fountain of Discontent,* 70–71; R. J. M. Blackett, *Divided Hearts: Britain and the American Civil War* (Baton Rouge: Louisiana State University, 2001), 123–24, 127.

34. Foreman, *World on Fire,* 102.

35. Stahr, *Seward,* 290–91; Van Deusen, *William Henry Seward,* 297; Peraino, *Lincoln in the World,* 115–16.

36. Adam I. P. Smith, "'The Stuff Our Dreams Are Made Of': Lincoln in the English Imagination," Carwardine and Sexton, eds., *Global Lincoln,* 35.

37. Case and Spence, *United States and France,* 62–63.

38. Martin B. Duberman, *Charles Francis Adams, 1807–1886* (Boston: Houghton Mifflin, 1960), 263–64, 268 (Adams), 275–76; Foreman, *World on Fire,* 98 (Russell), 104 (sharp edges).

39. Carroll, *Mercier,* 74–82; Brian Jenkins, *Lord Lyons: A Diplomat in an Age of Nationalism and War* (Montreal: McGill-Queen's University Press, 2014), 159–61; Ferris, *Desperate Diplomacy,* 46–47 (quote).

40. Jenkins, *Lord Lyons,* 158–59.

41. McPherson, *War That Forged a Nation,* 66; Ferris, *Desperate Diplomacy,* 64–70; Crook, *The North, the South, and the Powers,* 69–70.

42. Ferris, *Desperate Diplomacy,* 65 (quote), 69–70; Robin W. Winks, *Canada and the United States: The Civil War Years* (Baltimore: Johns Hopkins University Press, 1960), 46, 50; Van Deusen, *William Henry Seward,* 299–301.

43. Ferris, *Desperate Diplomacy,* 85–90; Jones, *Blue and Gray Diplomacy,* 57–59; McPherson, *War That Forged a Nation,* 68–72.

44. Crook, *The North, the South, and the Powers,* 66; Ferris, *Desperate Diplomacy,* 85–90; Case and Spencer, *United States and France,* 148–57.

45. Ferris, *Desperate Diplomacy,* 89–90.

46. McPherson, *War That Forged a Nation,* 126–27, 160, 164; Doyle, *Cause of All Nations,* 87.

47. White, *A. Lincoln,* 425–26.

48. Jones, *Blue and Gray Diplomacy,* 61 (races); McPherson, *Battle Cry of Freedom,* 339–48; White, *A. Lincoln,* 432–35.

49. McPherson, *War That Forged a Nation,* 125.

50. Norman A. Graebner, "Northern Diplomacy and European Neutrality," Donald, ed., *Why the North Won the Civil War,* 61; Doyle, *Cause of All Nations,* 46; McPherson, *War That Forged a Nation,* 72 (Cecil); Fry, *Dixie Looks Abroad,* 89–90 (Palmerston).

51. White, *A. Lincoln,* 437–38, 442–43, (all quotes from White); McPherson, *War That Forged a Nation,* 123–24, 136–38.

52. McPherson, *War That Forged a Nation,* 136 (Tardy George); White, *A. Lincoln,* 452 (liberating)-53.

53. Ferris, *Desperate Diplomacy,* 96, 106, 143.

54. Ferris, *Desperate Diplomacy,* 97–116, 99 (treasonable); Foreman, *World on Fire,* 137–38, 160–61.

55. White, *A. Lincoln,* 565 (Lincoln); Jenkins, *Lord Lyons,* 167–68 (other quotes); Ferris, *Desperate Diplomacy,* 117–18.

56. Jones, *Blue and Gray Diplomacy,* 75–80; Ferris, *Desperate Diplomacy,* 154–70; Crook, *The North, the South, and the Powers,* 93; Foreman, *World on Fire,* 153–54; Alfred Jackson Hanna and Kathryn Abbey Hanna, *Napoleon III and Mexico:*

American Triumph over Monarchy (Chapel Hill: University of North Carolina Press, 1971), 38–40.

57. Foreman, *World on Fire,* 147, 158, 221–22, 146; Fry, *Sanford,* 41–46; Frank J. Merli, *Great Britain and The Confederate Navy, 1861–1865* (Bloomington: Indiana University Press, 1970), 58–72; Frank Lawrence Owsley, revised edition by Harriet Chappell Owsley, *King Cotton Diplomacy: Foreign Relations of the Confederate States of America* (Chicago: University of Chicago Press, 1959), 49, 63, 395–97; Charles M. Hubbard, *The Burden of Confederate Diplomacy* (Knoxville: University of Tennessee Press, 1998).

58. Jones, *Blue and Gray Diplomacy,* 88.

59. Ferris, *Trent Affair,* 32 (*Transcript*); Warren, *Fountain of Discontent,* 37 (Welles); Van Deusen, *William Henry Seward,* 309 (House of Representatives).

60. Ferris, *Trent Affair,* 47 (*Daily Post and News*), 48 (*Times*); Peraino, *Lincoln in the World,* 125 (frantic).

61. Crook, *The North, the South, and the Powers,* 125; Peraino, *Lincoln in the World,* 125; Ferris, *Trent Affair,* 53, 61, 108; Foreman, *World on Fire,* 183.

62. Winks, *Canada and the United States,* 80–83; Warren, *Fountain of Discontent,* 128–30; Crook, *The North, the South, and the Powers,* 140–47; Jenkins, *Lord Lyons,* 180.

63. Winks, *Canada and the United States,* 80 (quote)-83.

64. Sexton, *Dollar Diplomacy,* 12, 89 (*Economist*), 96–98.

65. Sexton, *Dollar Diplomacy,* 98–99 (quote); Foreman, *World on Fire,* 189–90.

66. Jones, *Blue and Gray Diplomacy,* 98.

67. Jones, *Blue and Gray Diplomacy,* 105 (Lyons); Peraino, *Lincoln in the World,* 143 (Lincoln).

68. Warren, *Fountain of Discontent,* 38 (white elephants), 170 (arranged); Peraino, *Lincoln in the World,* 146 (trouble); Jay Monaghan, *Diplomat in Carpet Slippers: Abraham Lincoln Deals with Foreign Affairs* (1945, reprint ed.; Freeport, New York: Books for Libraries, 1972), 187 (bulldog).

69. Warren, *Fountain of Discontent,* 174–75; Foreman, *World on Fire,* 191; Carroll, *Mercier,* 108.

70. Ferris, *Trent Affair,* 102–3, 171 (fatal); Foreman, *World on Fire,* 189 (impediment); Peraino, *Lincoln in the World,* 147 (watch).

71. Warren, *Fountain of Discontent,* 178–79; Ferris, *Trent Affair,* 172–77; Foreman, *World on Fire,* 193.

72. Ferris, *Trent Affair,* 132 (Lyons); Jenkins, *Lord Lyons,* 180–83; *Stahr, Seward,* 313–17; Jones, *Blue and Gray Diplomacy,* 105–6.

73. Ferris, *Trent Affair,* 135 (sudden), 179–81; Stahr, *Seward,* 316 (Weed); Crook, *The North, the South, and the Powers,* 159; Case and Spencer, *United States and France,* 220–22.

74. Peraino, *Lincoln in the World,* 155–57; Stahr, *Seward,* 315–16; Ferris, *Trent Affair,* 175–79; Crook, *The North, the South, and the Powers,* 156–58.

75. Ferris, *Trent Affair,* 183 (concrete and diverted)-85; Crook, *The North, the South, and the Powers,* 161 (contraband)-62.

76. Ferris, *Trent Affair,* 183–85 (quote); Jones, *Blue and Gray Diplomacy,* 106–7; Crook, *The North, the South, and the Powers,* 161–62.

77. Stahr, *Seward,* 319; Peraino, *Lincoln in the World,* 158 (muzzle).

78. Stahr, *Seward,* 320 (Lincoln); Peraino, *Lincoln in the World,* 157 (self-important); Howard Jones, *Union in Peril: The Crisis over British Intervention in the American Civil War* (Chapel Hill: University of North Carolina Press, 1992), 91–92 (record).

79. Goodwin, *Team of Rivals,* 400–401.

80. Warren, *Fountain of Discontent,* 206 (quote)-207; Ferris, *Trent Affair,* 188.

81. Ferris, *Trent Affair,* 189; Stahr, *Seward,* 322; on Lincoln's contacting the press at this juncture, see Peraino, *Lincoln in the World,* 149, for his discussion with John Forney of the *Philadelphia Press;* see also, Case and Spencer, *France and the United States,* 231–32.

82. Warren, *Fountain of Discontent,* 184 (monument); Ferris, *Trent Affair,* 183 (*political* paper and *diplomatic* document); Monaghan, *Diplomat in Carpet Slippers,* 193 (Seward and Train); Crook, *The North, the South, and the Powers,* 165–67; Donald, *Sumner,* 2:42–44; for a more positive appraisal of Seward's interpretation of relevant international law, see Jones, *Blue and Gray Diplomacy,* 106–8.

83. Ferris, *Trent Affair,* 191 (clerk), 198 (Russell); Peraino, *Lincoln in the World,* 161 (Palmerston); Duberman, *Adams,* 284–85 (Russell and Bright); Jones, *Blue and Gray Diplomacy,* 111 (editor).

3. The Recognition and Cabinet Crises, 1862

1. Goodwin, *Team of Rivals,* 495.

2. Donald, *Sumner,* 2:87 (paralyzing); Van Deusen, *William Henry Seward,* 342 (low); Goodwin, *Team of Rivals,* 487 (sponge).

3. Stahr, *Seward,* 357 (Seward), 358 (get along); Goodwin, *Team of Rivals,* 488 (trusted); Philip Shaw Paludan, *The Presidency of Abraham Lincoln* (Lawrence: University Press of Kansas, 1994), 168 (fond, comfort); Brian Jenkins, *Britain and the War for the Union* (2 vols; Montreal: McGill-Queen's University Press, 1975, 1980), 2:191 (Lyons); Jenkins, *Lord Lyons,* 217 (Lyons).

4. Goodwin, *Team of Rivals,* 490, 493; Van Deusen, *William Henry Seward,* 348.

5. Van Deusen, *William Henry Seward,* 342 (Adams); Jenkins, *Britain and the War for the Union,* 2:21 (Seward description); Ferris, *Trent Affair,* 201 (Seward).

6. White, *A. Lincoln,* 476.

7. Gienapp, *Abraham Lincoln and Civil War America,* 98.

8. Peraino, *Lincoln in the World,* 200.

9. Gienapp, *Abraham Lincoln and Civil War America,* 99–100 (limited, hands); McPherson, *War That Forged a Nation,* 47 (hard war); White, *A. Lincoln,* 471–72 (other quotes).

10. Paludan, *Presidency of Abraham Lincoln,* 129; McPherson, *Battle Cry of Freedom,* 418–22; Crook, *The North, the South, and the Powers,* 185.

11. White, *A. Lincoln,* 447, 480 (quotes); McPherson, *Battle Cry of Freedom,* 462–71.

12. Case and Spencer, *United States and France,* 250 (Seward); McPherson, *War That Forged a Nation,* 69–70; McPherson, *Battle Cry of Freedom,* 378–82; Owsley, *King Cotton Diplomacy,* 232–67.

13. McPherson, *Battle Cry of Freedom,* 378–82, 381 (quote).

14. Blumenthal, *Reappraisal of Franco-American Relations,* 124.

15. McPherson, *War That Forged a Nation,* 71 (Russell); Case and Spencer, *United States and France,* 263–64; Jenkins, *Britain and the War for the Union,* 1:255; Hubbard, *Burden of Confederate Diplomacy,* 80.

16. Jenkins, *Britain and the War for the Union,* 2:76–77; Stuart L. Bernath, *Squall across the Atlantic: American Civil War Prize Cases and Diplomacy* (Berkeley: University of California Press, 1970), 4–5, 119; Samuel B. Thompson, *Confederate Purchasing Operations Abroad* (Chapel Hill: University of North Carolina Press, 1935), 5–9, 50–51; Richard I. Lester, *Confederate Finance and Purchasing in Great Britain* (Charlottesville: University of Virginia Press, 1975), 199.

17. Beckert, *Empire of Cotton,* 260 (pro-Confederate); Jenkins, *Britain and the War for the Union,* 2:76 (Russell), 199.

18. Merli, *Great Britain and the Confederate Navy,* 63, 68–69, 72–73; Jones, *Blue and Gray Diplomacy,* 191–99.

19. Sexton, *Dollar Diplomacy,* 106 (FEA); Jenkins, *Britain and the War for the Union,* 2:115 (Seward); Jones, *Blue and Gray Diplomacy,* 191–99.

20. Jones, *Blue and Gray Diplomacy,* 128 (Seward); Case and Spencer, *United States and France,* 250–96.

21. Jenkins, *Britain and the War for the Union,* 2:25, 30–31; Van Deusen, *William Henry Seward,* 323.

22. Jones, *Lincoln and a New Birth of Freedom,* 85; Jones, *Blue and Gray Diplomacy,* 152.

23. For quotes, Doyle, *Cause of All Nations,* 219; Stahr, *Seward,* 351; Jones, *Blue and Gray Diplomacy,* 152; see also Crook, *The North, the South, and the Powers,* 208; Case and Spencer, *United States and France,* 277.

24. Jenkins, *Britain and the War for the Union,* 2:17 (Hotze); Carroll, *Mercier,* 173–74 (Mercier); Case and Spencer, *United States and France,* 283, 295 (Thouvenel); Crook, *The North, the South, and the Powers,* 207, (threat), 213; Jones, *Blue and Gray Diplomacy,* 143, 147 (benefits).

25. Case and Spencer, *United States and France,* 290–93, 292 (Seward); Jenkins, *Britain and the War for the Union,* 2:27–28, 115 (Lincoln); Foreman, *World on Fire,* 273.

26. Bernath, *Squall across the Atlantic,* 13–14; Jenkins, *Britain and the War for the Union,* 2:273.

27. Bernath, *Squall across the Atlantic,* 99 and *passim.*

28. Bernath, *Squall across the Atlantic,* 12–17, 53–54, 113, 167 (evasion); Jenkins, *Britain and the War for the Union,* 2:116 (reasonable)-17.

29. Bernath, *Squall across the Atlantic,* 108–10, 160 (Russell), 162 (Lyons); Crook, *The North, the South, and the Powers,* 261.

30. Case and Spencer, *United States and France,* 277; Carroll, *Mercier,* 146–80.

31. Jenkins, *Britain and the War for the Union,* 2:18 (*Mobile Advertiser and Register*); Case and Spencer, *United States and France,* 278 (Seward); Blumenthal, *Reappraisal of Franco-American Relations,* 140–42, 140 (impudent).

32. Carroll, *Mercier,* 161; Case and Spencer, *United States and France,* 279–80; Crook, *The North, the South, and the Powers,* 181; Hubbard, *Burden of Confederate Diplomacy,* 91–98.

33. White, *A. Lincoln,* 507–8 (quotes); Goodwin, *Team of Rivals,* 477–79.

34. Donald, *Sumner,* 1:383 (bishop); 2:58 (*inertiae*); Paludan, *Presidency of Abraham Lincoln,* 26 (statutes); Goodwin, *Team of Rivals,* 462 (Seward); Jenkins, *Britain and the War for the Union,* 2:31–32 (Seward).

35. Case and Spencer, *United States and France,* 301, 307; Jones, *Lincoln and a New Birth of Freedom,* 100–103, 100 (*London Morning Herald*).

36. Owsley, *King Cotton Diplomacy,* 16, 24.

37. Case and Spencer, *United States and France,* 161, 169, 179–80; Beckert, *Empire of Cotton,* 248; Jones, *Blue and Gray Diplomacy,* 130, 163, 209.

38. Crook, *The North, the South, and the Powers,* 204; Foreman, *World on Fire,* 273, 278; Jones, *Blue and Gray Diplomacy,* 163; Beckert, *Empire of Cotton,* 247–48.

39. Ferris, *Desperate Diplomacy,* 40 (Lyons); Merli, *Great Britain and the Confederate Navy,* 258 (*Times*); Beckert, *Empire of Cotton,* 255–57; Fry, *Dixie Looks Abroad,* 82–83; Eugene A. Brady, "A Reconsideration of the Lancashire 'Cotton Famine,'" *Agriculture History* 37 (July 1963): 156–62; Crook, *The North, the South, and the Powers,* 199–206; Case and Spencer, *United States and France,* 158–89, 374–81. For an excellent recent analysis of US slaveholders' confidence in "King Cotton" and the "Emperor Slavery," see Karp, *Vast Southern Empire,* 127, 129, 137–39, 141, 180, 229.

40. Fry, *Dixie Looks Abroad,* 83; Case and Spencer, *United States and France,* 158–59; Blumenthal, *Reappraisal of Franco-American Relations,* 153–56.

41. Crook, *The North, the South, and the Powers,* 215–16 (Palmerston); Jones, *Blue and Gray Diplomacy,* 170–73 (Palmerston); Case and Spencer, *United States and France,* 275 (Napoleon), 295 (Thouvenel).

42. Case and Spencer, *United States and France,* 301 (Napoleon), 307, 309, 312–13 (Thouvenel); Owsley, *King Cotton Diplomacy,* 310.

43. Jones, *Blue and Gray Diplomacy,* 199, 203, 208, 215 (Palmerston); 218 (recognition)-19; Crook, *The North, the South, and the Powers,* 222–23.

44. Jones, *Blue and Gray Diplomacy,* 213 (Seward), 217 (Palmerston); Carroll, *Mercier,* 214 (Seward); Foreman, *World on Fire,* 295 (Palmerston).

45. Van Deusen, *William Henry Seward,* 324 (service); Stahr, *Seward,* 333 (federal arms)-34; Walter Stahr, *Stanton: Lincoln's War Secretary* (New York: Simon and Schuster, 2017), 188.

46. Jenkins, *Britain and the War for the Union,* 2:31 (vigor); Doyle, *Cause of All Nations,* 177–81; Foreman, *World on Fire,* 283–84.

47. Doyle, *Cause of All Nations,* 177 (Seward)-81; Foreman, *World on Fire,* 283–84 (Seward).

48. Mahin, *One War at a Time,* 27 (Russell), 52 (*Times*); Doyle, *Cause of All Nations,* 129.

49. White, *A. Lincoln,* 493, 504; Case and Spencer, *United States and France,* 323; Paludan, *Presidency of Abraham Lincoln,* 151; Blackett, *Divided Hearts,* 230.

50. Peraino, *Lincoln in the World,* 192; Jones, *Lincoln and a New Birth of Freedom,* 64–66.

51. Foreman, *World on Fire,* 239 (Lyons); Jenkins, *Lord Lyons,* 191–92; Stahr, *Seward,* 337–38.

52. Jones, *Lincoln and a New Birth of Freedom,* 64–65 (quote); Peraino, *Lincoln in the World,* 196–97; White, *A. Lincoln,* 492.

53. Goodwin, *Team of Rivals,* 464.

54. For Lincoln quotes, see Peraino, *Lincoln in the World,* 170, 198 (Lincoln); McPherson, *Battle Cry of Freedom,* 500; Jones, *Lincoln and a New Birth of Freedom,* 69; see also Paludan, *Presidency of Abraham Lincoln,* 143–48; Michael S. Green, *Freedom, Union, and Power: Lincoln and His Party during the Civil War* (New York: Fordham University Press, 2004), 151–52, 161.

55. Paludan, *Presidency of Abraham Lincoln,* 17 (deeprooted); Louise L. Stevenson, *Lincoln in the Atlantic World* (New York: Cambridge University Press, 2015), 166, 183–84; see also Green, *Freedom, Union, and Power,* 150–52.

56. Stahr, *Seward,* 344 (Brooks); Van Deusen, *William Henry Seward,* 330–33 (weakness); Jenkins, *Britain and the War for the Union,* 2:132 (paper); Goodwin, *Team of Rivals,* 467–68.

57. Stahr, *Seward,* 343; Goodwin, *Team of Rivals,* 468.

58. Goodwin, *Team of Rivals,* 469–70; Gienapp, *Abraham Lincoln and Civil War America,* 111–12; White, *A. Lincoln,* 510–11.

59. May, *Slavery, Race and Conquest in the Tropics,* 261, 263, 265.

60. Gienapp, *Abraham Lincoln and Civil War America,* 113; Stevenson, *Lincoln in the Atlantic World,* 165–66.

61. Paludan, *Presidency of Abraham Lincoln,* 151–52; White, *A. Lincoln,* 512.

62. Stahr, *Seward,* 341, 346.

63. Peraino, *Lincoln in the World,* 207; Stahr, *Seward,* 347; Van Deusen, *William Henry Seward,* 333–34.

64. Doyle, *Cause of All Nations,* 243–44; Jones, *Lincoln and a New Birth of Freedom,* 119; Jones, *Blue and Gray Diplomacy,* 250.

65. Brauer, "The Slavery Problem in the Diplomacy of the American Civil War," 463; Jones, *Blue and Gray Diplomacy,* 231; Carroll, *Mercier,* 224; Case and Spencer, *United States and France,* 327–28.

66. Goldman, "'A Total Misconception,'" 114 (*Times*); Jones, *Blue and Gray Diplomacy,* 232 (*Times*); Blackett, *Divided Hearts,* 29 (*Punch*); Case and Spencer, *United States and France,* 330–31.

67. Foreman, *World on Fire,* 321 (Gladstone), 329–30; Jones, *Lincoln and a New Birth of Freedom,* 122 (*Economist*); Jones, *Blue and Gray Diplomacy,* 241 (Russell)-74; Jenkins, *Britain and the War for the Union,* 2:171–72; Crook, *The North, the South, and the Powers,* 233–34.

68. Crook, *The North, the South, and the Powers,* 251–52; Norman Saul, *Distant Friends: The United States and Russia, 1763–1867* (Lawrence: University Press of Kansas, 1991), 325.

69. Jones, *Blue and Gray Diplomacy,* 243–44, 268 (Lewis)-70; Crook, *The North, the South, and the Powers,* 234–40.

70. Kinley J. Brauer, "British Mediation and the American Civil War: A Reconsideration," *Journal of Southern History* 38 (February 1972): 58–59 (Palmerston); Jones, *Blue and Gray Diplomacy,* 244 (Palmerston); Jones, *Lincoln and a New Birth of Freedom,* 122 (Jones), 124 (Adams).

71. Jones, *Blue and Gray Diplomacy,* 274–75.

72. Jones, *Blue and Gray Diplomacy,* 279 (*Morning Star*); Doyle, *Cause of All Nations,* 244 (revolting)-46, 249; Blackett, *Divided Hearts,* 32–33, 54–55, 75, 94–95, 119–21, 132–37, 157–68, 188–89, 194–97, 211–12; R. J. M. Blackett, "Pressure from Without: African-Americans, British Public Opinion, and Civil War Diplomacy," May, ed., *The Union, the Confederacy, and the Atlantic Rim,* 83–114; Peraino, *Lincoln in the World,* 216–17; Stephen Tuffnell, "Expatriate Foreign Relations: Britain's American Community and Transnational Approaches to the U.S. Civil War," *Diplomatic History* 40 (September 2016): 635–63; Stevenson, *Lincoln in the Atlantic World,* 150–52; Case and Spencer, *United States and France,* 347.

73. Stevenson, *Lincoln in the Atlantic World,* 152–53; Doyle, *Cause of All Nations,* 245.

74. Paludan, *Presidency of Abraham Lincoln,* 163, 179, 184; McPherson, *War That Forged a Nation,* 169–70; White, *A. Lincoln,* 523–24.

75. Mahin, *One War at a Time,* 140 (Mason); McPherson, "'The Whole Family of Man,'" 159 (C. F. Adams); Peraino, *Lincoln in the World,* 218 (Seward), 219 (H. Adams); Jenkins, *Lord Lyons,* 219 (Russell).

4. Victory and the Death of the Partnership, 1863–1865

1. Peraino, *Lincoln in the World,* 281 (quote); Gienapp, *Abraham Lincoln and Civil War America,* 183–84, 193.

2. Stahr, *Seward,* 243 (thin), 431–33, 432 (Lincoln and Stanton); Stahr, *Stanton,* 408 (Stanton)-9; Van Deusen, *William Henry Seward,* 411–12.

3. Goodwin, *Team of Rivals,* 609; Gienapp, *Abraham Lincoln and Civil War America,* 186.

4. Goodwin, *Team of Rivals,* 718 (Seward), 728; Gienapp, *Abraham Lincoln and Civil War America,* 200 (fear and Lincoln); Stevenson, *Lincoln in the Atlantic World,* 80–82.

5. Goodwin, *Team of Rivals,* 735–37 (quotes); Stahr, *Seward,* 435–38; Van Deusen, *William Henry Seward,* 413–15.

6. Stahr, *Seward,* 438; Foreman, *World on Fire,* 800.

7. Stahr, *Seward,* 367 (Hay); Goodwin, *Team of Rivals,* 668–69 (Welles).

8. Goodwin, *Team of Rivals,* 669 (vote); Stahr, *Seward,* 366–67 (vices, Lincoln); Van Deusen, *William Henry Seward,* 371.

9. McPherson, *Battle Cry of Freedom,* 570–74, 639–44.

10. McPherson, *Battle Cry of Freedom,* 591 (Lincoln)-625; Hahn, *Nation without Borders,* 256–57.

11. Paludan, *Presidency of Abraham Lincoln,* 203 (Lincoln), 205; Gienapp, *Abraham Lincoln and Civil War America,* 135.

12. Paludan, *Presidency of Abraham Lincoln,* 206.

13. Gienapp, *Abraham Lincoln and Civil War America,* 140.

14. Paludan, *Presidency of Abraham Lincoln,* 213, 260 (Lincoln); Green, *Freedom, Union, and Power,* 235–36; McPherson, *Battle Cry of Freedom,* 588–90; Goodwin, *Team of Rivals,* 529.

15. Case and Spencer, *United States and France,* 386–89 (Drouyn).

16. Carroll, *Mercier,* 251–52 (Vallandigham); Case and Spencer, *United States and France,* 393–95; Jones, *Blue and Gray Diplomacy,* 288.

17. Carroll, *Mercier,* 252–63, 259 (negotiations); Case and Spencer, *United States and France,* 393–95 (Jewett-Greeley affair); Stahr, *Seward,* 363–64.

18. Case and Spencer, *United States and France,* 395–97, 396 (Seward); Jones, *Blue and Gray Diplomacy,* 289–90 (*Herald*); Carroll, *Mercier,* 261–65.

19. Donald, *Sumner,* 2:100–101.

20. Ibid., 98, 103 (protest).

21. Stahr, *Seward,* 338 for quotes.

22. Donald, *Sumner,* 2:104–5.

23. Case and Spencer, *United States and France,* 408–19, 408 (awkward), 417 (resolved); Crook, *The North, the South, and the Powers,* 426.

24. Case and Spencer, *United States and France,* 408–19; Crook, *The North, the South, and the Powers,* 309–14.

25. Crook, *The North, the South, and the Powers,* 309 (fiasco); Case and Spencer, *United States and France,* 425 (diplomatic threat).

26. Case and Spencer, *United States and France,* 422–24.

27. Bernath, *Squall across the Atlantic,* 5, 34 (quote)-35.

28. Bernath, *Squall across the Atlantic,* 108–10; Crook, *The North, the South, and the Powers,* 261.

29. Jenkins, *Britain and the War for the Union,* 2:261 (Aspinwall and Forbes); Bernath, *Squall across the Atlantic,* 68 (*Times*).

30. Jenkins, *Britain and the War for the Union,* 2:263 (Lyons)-65 (Russell); Bernath, *Squall across the Atlantic,* 67–70.

31. Van Deusen, *William Henry Seward,* 355 (Lincoln); Foreman, *World on Fire,* 375–76 (Lyons, bluster); Mahin, *One War at a Time,* 175 (Lyons, negotiation); Carroll, *Mercier,* 313–14.

32. Mahin, *One War at a Time,* 186 (Lincoln); Bernath, *Squall across the Atlantic,* 111–12.

33. Bernath, *Squall across the Atlantic,* 71–72; Mahin, *One War at a Time,* 187–88.

34. Bernath, *Squall across the Atlantic,* 75–84.

35. Bernath, *Squall across the Atlantic,* 20.

36. Bernath, *Squall across the Atlantic,* 21, 29–33, 32 (quote); Stevenson, *Lincoln in the Atlantic World,* 180–83.

37. Crook, *The North, the South, and the Powers,* 293–94.

38. Sexton, *Dollar Diplomacy,* 107 (Welles); Mahin, *One War at a Time,* 177 (Adams); for Lyons, Russell, and Palmerston, see Jenkins, *Britain and the War for the Union,* 2:248; Jenkins, *Lyons,* 223; Foreman, *World on Fire,* 408, 413, 520.

39. Duberman, *Adams,* 311 (Adams); Jenkins, *Britain and the War for the Union,* 2:248, 278; Merli, *Great Britain and the Confederate Navy,* 196–208. Russell had decided to hold the rams prior to receiving Adams's September 5 note.

40. Merli, *Great Britain and the Confederate Navy,* 118, 119 (quote), 195–96; Jenkins, *Lord Lyons,* 237–38; Jenkins, *Britain and the War for the Union,* 2:282–83; Warren F. Spencer, *The Confederate Navy in Europe* (University, AL: University of Alabama Press, 1983), 125; Crook, *The North, the South, and the Powers,* 294–98.

41. Merli, *Great Britain and the Confederate Navy,* 58–59, 70–71, 160–61, 173–77, 176 (apparently); Spencer, *Confederate Navy in Europe,* 99–103; Crook, *The North, the South, and the Powers,* 298–301.

42. Merli, *Great Britain and the Confederate Navy,* 151, 167.

43. Jenkins, *Britain and the War for the Union,* 2:289–90 (policy), 291 (commonsense), 299–304, 306; Spencer, *Confederate Navy in Europe,* 119 (moment).

44. Donald, *Sumner,* 2:128–34, 129 (Sumner); Jenkins, *Britain and the War for the Union,* 2:298–300 (Sumner, Russell, and British press); Stahr, *Seward,* 376–77 (Seward).

45. Case and Spencer, *United States and France,* 427–36; Spencer, *Confederate Navy in Europe,* 147–63.

46. Case and Spencer, *United States and France,* 436–54, 453 (remanstrances); Spencer, *Confederate Navy in Europe,* 170–71.

47. Case and Spencer, *United States and France,* 434–460 (Seward).

48. Case and Spencer, *United States and France,* 440–77, 477 (Seward); Spencer, *Confederate Navy in Europe,* 172–73.

49. Stahr, *Seward,* 379 (Lyons); Donald, *Sumner,* 2:135 (Russell); Van Deusen, *William Henry Seward,* 375 (Mercier); Peraino, *Lincoln in the World,* 261 (Mercier); Foreman, *World on Fire,* 511 (Palmerston); Jenkins, *Britain and the War for the Union,* 2:231–32.

50. Albert A. Woldman, *Lincoln and the Russians* (Cleveland: The World Publishing Company, 1952), 124–25, 129, 134.

51. Saul, *Distant Friends,* 341–52, 351; Peraino, *Lincoln in the World,* 260–61; Stahr, *Seward,* 377–78; Foreman, *World on Fire,* 545–46.

52. Woldman, *Lincoln and the Russians,* 146 (Hay); Peraino, *Lincoln in the World,* 261; Saul, *Distant Friends,* 345–53; Crook, *The North, the South, and the Powers,* 317–18; Stahr, *Seward,* 377.

53. White, *A. Lincoln,* 601–9, 605–7 (Lincoln), 609 (Everett); Stahr, *Seward,* 386; Paludan, *Presidency of Abraham Lincoln,* 228–30; Gienapp, *Abraham Lincoln and Civil War America,* 148.

54. Nichols, *Lincoln and the Indians,* 186–87; Nichols, "Lincoln and the Indians," Etulain, ed. *Lincoln Looks West,* 223.

55. Etulain, "Abraham Lincoln and the Trans-Mississippi West," 51–52; Nichols, *Lincoln and the Indians,* 50, 144, 153–54, 159, 164, 193–207; Nichols, "Lincoln and the Indians," 224–26; Hahn, *Nation without Borders,* 284; Durwood Ball, "Liberty, Empire, and Civil War in the American West," in *Empire and Liberty: The Civil War and the West,* ed. Virginia Scharff (Oakland: University of California Press, 2015), 69, 78–79, 81; Kent Blansett, "When the Stars Fell from the Sky: The Cherokee Nation and Autonomy in the Civil War," Scharff, ed., *Empire and Liberty,* 96–98. For US-Indian relations as foreign relations, see Brian Delay, "Indian Polities, Empire, and the History of American Foreign Relations," *Diplomatic History* 39 (November 2015): 927–42; Arthur N. Gilbert, "The American Indian and United States Diplomatic History," *History Teacher* 8 (February 1975): 229–41; Nathan J. Citino, "The Global Frontier: Comparative History and the Frontier-Borderlands Approach," in *Explaining the History of American Foreign Relations,* ed. Frank Costigliola and Michael J. Hogan, 3rd ed. (New York: Cambridge University Press, 2016), 168–87; James O. Gump, *The Dust Rose Like Smoke: The Subjugation of the Zulu and the Sioux* (Lincoln: University of Nebraska Press, 1994); Nugent, *Habits of Empire.*

56. Nichols, *Lincoln and the Indians,* 192–95; Etulain, "Abraham Lincoln and the Trans-Mississippi West," 27–29; Hahn, *Nation without Borders,* 242.

57. Nichols, *Lincoln and the Indians,* 27–33; Fry, *Dixie Looks Abroad,* 100–101.

58. Nichols, *Lincoln and the Indians,* 33–63; Hahn, *Nations without Borders,* 281–85.

59. Nichols, "Lincoln and the Indians," 214–15.

60. Nichols, *Lincoln and the Indians,* 215–19, 223–27; Walter L. Hixson, *American Settler Colonialism: A History* (New York: Palgrave Macmillan, 2013), 118. Thirty-eight of the Indians were ultimately executed.

61. Nichols, *Lincoln and the Indians,* 133 (impact), 161 (context); Delay, "Indian Polities, Empire, and the History of American Foreign Relations," 935 (empire); Haupton, *Between Two Fires,* 25–28, 189–92.

62. Gienapp, *Abraham Lincoln and Civil War America,* 155 (Davis); Goodwin, *Team of Rivals,* 564 (Chase), 605 (Chase for President, Chase); White, *A. Lincoln,* 615.

63. Goodwin, *Team of Rivals,* 607 (Chase), 607 (*Times*), 608 (Chase), 680 (fever); Paludan, *Presidency of Abraham Lincoln,* 267 (fly)-69; White, *A. Lincoln,* 636 (embarrassment).

64. White, *A. Lincoln,* 636–39, 638 (Raymond); Hahn, *Nation without Borders,* 295 (Lincoln).

65. Goodwin, *Team of Rivals,* 652.

66. Paludan, *Presidency of Abraham Lincoln,* 290–91.

67. Winks, *Canada and the United States,* 146, 244–55, 253 (Seward); Jenkins, *Britain and the War for the Union,* 2:350–53.

68. Winks, *Canada and the United States,* 265–75, 288–93, 289 (prostitute); Jenkins, *Britain and the War for the Union,* 2:356–57.

69. Winks, *Canada and the United States,* 298–301, 310–18; Jenkins, *Britain and the War for the Union,* 2:357.

70. Winks, *Canada and the United States,* 318.

71. Mahin, *One War at a Time,* 196 (Lincoln); Winks, *Canada and the United States,* 302 (Dix), 317 (Sumner), 318–20, 359–60; Jenkins, *Britain and the War for the Union,* 2:359–60.

72. Mahin, *One War at a Time,* 247 (Seward); Monaghan, *Diplomat in Carpet Slippers,* 393 (Lincoln); Jenkins, *Lord Lyons,* 237; Winks, *Canada and the United States,* 318, 326–27.

73. Jenkins, *Britain and the War for the Union,* 2:357, 359 (Seward), 367; Winks, *Canada and the United States,* 306–8, 320, 329–30, 362.

74. Hanna and Hanna, *Napoleon III and Mexico,* 58–68, 77–85.

75. Hanna and Hanna, *Napoleon III and Mexico,* 103, 116, 294, 297, 306, 308–19; Crook, *The North, the South, and the Powers,* 338, 345; Case and Spencer, *United States and France,* 411, 455, 508, 555; Jones, *Blue and Gray Diplomacy,* 308–15; Doyle, *Cause of All Nations,* 202.

76. Crook, *The North, the South, and the Powers,* 345 (competence), 351–52; Hanna and Hanna, *Napoleon III and Mexico,* 58–67; Peraino, *Lincoln in the World,* 254–59, 270, 276; Jones, *Blue and Gray Diplomacy,* 311.

77. Mahin, *One War at a Time,* 224–27 (Seward); Peraino, *Lincoln in the World,* 270, 276.

78. Carroll, *Mercier,* 283 (Mercier); Hanna and Hanna, *Napoleon III and Mexico,* 73–74, 120–23.

79. Hanna and Hanna, *Napoleon III and Mexico,* 114 (Napoleon), 126–37, 145; Peraino, *Lincoln in the World,* 267 (Archdupe).

80. Jones, *Blue and Gray Diplomacy,* 313 (Lincoln)-16; Case and Spencer, *United States and France,* 455, 508.

81. Peraino, *Lincoln in the World,* 269 (*Herald*); Mahin, *One War at a Time,* 231–33 (other quotes).

82. Mahin, *One War at a Time,* 234 (Lincoln), 272 (Seward); Crook, *The North, the South, and the Powers,* 343 (Seward); Peraino, *Lincoln in the World,* 274.

83. Goodwin, *Team of Rivals,* 690–95, 691 (Lincoln).

84. Goodwin, *Team of Rivals,* 692–93; Stahr, *Seward,* 421–23; White, *A. Lincoln,* 657.

85. For Confederate diplomacy, see May, "Irony of Confederate Diplomacy," 69, 87–95, 100, 102–5; Fry, *Dixie Looks Abroad,* 75–105; Jones, *Blue and Gray Diplomacy;* Owsley, *King Cotton Diplomacy;* Henry Blumenthal, "Confederate Diplomacy: Popular Notions and International Realities," *Journal of Southern History* 32

(May 1966): 151–71; Hubbard, *Burden of Confederate Diplomacy;* Charles P. Cullop, *Confederate Propaganda in Europe, 1861–1865* (Coral Gables: University of Miami Press, 1969); and Jay Sexton, *The Monroe Doctrine: Empire and Nation in Nineteenth-Century America* (New York: Hill and Wang, 2011), 138; for southern belief in the power and influence of the "Emperor Slavery" as the superior form of labor in the tropics, see Karp, *Vast Southern Empire.*

5. Seward and Empire, 1865–1869

1. Van Deusen, *William Henry Seward,* 562–63; Stahr, *Seward,* 539.

2. Stahr, *Seward,* 534–541 (rest); Van Deusen, *William Henry Seward,* 553–61; Sexton, "William H. Seward in the World," 400–402.

3. Hans L. Trefousse, *Andrew Johnson: A Biography* (New York: W.W. Norton, 1989), 13–30, 45; Albert Castel, *The Presidency of Andrew Johnson* (Lawrence: Regents Press of Kansas, 1979), 4–5.

4. Trefousse, *Andrew Johnson,* 32–83, 22 (zest), 34 (dressed).

5. Trefousse, *Andrew Johnson,* 38–39, 48–49, 61 (people), 62 (maverick), 63 (poor man); 70–72, 88–119; Castel, *Presidency of Andrew Johnson,* 5–6.

6. Trefousse, *Andrew Johnson,* 130–37.

7. Trefousse, *Andrew Johnson,* 207; Stahr, *Seward,* 509–13; Van Deusen, *William Henry Seward,* 79–81; Castel, *Presidency of Andrew Johnson,* 19, 42, 120, 144, 200.

8. Van Deusen, *William Henry Seward,* 407; Castel, *Presidency of Andrew Johnson,* 79–80; Stahr, *Seward,* 462–63.

9. Castel, *Presidency of Andrew Johnson,* 28–29, 44–47, 60, 66–70, 90–95, 99–100, 152; Trefousse, *Andrew Johnson,* 219–24, 242–43, 263, 271, 277; Hahn, *Nation without Borders,* 299–314; Van Deusen, *William Henry Seward,* 387, 435–47, 451, 469; Stahr, *Seward,* 446–52, 478–79.

10. Ibid.

11. Trefousse, *Andrew Johnson,* 264 (kill), 267 (Fessenden); Stahr, *Seward,* 473 (*Nation*), 474 (*Tribune*), 482 (Weed), 493 (suicide); Van Deusen, *William Henry Seward,* 462, 474–75 (dead carcass).

12. Immerman, *Empire for Liberty,* 121.

13. Case and Spencer, *United States and France,* 586; Hanna and Hanna, *Napoleon III and Mexico,* 145.

14. Thomas David Schoonover, *Dollars over Dominion: The Triumph of Liberalism in Mexican-United States Relations, 1861–1867* (Baton Rouge: Louisiana State University Press, 1978), 193 (Grant).

15. Sexton, *Monroe Doctrine,* 154–57; Schoonover, *Dollars over Dominion,* 193–200; Hanna and Hanna, *Napoleon III and Mexico,* 238–40; Hahn, *Nation without Borders,* 363.

16. Gretchen Murphy, *Hemispheric Imaginings: The Monroe Doctrine and Narratives of U.S. Empire* (Durham: Duke University Press, 2005), 100 (public discourse);

Schoonover, *Dollars over Dominion,* 106–8, 128 (Romero), 193–94; Hanna and Hanna, *Napoleon III and Mexico,* 239–40.

17. Mahin, *One War at a Time,* 234 (Johnson); Peraino, *Lincoln in the World,* 274; Hanna and Hanna, *Napoleon III and Mexico,* 240–41; Schoonover, *Dollars over Dominion,* 214–15.

18. Hanna and Hanna, *Napoleon III and Mexico,* 240–41, 274 (cogwheels); Mahin, *One War at a Time,* 271 (Seward); Stahr, *Seward,* 443 (Welles).

19. Schoonover, *Dollars over Dominion,* 179–80 (Romero).

20. Hanna and Hanna, *Napoleon III and Mexico,* 242–47, 243 (Seward).

21. Hanna and Hanna, *Napoleon III and Mexico,* 264–65; Schoonover, *Dollars over Dominion,* 215–16; Van Deusen, *William Henry Seward,* 490.

22. Hanna and Hanna, *Napoleon III and Mexico,* 266–67 (Johnson), 267–68 (Seward); Stahr, *Seward,* 445; Van Deusen, *William Henry Seward,* 490.

23. Van Deusen, *William Henry Seward,* 492 (Russell); Mahin, *One War at a Time,* 276 (Grant and Sheridan); Hanna and Hanna, *Napoleon III and Mexico,* 271, 277; Schoonover, *Dollars over Dominion,* 196–98.

24. Stephen J. Valone, "'Weakness Offers Temptation': William H. Seward and the Reassertion of the Monroe Doctrine," *Diplomatic History* 19 (Fall 1995): 489–95, 591 (reports); 592 and 595 (Seward).

25. Valone, "'Weakness Offers Temptation,'" 591 (Seward), 596 (Bigelow).

26. Schoonover, *Dollars over Dominion,* 239 (Seward); Hanna and Hanna, *Napoleon III and* Mexico, 285–89, 288 (Sherman).

27. Schoonover, *Dollars over Dominion,* 238 (*Tribune*); Robert L. Beisner, *From the Old Diplomacy to the New, 1865–1900,* rev. ed. (Arlington Heights, IL: Harlan Davidson, 1986), 43 (graciously); Sexton, *Monroe Doctrine,* 141 (challenge); Mahin, *One War at a Time,* 285 (Bancroft).

28. Stahr, *Seward,* 547 (foundations); LaFeber, *American Search for Opportunity,* 15 (Welles), 19 (national policy); Paolino, *Foundations of the American Empire,* 118 (system of negotiations); Beisner, *From the Old Diplomacy to the New,* 45–46, 48 (Adams and other characterizations of Seward's motives and imperial policies); David C. Hendrickson, *Union, Nation, or Empire: The American Debate over International Relations, 1789–1941* (Lawrence: University Press of Kansas, 2009), 285–89.

29. Nugent, *Habits of Empire,* 251 (Seward); LaFeber, *New Empire,* 26.

30. Van Deusen, *William Henry Seward,* 517 (Great American Route); LaFeber, *American Search for Opportunity,* 14 (foothold); for other quotes, see Paolino, *Foundations of the American Empire,* 26–28, 127, 129, 142. The Alaska "foothold" quote (LaFeber, 14) was by Frederick W. Seward, the assistant secretary of state. It has been interspersed with those directly from William H. Seward, since as the first assistant secretary of state, he was a reliable and accurate proponent of the elder Seward's philosophy and imperial objectives. Although Seward would no doubt have been uncomfortable with the comparison, it is interesting to note how much his primary objective of dominating Asian trade and possibly annexing Hawaii resembled the

foreign policy of John Tyler, the nation's most actively pro-slavery president. See, Crapol, *John Tyler,* 130, 141, 155, 168–69.

31. Lee A. Farrow, *Seward's Folly: A New Look at the Alaska Purchase* (Fairbanks: University of Alaska Press, 2016), 23 (Seward); Howard I. Kushner, *Conflict on the Northwest Coast: American-Russian Rivalry in the Pacific Northwest, 1790–1867* (Westport, CT: Greenwood Press, 1975), 110–11; Immerman, *Empire for Liberty,* 124–25. The name Alaska was derived from the word meaning "mainland" in the Aleut language. The Aleut people lived in the western part of the Russian American territory. Either Seward or Sumner selected this name; see Van Deusen, *William Henry Seward,* 544; Donald, *Sumner,* 2:310.

32. Ronald J. Jensen, *The Alaska Purchase and Russian-American Relations* (Seattle: University of Washington Press, 1975), 25–35.

33. Jensen, *Alaska Purchase,* 38, 45 (Seward); Saul, *Distant Friends,* 325, 333, 336–39.

34. Paul S. Holbo, *Tarnished Expansion: The Alaska Scandal, the Press, and Congress, 1867–1871* (Knoxville: University of Tennessee Press, 1983), 5–7; Jensen, *Alaska Purchase,* 15–61, 68; Kushner, *Conflict on the Northwest Coast,* 117–42; Saul, *Distant Friends,* 270–71, 273–77, 388–96.

35. Jensen, *Alaska Purchase,* 69–70.

36. Stahr, *Seward,* 484 (not inclined); Jensen, *Alaska Purchase,* 70–73, 71 (secrecy).

37. Stahr, *Seward,* 484–85; Jensen, *Alaska Purchase,* 70–73; Ted C. Hinckley, "William H. Seward Visits His Purchase," *Oregon Historical Quarterly* 72 (June 1971): 127–47; Stuart Banner, *Possessing the Pacific: Land, Settlers, and Indigenous People from Australia to Alaska* (Cambridge: Harvard University Press, 2007), 293 (uncivilized native tribes), 295; Frederick W. Seward, *Seward at Washington as Senator and Secretary of State: A Memoir of His Life, with Selections from his Letters, 1861–1872* (New York: Derby and Miller, 1891), 426, 429, 433 for other quotes, which are by F. W. Seward, but reflect his father's views. See also, Haupton, *Between Two Fires,* 11, for W. H. Seward on the need for Native American removal in areas south of Kansas in 1860.

38. Jensen, *Alaska Purchase,* 75–76.

39. Donald, *Sumner,* 2:304.

40. Donald, *Sumner,* 2:304–5; Nugent, *Habits of Empire,* 245–46.

41. Jensen, *Alaska Purchase,* 80 (Sumner).

42. Stahr, *Seward,* 492–93 (careless and speaks); Paolino, *Foundations of the American Empire,* 116–17.

43. Jensen, *Alaska Purchase,* 87 (Terrapin and seductive dinners); Donald, *Sumner,* 2:306 (symposium).

44. Jensen, *Alaska Purchase,* 80–82; Stahr, *Seward,* 487–89; Farrow, *Seward's Folly,* 56–60.

45. Holbo, *Tarnished Expansion,* 12 (failures and icehouse); Stahr, *Seward,* 488 (folly); Farrow, *Seward's Folly,* 60–62.

46. Jensen, *Alaska Purchase,* 86; Stahr, *Seward,* 489.

47. Jensen, *Alaska Purchase,* 87–88 (bungler); LaFeber, *American Search for Opportunity,* 15 (clown); Stahr, *Seward,* 491; Michael S. Green, "Eastern and Western Empire: Thaddeus Stevens and the Greater Reconstruction," in *The Worlds of James Buchanan and Thaddeus Stevens,* ed. Michael Birkner, Randall Miller, and John Quist (forthcoming from Louisiana State University Press, 2018).

48. Donald, *Sumner,* 2:306–9, 307 (Fessenden); Jensen, *Alaska Purchase,* 88–92.

49. Donald, *Sumner,* 2:309 (Sumner); Jensen, *Alaska Purchase,* 88–92.

50. Van Deusen, *William Henry Seward,* 544.

51. Farrow, *Seward's Folly,* 71–72, 101 (*Times* and *Morning Chronicle*); Jensen, *Alaska Purchase,* 100–103, 123 (Orth); Kushner, *Conflict on the Northwest Coast,* 152–53; Van Deusen, *William Henry Seward,* 543.

52. Farrow, *Seward's Folly,* 101 (coerced); Holbo, *Tarnished Expansion,* 25 (pass this appropriation); Stahr, *Seward,* 496 (own motion); Jensen, *Alaska Purchase,* 114 (Walrussia).

53. Jensen, *Alaska Purchase,* 105 (talkers and life-long)-6; Holbo, *Tarnished Expansion,* 24.

54. Farrow, *Seward's Folly,* 95 (persistently); Holbo, *Tarnished Expansion,* 18–19, 21, 49; Jensen, *Alaska Purchase,* 111–13, 115–18, 122–31.

55. Holbo, *Tarnished Expansion,* 47–49, 69 (Seward), 88 (tainted); Stahr, *Seward,* 518 (Seward); Jensen, *Alaska Purchase,* 128–29.

56. Stahr, *Seward,* 496 (*Hartford Courant*).

57. Stahr, *Seward,* 498–500, 499 (quotes); Mahin, *One War at a Time,* 287; Donald, *Sumner,* 2: 374–76, 392; Charles S. Campbell, *The Transformation of American Foreign Relations, 1865–1900* (New York: Harper & Row, 1976), 8–10.

58. Van Deusen, *William Henry Seward,* 526–28; Paolino, *Foundations of the American Empire,* 118–25; Immerman, *Empire for Liberty,* 126–27.

59. Van Deusen, *William Henry Seward,* 527 (outlandish); Paolino, *Foundations of the American Empire,* 120–28; Stahr, *Seward,* 519–20.

60. Paolino, *Foundations of the American Empire,* 121–28; Van Deusen, *William Henry Seward,* 529–31; Stahr, *Seward,* 520.

61. Paolino, *Foundations of the American Empire,* 129 (Panama route), 130–44, 136 (men of wealth); Stahr, *Seward,* 523–24 (transcendently); Van Deusen, *William Henry Seward,* 517.

62. Stahr, *Seward,* 500 (Seward); Campbell, *Transformation of American Foreign Relations,* 16; Donald Marquard Dozer, "Anti-Expansionism during the Johnson Administration," *Pacific Historical Review* 12 (September 1943): 272–73.

63. Paolino, *Foundations of the American Empire,* 145–203, 146–47, 152 (Seward); Sexton, "William H. Seward in the World," 417; Van Deusen, *William Henry Seward,* 519–25.

64. LaFeber, *American Search for Opportunity,* 18 (Seward); Warren I. Cohen, *America's Response to China: A History of Sino-American Relations,* 4th ed. (New York: Columbia University Press, 2000), 27; Michael H. Hunt, *The Making of a*

Special Relationship: The United States and China to 1914 (New York: Columbia University Press, 1983), 57–58.

65. Paolino, *Foundations of the American Empire,* 146–69, 156 (free immigration), 157 (mature, Paolino's language); Van Deusen, *William Henry Seward,* 523–25; Stahr, *Seward,* 520–21. Much as Japan did in Korea, China claimed jurisdiction over Formosa, although it exercised little control over the island's inhabitants. When Formosa natives attacked western ships and killed thirteen crew members from the American ship *Rover* in 1867, Seward demonstrated the same willingness to use force to protect American commerce.

66. Van Deusen, *William Henry Seward,* 519 (semi-barbarous); Paolino, *Foundations of the American Empire,* 170, 172 (Seward).

67. Paolino, *Foundations of the American Empire,* 170–203; Walter LaFeber, *The Clash: A History of U.S.-Japanese Relations* (New York: W.W. Norton, 1997), 25–28.

68. Stahr, *Seward,* 547 (foundations); Van Deusen, *William Henry Seward,* 530 (ambition); Dozer, "Anti-Expansionism during the Johnson Administration," 265 (dollars).

69. Dozer, "Anti-Expansionism during the Johnson Administration," 255–75, 264 (Welles), 265 (room); Campbell, *Transformation of American Foreign Relations,* 16; Paolino, *Foundations of the American Empire,* 209.

70. LaFeber, *New Empire,* 31 (Adams); Campbell, *Transformation of American Foreign Relations,* 24 (art of the possible).

71. Immerman, *Empire for Liberty,* 127 (road map); Richard W. Van Alstyne, *The Rising American Empire* (Oxford, UK: Basil Blackwell, 1960): 176 (central figure); LaFeber, *New Empire,* 24 (prince); Paolino, *Foundations of the American Empire,* 211; Sexton, "William H. Seward in the World," 398–99; Thomas Schoonover, "Napoleon Is Coming! Maximilian Is Coming?: The International History of the Civil War in the Caribbean Basin," May, ed., *The Union, the Confederacy, and the Atlantic Rim,* 128–29.

BIBLIOGRAPHIC ESSAY

For a complete listing of sources used, see the notes. There is, of course, an overwhelming biographical literature on Lincoln. I have drawn primarily on Ronald C. White Jr., *A. Lincoln: A Biography* (New York: Random House, 2009); William E. Gienapp, *Abraham Lincoln and Civil War America* (New York: Oxford University Press, 2002); Doris Kearns Goodwin, *Team of Rivals: The Political Genius of Abraham Lincoln* (New York: Simon and Schuster, 2005); Michael S. Green, *Lincoln and the Election of 1860* (Carbondale and Edwardsville: Southern Illinois University Press, 2011); Michael S. Green, *Freedom, Union, and Power: Lincoln and His Party during the Civil War* (New York: Fordham University Press, 2004); Philip Shaw Paludan, *The Presidency of Abraham Lincoln* (Lawrence: University Press of Kansas, 1994); William Lee Miller, *Lincoln's Virtues: An Ethical Biography* (New York: Alfred A. Knopf, 2002); and Louise L. Stevenson, *Lincoln in the Atlantic World* (New York: Cambridge University Press, 2015) for basic biographical materials, Lincoln's rise to power, and his overall management of the Civil War.

In *Lincoln's Melancholy: How Depression Challenged a President and Fueled His Greatness* (Boston: Houghton Mifflin Company, 2005), Joshua Wolf Shenk provides keen insight into a prominent facet of Lincoln's health and life. Shenk's *Powers of Two: Finding the Essence of Innovation in Creative Pairs* (Boston: Houghton Mifflin Company, 2014) is similarly helpful in understanding the Lincoln-Seward partnership, although he does not include them among his examples. For more specific attention to the relationship, see David Herbert Donald, *"We Are Lincoln Men": Abraham Lincoln and His Friends* (New York: Simon and Schuster, 2003), chapter 5; Norman B. Ferris, "Lincoln and Seward in Civil War Diplomacy: Their Relationship at the Outset Reexamined," *Journal of the Abraham Lincoln Association* 12 (1991): 21–42; and Walter Stahr, "Seward and Lincoln: A Second

Look," in *Exploring Lincoln: Great Historians Appraise our Greatest President,* ed. Harold Holzer (New York: Fordham University Press, 2015), 49–65.

For more specialized examinations of Lincoln and foreign policy, see especially Howard Jones, *Abraham Lincoln and a New Birth of Freedom* (Lincoln: University of Nebraska Press, 1999); Kevin Peraino, *Lincoln in the World: The Making of a Statesman and the Dawn of American Power* (New York: Crown Publishers, 2013); Robert E. May, *Slavery, Race, and Conquest in the Tropics: Lincoln, Douglas, and the Future of Latin America* (New York: Cambridge University Press, 2013); the broad ranging and perceptive essays in Richard Carwardine and Jay Sexton, eds., *The Global Lincoln* (New York: Oxford University Press, 2011); and James M. McPherson, "'The Whole Family of Man': Lincoln and the Last Best Hope Abroad," in *The Union, the Confederacy, and the Atlantic Rim,* ed. Robert E. May, rev. ed. (Gainesville: University of Florida Press, 2013), 145–72. Jay Monaghan's *Diplomat in Carpet Slippers; Abraham Lincoln Deals with Foreign Affairs,* reprint ed. (Freeport, NY: Books for Libraries Press, 1972) and Albert A. Woldman (Cleveland: The World Publishing Company, 1952) are older, but still useful studies. On Lincoln, American westward expansion, and its imperial impacts, see Richard W. Etulain, "Abraham Lincoln and the Trans-Mississippi West: An Introductory Overview" in *Lincoln Looks West: From the Mississippi to the Pacific,* ed. Richard W. Etulain (Carbondale: Southern Illinois University Press, 2010), 1–67; David A. Nichols, *Lincoln and the Indians: Civil War Policy and Politics* (Columbia: University of Missouri Press, 1978); Nichols, "Lincoln and the Indians," Etulain, ed., *Lincoln Looks West,* 210–19; Laurence M. Haupton, *Between Two Fires: American Indians in the Civil* War (New York: The Free Press, 1995); Michael S. Green, "Lincoln, Native Americans, and the Greater Reconstruction: What Might Have Been," Paper presented at the Western Historical Association Conference (San Diego, November 4, 2017); and Walter L. Hixson, *American Settler Colonialism: A History* (New York: Palgrave Macmillan, 2013). For US-Indian relations as foreign relations, see Brian Delay, "Indian Polities, Empire, and the History of American Foreign Relations," *Diplomatic History* 39 (November 2015): 927–42 and Arthur N. Gilbert, "The American Indian and United States Diplomatic History," *History Teacher* 8 (February 1975): 229–41.

Two excellent biographers have examined Seward, his private life, political career, and tenure as secretary of state: Glyndon G. Van Deusen, *William Henry Seward* (New York: Oxford University Press, 1967) and Walter Stahr, *Seward: Lincoln's Indispensable Man* (New York: Simon and Schuster, 2012). For important, more specialized studies of Seward's foreign policies, see Ernest N. Paolino, *The Foundations of the American Empire: William Henry Seward and U.S. Foreign Policy* (Ithaca: Cornell University Press, 1973); Norman B. Ferris, *Desperate Diplomacy: William H. Seward's Foreign Policy, 1861* (Knoxville: University of

Tennessee Press, 1976); Gordon H. Warren, "Imperial Dreamer: William Henry Seward and American Destiny," in *Makers of American Diplomacy: From Benjamin Franklin to Alfred Thayer Mahan,* ed. Frank J. Merli and Theodore A. Wilson (New York: Charles Scribner's and Sons, 1974), 195–221; Stephen J. Valone, "'Weakness Offers Temptation': William H. Seward and the Reassertion of the Monroe Doctrine," *Diplomatic History* 19 (Fall 1995): 583–99; Richard H. Immerman, *Empire for Liberty: A History of American Imperialism from Benjamin Franklin to Paul Wolfowitz* (Princeton: Princeton University Press, 2010), chapter 3; and Jay Sexton, "William H. Seward in the World," *Journal of the Civil War Era* 4 (September 2014): 398–430.

I have benefited from a rich literature on sectional foreign policy competition, its imperial dimensions, and the coming of the Civil War. That literature includes William Earl Weeks, *The New Cambridge History of American Foreign Relations, Volume 1, Dimensions of the Early American Empire, 1754–1865,* 2nd ed. (New York: Cambridge University Press, 2013); Jay Sexton, "'The Imperialism of the Declaration of Independence' in the Civil War Era," in *Empire's Twin: U.S. Anti-Imperialism from the Founding Era to the Age of Terrorism,* ed. Ian Tyrrell and Jay Sexton (Ithaca: Cornell University Press, 2015), 21–40; Robert E. May, *The Southern Dream of a Caribbean Empire, 1854–1861* (Athens: University of Georgia Press, 1889); May, *Slavery, Race, and Conquest in the Tropics* (cited above); Edward P. Crapol, *John Tyler: The Accidental President* (Chapel Hill: University of North Carolina Press, 2006); Thomas R. Hietala, *Manifest Design: American "Exceptionalism" & Empire,* rev. ed. (Ithaca: Cornell University Press, rev. ed., 2003); Michael A. Morrison, *Slavery and the American West: The Eclipse of Manifest Destiny and the Coming of the Civil War* (Chapel Hill: University of North Carolina Press, 1997); Brian Schoen, *The Fragile Fabric of Union: Cotton, Federal Politics and the Global Origins of the Civil War* (Baltimore: Johns Hopkins University Press, 2009); Walter Johnson, *River of Dark Dreams: Slavery and Empire in the Cotton Kingdom* (Cambridge: Harvard University Press, 2013); and Matthew Karp, *This Vast Southern Empire: Slaveholders at the Helm of American Foreign Policy* (Cambridge: Harvard University Press, 2016).

For an understanding of the overall Civil War period, I consulted James M. McPherson, *Battle Cry of Freedom: The Civil War Era* (New York: Oxford University Press, 1988) and McPherson, *The War That Forged a Nation: Why the Civil War Still Matters* (New York: Oxford University Press, 2015). McPherson's insights on Lincoln's progressive mastery of military strategies were essential.

The starting point for overall analysis of Civil War foreign relations is Howard Jones's masterful *Blue and Gray Diplomacy: A History of Union and Confederate Foreign Relations* (Chapel Hill: University of North Carolina Press, 2010). Don H. Doyle's *The Cause of All Nations: An International History of the American*

Civil War (New York: Basic Books, 2015) is an informative and provocative work. D. P. Crook, *The North, the South, and the Powers, 1861–1865* (New York: John Wiley & Sons, 1974) and the condensed version, *Diplomacy during the American Civil War* (New York: John Wiley & Sons, 1975) provide important international perspectives and comprehensive coverage. Dean B. Mahin, *One War at a Time: The International Dimensions of the American Civil War* (Washington, D.C.: Brassey's, 1999) includes important insights and illustrative quotes. Robert E. May, ed., *The Union, the Confederacy, and the Atlantic Rim* (cited above) includes May's informative introduction and excellent articles by McPherson, Jones, R. J. M. Blackett, and Thomas Schoonover; and Jay Sexton, *Debtor Diplomacy: Finance and American Foreign Relations in the Civil War Era, 1837–1873* (Oxford, UK: Oxford University Press, 2005) affords a unique and provocative perspective.

Steven Hahn locates the war in a more expansive chronological perspective and contributes to an imperial analysis of the nation's westward expansion and foreign policies in the nineteenth century in *A Nation without Borders: The United States and Its World in an Age of Civil Wars, 1830–1910* (New York: Viking, 2016). Other studies framing the war and its significance in broad, international terms include Doyle, *Cause of All Nations,* cited above; David M. Potter, *The South and the Sectional Crisis* (Baton Rouge: Louisiana State University Press, 1968); Thomas Bender, *A Nation among Nations: America's Place in World History* (New York: Hill and Wang, 2006); David Armitage, Thomas Bender, Leslie Butler, Don H. Doyle, Susan-Mary Grant, Charles S. Maier, Jörg Nagler, Paul Quigley, and Jay Sexton, "Interchange: Nationalism and Internationalism in the Era of the Civil War," *Journal of American History* 98 (September 2011): 79–95; Jay Sexton, "Toward a Synthesis of Foreign Relations in the Civil War Era, 1848–77," *American Nineteenth Century History* 5 (Autumn 2004): 50–73; and Douglas R. Egerton, "Rethinking Atlantic Historiography in a Postcolonial Era: The Civil War in a Global Perspective," *Journal of the Civil War Era,"* 1 (March 2011): 79–95.

For studies of individual European countries and the Civil War, see Brian Jenkins, *Britain and the War for the Union* (2 vols; Montreal: McGill-Queen's University Press, 1975, 1980); R. J. M. Blackett, *Divided Hearts: Britain and the American Civil War* (Baton Rouge: Louisiana State University Press, 2001); Amanda Foreman, *A World on Fire: Britain's Role in the American Civil War* (New York: Random House, 2010); Lynn M. Case and Warren F. Spencer, *The United States and France: Civil War Diplomacy* (Philadelphia: University of Pennsylvania Press, 1970); Henri Blumenthal, *A Reappraisal of Franco-American Relations, 1830–1871* (Chapel Hill: University of North Carolina Press, 1959); Warren H. Bowen, *Spain and the American Civil War* (Columbia: University of Missouri

Press, 2011); and Robin W. Winks, *Canada and the United States: The Civil War Years* (Baltimore: Johns Hopkins University Press, 1960).

Examinations of critical moments or episodes include Norman B. Ferris, *The Trent Affair: A Diplomatic Crisis* (Knoxville: University of Tennessee Press, 1977); Gordon H. Warren, *Fountain of Discontent: The Trent Affair and Freedom of the Seas* (Boston: Northeastern University Press, 1981); Howard Jones, *Union in Peril: The Crisis over British Intervention in the American Civil War* (Chapel Hill: University of North Carolina Press, 1992); Kinley J. Brauer, "British Mediation and the American Civil War: A Reconsideration," *Journal of Southern History* 38 (February 1972): 49–64; Alfred Jackson Hanna and Kathryn Abbey Hanna, *Napoleon III and Mexico: American Triumph over Monarchy* (Chapel Hill: University of North Carolina Press, 1971); Thomas David Schoonover, *Dollars over Dominion: The Triumph of Liberalism in Mexican-United States Relations, 1861–1867* (Baton Rouge: Louisiana State University Press, 1978), which also examines the French intervention in Mexico.

For biographies of other key individuals, see Martin B. Duberman, *Charles Francis Adams, 1807–1886* (Boston: Houghton Mifflin, 1960); David Herbert Donald, *Sumner* (New York: Da Capo Press, 1996); Brian Jenkins, *Lord Lyons: A Diplomat in an Age of Nationalism and War* (Montreal: McGill-Queen's University Press, 2014); and Daniel B. Carroll, *Henri Mercier and the American Civil War* (Princeton: Princeton University Press, 1971).

Confederate diplomacy has received excellent scholarly attention. See Robert E. May, "The Irony of Confederate Diplomacy: Visions of Empire, the Monroe Doctrine, and the Quest for Nationhood," *Journal of Southern History* 83 (February 2017): 69–106; Jones, *Blue and Gray Diplomacy* (cited above); Frank L. Owsley, *King Cotton Diplomacy: Foreign Relations of the Confederate States of America,* 2nd ed., revised by Harriet Chappell Owsley (Chicago: University of Chicago Press, 1959); Henry Blumenthal, "Confederate Diplomacy: Popular Notions and International Realities," *Journal of Southern History* 32 (May 1966): 151–71; Joseph A. Fry, *Dixie Looks Abroad: The South and U.S. Foreign Relations, 1787–1973* (Baton Rouge: Louisiana State University Press, 2002), chapter 3; Charles M. Hubbard, *The Burden of Confederate Diplomacy* (Knoxville: University of Tennessee Press, 1998); and Charles P. Cullop, *Confederate Propaganda in Europe, 1861–1865* (Coral Gables: University of Miami Press, 1969).

More specialized studies of Confederate shipbuilding and purchasing efforts in Europe and general maritime issues include Stuart L. Bernath, *Squall across the Atlantic: American Civil War Prize Cases and Diplomacy* (Berkeley: University of California Press, 1970); Frank J. Merli, *Great Britain and the Confederate Navy, 1861–1865* (Bloomington: Indiana University Press, 1970); Richard L. Lester,

Confederate Finance and Purchasing in Great Britain (Charlottesville: University of Virginia Press, 1975); Warren F. Spencer, *The Confederate Navy in Europe* (University, AL: University of Alabama Press, 1983); and Samuel B. Thompson, *Confederate Purchasing Operations* (Chapel Hill: University of North Carolina Press, 1935).

For the political context and Seward's relations with President Andrew Johnson from 1865 through 1869, I depended on the Seward biographies cited above; Hans L. Trefousse, *Andrew Johnson: A Biography* (New York: W.W. Norton, 1989); and Albert Castel, *The Presidency of Andrew Johnson* (Lawrence: Regents Press of Kansas, 1979).

For Seward's expansionist agenda and efforts and their place in nineteenth-century US imperialism, see Paolino, *Foundations of the American Empire*; the Seward biographies; Edward P. Crapol, "Coming to Terms with Empire: The Historiography of Late-Nineteenth-Century American Foreign Relations," *Diplomatic History* 16 (October 1992): 573–97; Walter La Feber, *The New Empire: An Interpretation of American Expansion, 1860–1898* (Ithaca: Cornell University Press, 1998); La Feber, *The New Cambridge History of American Foreign Relations: Volume 2, The American Search for Opportunity, 1865–1913,* 2nd ed. (New York: Cambridge University Press, 2015); Immerman, *Empire for Liberty*; Charles S. Campbell, *The Transformation of American Foreign Relations, 1865–1900* (New York: Harper & Row, 1976); and Donald Marquard Dozer, "Anti-Expansionism during the Johnson Administration," *Pacific Historical Review* 12 (September 1943): 253–75. Campbell, Robert L. Beisner, *From the Old Diplomacy to the New, 1865–1900* (Arlington Heights, IL: Harlan Davidson, 1986) and David C. Hendrickson, *Union, Nation, or Empire: The American Debate over International Relations, 1789–1941* (Lawrence: University Press of Kansas, 2009) question whether Seward had a coherent expansionist agenda and whether it was subsequently implemented. For the purchase of Alaska and the implications for indigenous Alaskans, see Ronald J. Jensen, *The Alaska Purchase and Russian-American Relations* (Seattle: University of Washington Press, 1975); Howard I. Kushner, *Conflict on the Northwest Coast: American-Russian Rivalry in the Pacific Northwest, 1790–1867* (Westport, CT: Greenwood Press, 1975); Paul S. Holbo, *Tarnished Expansion: The Alaska Scandal, the Press, and Congress, 1867–1871* (Knoxville: University of Tennessee Press, 1983); Lee A. Farrow, *Seward's Folly: A New Look at the Alaska Purchase* (Fairbanks: University of Alaska Press, 2016); Stuart Banner, *Possessing the Pacific: Land, Settlers, and Indigenous People from Australia to Alaska* (Cambridge: Harvard University Press, 2007); and Ted C. Hinkley, "William H. Seward Visits His Purchase," *Oregon Historical Quarterly* 72 (June 1971): 127–47.

INDEX

Studies in Conflict, Diplomacy, and Peace

Series Editors: George C. Herring, Andrew L. Johns, and Kathryn C. Statler

This series focuses on key moments of conflict, diplomacy, and peace from the eighteenth century to the present to explore their wider significance in the development of U.S. foreign relations. The series editors welcome new research in the form of original monographs, interpretive studies, biographies, and anthologies from historians, political scientists, journalists, and policymakers. A primary goal of the series is to examine the United States' engagement with the world, its evolving role in the international arena, and the ways in which the state, nonstate actors, individuals, and ideas have shaped and continue to influence history, both at home and abroad.

Advisory Board Members

Books in the Series

Truman, Congress, and Korea: The Politics of America's First Undeclared War
Larry Blomstedt

The Gulf: The Bush Presidencies and the Middle East
Michael F. Cairo

Reagan and the World: Leadership and National Security, 1981–1989
Edited by Bradley Lynn Coleman and Kyle Longley

American Justice in Taiwan: The 1957 Riots and Cold War Foreign Policy
Stephen G. Craft

Diplomatic Games: Sport, Statecraft, and International Relations since 1945
Edited by Heather L. Dichter and Andrew L. Johns

Nothing Less Than War: A New History of America's Entry into World War I
Justus D. Doenecke

Aid under Fire: Nation Building and the Vietnam War
Jessica Elkind

Enemies to Allies: Cold War Germany and American Memory
Brian C. Etheridge

Grounded: The Case for Abolishing the United States Air Force
Robert M. Farley

Lincoln, Seward, and US Foreign Relations in the Civil War Era
Joseph A. Fry

The American South and the Vietnam War: Belligerence, Protest, and Agony in Dixie
Joseph A. Fry

Obama at War: Congress and the Imperial Presidency
Ryan C. Hendrickson

US Presidential Elections and Foreign Policy: Candidates, Campaigns, and Global Politics from FDR to Bill Clinton
Edited by Andrew Johnstone and Andrew Priest

The Cold War at Home and Abroad: Domestic Politics and US Foreign Policy since 1945
Edited by Andrew L. Johns and Mitchell B. Lerner

Paving the Way for Reagan: The Influence of Conservative Media on US Foreign Policy
Laurence R. Jurdem

The Conversion of Senator Arthur H. Vandenberg: From Isolation to International Engagement
Lawrence S. Kaplan

Harold Stassen: Eisenhower, the Cold War, and the Pursuit of Nuclear Disarmament
Lawrence S. Kaplan

Nixon's Back Channel to Moscow: Confidential Diplomacy and Détente
Richard A. Moss

Peacemakers: American Leadership and the End of Genocide in the Balkans
James W. Pardew

The Currents of War: A New History of American-Japanese Relations, 1899–1941
Sidney Pash

Eisenhower and Cambodia: Diplomacy, Covert Action, and the Origins of the Second Indochina War
William J. Rust

So Much to Lose: John F. Kennedy and American Policy in Laos
William J. Rust

Foreign Policy at the Periphery: The Shifting Margins of US International Relations since World War II
Edited by Bevan Sewell and Maria Ryan

Lincoln Gordon: Architect of Cold War Foreign Policy
Bruce L. R. Smith

Thomas C. Mann: President Johnson, the Cold War, and the Restructuring of Latin American Foreign Policy
Thomas Tunstall Allcock